Instructional Technology in Early Childhood

Instructional Technology in Early Childhood

Teaching in the Digital Age

by

Howard P. Parette, Jr., Ed.D.
Illinois State University
Normal

and

Craig Blum, Ph.D.
Illinois State University
Normal

with invited contributors

·P·A·U·L·H·
BROOKES
PUBLISHING Co.®

Baltimore • London • Sydney

Paul H. Brookes Publishing Co.
Post Office Box 10624
Baltimore, Maryland 21285-0624

www.brookespublishing.com

Typeset by Integrated Publishing Solutions, Grand Rapids, Michigan.
Manufactured in the United States of America by
Sheridan Books, Chelsea, Michigan.

The individuals described in this book are composites or real people whose situations are masked and are based on the author's experiences. In all instances, names and identifying details have been changed to protect confidentiality.

Cover photo ©iStockphoto.com/Dean Mitchell

The slogan "Every kiss begins with Kay" on page 124 is a registered trademark of Kay Jewelers.

Library of Congress Cataloging-in-Publication Data

Parette, Howard P.
   Instructional technology in early childhood : teaching in the digital age / by Howard P. Parette, Jr.,
Ed.D., and Craig Blum, Ph.D.
     pages   cm
   Includes index.
   ISBN-13: 978-1-59857-245-2
   ISBN-10: 1-59857-245-8
   1. Early childhood education—Computer-assisted instruction.   2. Educational technology—United
States.   3. Early childhood education—Curricula—United States.   I. Blum, Craig H.   II. Title.
   LB1139.35.C64P37   2013
   372.210785--dc23
                                                                       2013001004

British Library Cataloguing in Publication data are available from the British Library.

2017   2016   2015   2014   2013

10   9   8   7   6   5   4   3   2   1

Contents

Preface

Technology has increasingly become an important aspect of 21st-century life for young children and their families, as well as that of early childhood education professionals who are seeking to understand its role in developmentally appropriate practice. Now that the National Association for the Education of Young Children and Fred Rogers Center have published the 2012 position statement, *Technology and Interactive Media as Tools in Early Childhood Programs Serving Children from Birth through Age 8,* there is increased interest in how practitioners may meaningfully *integrate* instructional technology into planned classroom activities and *document* its impact on children's learning. In addition, given the increasing presence of young children with disabilities in today's early childhood classrooms, the role of problem solving to identify and use assistive technology to include these children in small and large group activities is particularly important. This textbook addresses these current educational issues by providing a conceptual framework—EXPECT IT-PLAN IT-TEACH IT-SOLVE IT—that is a practical approach to thoughtfully connecting planned activities to both instructional and assistive technologies. Drawing on a research base regarding well-recognized instructional methodologies, assessment strategies, and universal design for learning principles, the framework links technology to the development of planned classroom activities, while also enabling the practitioner to make decisions about assistive technologies by understanding the DO-SAY-REMEMBER demands placed on children to effectively and efficiently complete steps in planned activities. While examples of an array of both readily available and commercially acquired instructional and assistive technologies are provided throughout, the emphasis of this textbook is the "process." Practitioners need structure regarding how planning for technology integration occurs, and this textbook provides an alternative to the current trial and error approaches that often characterize practice in early childhood education settings. Admittedly, technologies are constantly changing and their use in early childhood planned activities is not an "end"; they are, however, an effective and efficient means to support the delivery of instruction, and ensure that young children with disabilities are included in the curriculum. As such, it is felt that this conceptual framework provides firm guidance for the field in our collective efforts to use 21st-century tools with young children. We hope that you find this framework meaningful, as well, and that it helps you to make a difference in the learning experiences of children!

About the Authors

Howard P. Parette, Jr., Ed.D., is Professor and Director of the Special Education Assistive Technology (SEAT) Center, Department of Special Education, at Illinois State University, and formerly Kara Peters Endowed Chair in Assistive Technology (2003–2011). Having an array of teaching experiences in his early career, including work in early intervention settings, he has taught both early childhood special education and special education courses at four institutions of higher learning, and was Dean of Graduate Studies and Research at Southeast Missouri State University (2000–2002). Recognized as University Researcher of the Year in 2009, he is also the founding editor of the online journal, *Assistive Technology Outcomes and Benefits*, a collaboration between the SEAT Center and the Assistive Technology Industry Association (2004 to present). He coauthored many grants and published hundreds of peer-reviewed articles, with a preponderance of scholarship focused on assistive technology issues, and, more recently, on the role of universal design for learning and readily available technology integration in 21st-century early childhood settings. In addition to teaching assistive technology courses for special education majors, he developed and teaches a unique course—Technology for Young Children with Disabilities—designed for early childhood education majors.

Craig Blum, Ph.D., has taught young children in Los Angeles and is currently Associate Professor in the Special Education Department at Illinois State University. He has taught and worked in many different types of settings ranging from adults with development disabilities, vocational training programs, mental health programs for young children with behavior disorders, inclusive education programs with children of all ages, and young children with developmental disabilities. Dr. Blum has provided extensive professional development to educators in schoolwide positive behavior support, and worked as part of research and professional development team on the Making a Difference for Assistive Technology project. There he worked to demonstrate the usefulness of readily available technology tools to teach phonological awareness to young children. Dr. Blum has codeveloped and established the reliability and validity of the Teacher Knowledge and Skills Survey of Positive Behavior Support. He assisted in providing the foundation for a statewide positive behavior support network in Washington State. He is actively involved in the Association for Positive Behavior Support and the work group for web site development. He has obtained federal grants on schoolwide positive behavior support and has coauthored numerous federally funded grants. He has worked on numerous federal and privately funded grants including Making a Difference for Assistive Technology, which focused on implementing a technology toolkit in an early childhood education center. He has coauthored a book, *Effective RTI Training and Practices*. He has coauthored 15 peer-reviewed articles or book chapters in journals such as *Early Childhood Education Journal, Journal of Positive Behavior Support, Teacher Education and Special Education, Teaching Exceptional Children,* and *Assessment for Effective Intervention*. He regularly presents both locally and nationally at conferences such as the Council for Exceptional Children Expo, Associate for Positive Behavior Support, and the Assistive Technology Industry Association.

Contributors

Christine Clark-Bischke, Ph.D.
Illinois State University, Normal,
Illinois

Carrie Anna Courtad, Ph.D.
Illinois State University, Normal,
Illinois

Yojanna Cuenca-Sanchez, Ph.D.
Illinois State University, Normal,
Illinois

Karen H. Douglas, Ph.D.
Illinois State University, Normal,
Illinois

Hedda Meadan, Ph.D.
University of Illinois, Champaign,
Illinois

Cori M. More, Ph.D.
Arizona State University, Phoenix,
Arizona

April L. Mustian, Ph.D.
Illinois State University, Normal,
Illinois

George R. Peterson-Karlan, Ph.D.
Illinois State University, Normal,
Illinois

Amanda C. Quesenberry, Ph.D.
Illinois State University, Normal,
Illinois

Jason C. Travers, Ph.D.
University of Massachusetts, Amhurst,
Massachusetts

Emily H. Watts, Ph.D.
Illinois State University, Normal,
Illinois

Foreword

TECHNOLOGY WITH YOUNG CHILDREN...TECHNOLOGY AND TEACHERS...TECHNOLOGY FOR TEACHING AND LEARNING

Technology is part of the everyday world young children are growing up in and the mobile, connected world their parents, families, and teachers live and work in. The rapid pace of innovation in technology and interactive media is transforming how we communicate and use information in our homes, offices, schools, and early childhood settings. Adults use smartphones, tablets, laptops, and other digital devices in many ways that are now second nature. They use these tools to communicate with one another, stay connected with family and friends on social media, keep track of their schedules, be informed of breaking news, get directions, check the weather, search for information and find answers to questions, listen to music and view videos, make reservations at a restaurant, buy movie tickets, or plan a vacation...just to name a few.

Young children are watching the important adults in their lives increasingly use and depend on these tools. In their own way, children are using many screens and screen media in school, in informal learning settings, at home, and for entertainment. Technology and interactive media are now tools of the culture, and early childhood educators, programs, and schools now have an opportunity to define how these tools will be used to compliment and enhance the relationships and educational experiences that are at the heart of the early years and are essential to healthy growth and development.

TECHNOLOGY AS A TOOL FOR LEARNING AND DEVELOPMENT

While there is justifiable excitement about the possibilities, there are also cautions for educators and parents. Years ago, Fred Rogers talked about inappropriate uses of technology when he said, "Let's not get so fascinated by what the technology can do that we forget what it can't do....It's through relationships that we grow best and learn best." The authors, who clearly share my fascination with technology, have honored Fred's commitment to relationships and healthy social/ emotional development by situating the use of technology and interactive media within an inclusive-classroom culture and context for teaching and learning that is based on the relationships between teachers and children, teachers and parents, and children with their peers.

This book offers much-needed guidance on the effective and appropriate use of technology and interactive media in early childhood classrooms. What makes the guidance provided by Parette, Blum, and the contributing authors so valuable and timely is that it is grounded in knowledge of how children grow, develop, and learn and offers an understandable framework for teachers to plan, implement, and reflect on technology integration alongside the familiar framework of developmentally appropriate practice.

TRANSLATING WHAT WE KNOW INTO WHAT TEACHERS DO

This book arrives soon after the 2012 Joint Position Statement called *Technology and Interactive Media as Tools in Early Childhood Programs Serving Young Children from Birth through Age 8* was issued by the National Association for the Education of Young Children and the Fred Rogers Center for Early Learning and Children's Media at Saint Vincent College. The position statement offers guidelines, based on research-based knowledge of how young children grow and learn, on both the opportunities and the challenges of the use of technology and interactive media in early childhood programs, schools, centers, family child care homes, and other settings serving children from birth through age 8.

The principles and guidelines of the position statement are clearly and intentionally in evidence throughout this book. Key ideas from the position statement that are reflected in the authors' approach and framework include the following:

- When used intentionally and appropriately, technology and interactive media are effective tools to support learning and development.

- Intentional use requires early childhood teachers and administrators to have information and resources regarding the nature of these tools and the implications of their use with children.

- Teachers need technology knowledge, proficiency, and digital literacy grounded in the principles of developmentally appropriate practice to select, use, integrate, and evaluate technology for the classroom.

The authors offer practical tips, real-life vignettes from home and school life that illustrate how young children use technology, and the essential role of the parent or teacher as technology mediator, and they connect what the research says to evidence-based practices and with child development principles and recommended practices. From the first page to the last, they create a classroom toolkit for technology integration and put valuable tools and strategies in the teacher's toolkit. Their framework, tools, and examples will empower teachers as technology problem solvers, decision makers, evaluators, and the "more capable other" to provide scaffolding for children's emerging technology skills and digital literacy. They provide a persuasive rationale for technology integration even while identifying barriers that can have an impact on the decisions school administrators and teachers make.

TECHNOLOGY PLAY TIME

One thing that is so compelling to early childhood educators and parents about multitouch screens and tablets is that they offer an easy and welcoming interface for children and are an invitation for joint engagement between the child and parent, child and teacher, or child with other children. In that same exciting sense of possibility, Parette, Blum, and the contributing authors have given early childhood educators an invitation to play and learn about—and with—technology tools, to add new tools to their toolkits, and to be proactive and purposeful with technology and interactive media.

HELPING ALL CHILDREN LEARN

They encourage readers to "EXPECT IT-PLAN IT-TEACH IT" and that framework will help teachers feel more confident and competent as they begin to integrate technology into the classroom. With this book as a guide, early childhood teachers can now take a playful and planful approach to technology that will enhance their own skills while offering young children appropriate experiences that compliment, extend and enhance classroom relationships, activities, experiences, teaching, and learning.

Chip Donohue, Ph.D.
Dean of Distance Learning and Continuing Education,
Erikson Institute Director of the TEC Center
(Technology in Early Childhood),
Erikson Institute Senior Fellow,
Fred Rogers Center for Early Learning and
Children's Media at Saint Vincent College
Latrobe, Pennsylvania

Acknowledgments

The inspiration for this work began decades ago with work in the field of early intervention, through experiences with leaders who helped shape understanding of the impact of technology when it is paired with well-conceptualized curricula and instructional approaches. Personal experiences with the Rural Infant Stimulation Environment program at the University of Alabama, under the leadership of its director, Dr. Loreta Holder, provided compelling evidence that an array of technologies were important educational supports for young children with physical disabilities. These experiences were further shaped through the work and tutelage of Louise Phillips, a leader in the field of early intervention, who developed and coordinated the Magnolia Project, the first inclusive public school preschool program funded under the Handicapped Children's Early Education Program. Children with disabilities in her classroom often used assistive technology to successfully participate in the curriculum with their typical peers. Later, through collaboration with Dr. Alan VanBiervliet at the University of Arkansas at Little Rock, even more opportunities unfolded to help craft a model statewide system of assistive technology service delivery and supporting curricula to guide all states seeking to serve persons with disabilities and their families. This latter experience, in particular, helped to shape an understanding of the influence of culture and its relationship to technology use by young children and families.

Our conceptual model of technology integration in 21st-century classrooms was further molded by experiences with early childhood education professionals at the Sarah Raymond School of Early Education in District 87, Bloomington, Illinois. The Making a Difference Through Assistive Technology (MDAT) project, funded by the Illinois Children's Healthcare Foundation, afforded us a rich, collaborative experience with teachers in 10 preschool classrooms. MDAT expanded our vision of professional development and how technology can be integrated daily into classrooms to support children's learning. The technology toolkits and the intensive and collaborative professional development provided by the MDAT project team remain a leading model for technology integration. Innovations, such as using PowerPoint as a vehicle to improve phonemic awareness, were part of the everyday experience at Sarah Raymond. We are grateful for the learning acquired that we have systematically disseminated to the field.

The conceptual framework—EXPECT IT-PLAN IT-TEACH IT—emerged over time as our understanding unfolded regarding how early childhood classroom activities were linked to a human factors approach for integrating technology in 21st-century classrooms. Reviewing the existing literature pertaining to developmentally appropriate practice and technology integration, coupled with our own experiences in teaching early childhood education preservice candidates, led us to conclude and strongly advocate that today's technologies are developmentally appropriate when thoughtfully connected to the curriculum. We would also like to thank all of those at Illinois State University connected to the Special Education Assistive Technology Center that provides an abundance of resources for early childhood education preservice teachers to learn the practice of integrating technology into early childhood settings. This resource is a rich living laboratory proving to be a useful incubator to develop the framework and ideas of the book.

Content for this textbook has systematically been embedded in a unique course designed for early childhood education majors—Technology and Young Children with Disabilities—taught each semester at Illinois State University since Spring 2011. Appreciation is extended to all those students during this time period who have helped to shape and test the EXPECT IT-PLAN IT-TEACH IT framework, allowing the editors to modify and refine their thinking about the practicality of the technology integration process using universal design for learning principles and problem solving to include young children with disabilities. Working with these future early childhood teachers and seeing them plan and present classroom activities supports our position that the model holds great potential for 21st-century classroom settings.

A special note of appreciation is extended to Jackie Hess and the Family Center on Technology and Disability, whose national mission of serving young children with disabilities and their families has provided an overarching vision that has guided our work. Their commitment to making a real difference with regard to both understanding and using technology in a 21st-century world is supported by this work demonstrating practical day-to-day classroom practices. The collegiality and encouragement of Bonnie Blagojevic, Center for Community Inclusion and Disability Studies at the University of Maine, is noted and we appreciate her efforts to connect us with the thinking of the National Association for the Education of Young Children (NAEYC) and its technology experts. We also appreciate the dedication of the NAEYC in supporting its Technology and Young Children Interest Forum, which has provided a rich source for contacts and information regarding technology integration in today's classroom settings.

*To all the hardworking and dedicated early childhood education
professionals and their students who are harnessing the power of
21st-century technologies in their homes, communities, and classroom environments*

*To our wives—Patty Parette and Nancy Blum—who have supported us throughout the
writing of this book; and to our children—Erin Wong, Sean Riches, and Andy Blum—
who have taught us about the miracle of human development*

*To our parents, who gave so much time and care to us as children, and who forever
changed our lives for the better*

1

The Role of Technology for Young Children in the 21st Century

Howard P. Parette, Jr., Craig Blum, and Amanda C. Quesenberry

After reading this chapter, you should be able to

- Describe the role of technology in the lives of young children
- Provide a rationale regarding technology integration as a developmentally appropriate practice
- Describe barriers to choices regarding integration of technology in the early childhood curriculum
- Describe elements of instructional technology
- Describe components of universal design for learning
- Identify characteristics and examples of readily available technologies
- Describe components of a classroom toolkit for technology integration

TECHNOLOGY IN THE LIVES OF YOUNG CHILDREN

While eating breakfast, 3-year-old Sean opens an application (or "app"), Teach Me Toddler, on his father's iPad and immediately becomes engaged in practicing letters, numbers, and shapes. A little mouse provides voice prompts to find something on the screen, and a checkmark appears when Sean makes an appropriate choice. After breakfast, Sean goes to the family computer and clicks on an icon for Zac Browser, an engaging browser designed for young children. When the browser launches, Sean is delighted to see the screen change to an undersea world where an animated submarine has become his cursor. Guiding the submarine to a games menu at the bottom of the screen, Sean smiles as his submarine changes to an animated butterfly, which he then directs to an icon representing a game called ABC Instruction. After clicking the Play button, an arrow prompts Sean to trace the letters of the alphabet.

Cherise, a 6-year-old kindergartner, sits at a computer terminal in her public library. She immediately clicks on the Firefox browser icon on her desktop, which takes her to the search engine Google. She types in the words *Handy Manny* and then clicks on the link that appears at the top of the search results. Because Handy Manny is used in her classroom at school, Cherise routinely visits this site to play games and watch Disney videos. She also watches Handy Manny and his friends on the television channel Disney Junior on weekday mornings before going to school. Cherise uses her Barbie digital camera to take several photos of the library so that she can share them during a show-and-tell activity in her classroom the next day.

Andy, who is 4 years old, and his mother sit in front of a laptop. Andy clicks on the Skype icon on the desktop using a child's mouse that his parents purchased for him. Andy's mother points to her father's name in a contact list that appears and says, "Click on Papa's name." Andy makes the selection and then follows his mother's prompt to "click on *Video Call*." Andy enthusiastically moves the cursor to a green Video Call button and clicks. A ringtone is heard and then a familiar face appears on the screen. "Hi, Andy," his grandfather says, as Andy smiles and reaches to hug the image on the screen.

Today, young children are growing up in a world where they are surrounded by a vast array of technologies. From morning to bedtime, young children use technologies to engage in home and community activities, prepare for school, participate in classroom activities, and interact with others in the world around them. Commercially acquired toys used in play activities are often technology-based, and children use many types of entertainment media in their homes. Computer usage by young children is increasingly common, and many families allow their children to access and engage with web-based interactive games and activities designed specifically for young children. In addition, mobile phones and other handheld devices are far more frequently used by families and regularly seen in television programs and movies, providing powerful models for young children regarding the role of technology in our lives. In these ways, technology use both influences and shapes the development of children's lives.

TECHNOLOGIES AS TOOLS FOR LEARNING

Technologies that have the potential to support children's learning in instructional settings are of particular importance to early childhood education professionals. Discussions about the role of technology in classroom settings are couched in the current understanding of *developmentally appropriate practice* (DAP). This term refers to the knowledge held by teachers regarding 1) how children develop and learn; 2) the strengths, needs, and interests of individual children; and 3) the social and cultural contexts in which children live (National Association for the Education of Young Children [NAEYC], 2009). In 1996, the NAEYC published a position statement that provided tepid support for the use of technology in DAP. Unfortunately, these early perceptions of technology and its role in the lives of young children were confounded by such diverse issues as violence in the media, the influence of hours of television viewing, and other concerns that were intermixed with the instructional uses of technology. Since that time, however, early childhood education professionals have developed both greater awareness and acceptance of the role of technology in the lives of young children. In 2012, NAEYC and the Fred Rogers Center for Early Learning and Children's Media at Saint Vincent College revised its position statement on technology, placing a stronger emphasis on its role as DAP in early childhood classrooms.

What the Research Says

The position statement from the NAEYC and the Fred Rogers Center (2012), *Technology in Early Childhood Programs Serving Children from Birth through Age 8*, defined technology broadly but primarily focused on principles and practices related to current technologies. The position statement summarized existing research in numerous areas, and key findings concluded that 1) developmentally appropriate technology can enhance children's cognitive and social abilities; 2) technology integration is effective when integrated into the "environment, curriculum, and daily routines" (p. 8); and 3) technology can help strengthen home–school connections.

For example, during her preschool circle time activity, Mrs. Hearns uses a digital projector connected to her desktop computer. Because she has Internet access, Mrs. Hearns is able to use many interactive games and learning activities that are located on accessible web sites. Children love the engaging games and activities, and they are particularly attracted to the vivid colors and animation features.

Mr. Bivens, a kindergarten teacher, uses a SMART Board to begin his large-group activity, which allows him to have children physically interact with teacher-made learning activities that he has downloaded from the SMART Activity Exchange. Students attend to how other children are participating in the activities using the SMART Board and call out words of encouragement to their classmates. Mr. Bivens has noticed a change in the attending behaviors of his students since he made the transition to the SMART Board.

Ms. Steele expects her students to transition quietly to the literacy center, sit at a table, listen to her instructions regarding the use of materials, and place their products in their respective student bins on a shelf. Because Casey is very distractible and has difficulty with routines, Ms. Steele gives him a laminated task sequence chart prior to his transition to the literacy center. The chart uses five Boardmaker symbols to represent the steps in the routine—go to the literacy center, sit, listen, make a drawing, and put things away. This chart provides structure so that Casey knows exactly what sequence he is expected to follow. Ms. Steel uses similar task charts for other activities to help Casey.

These examples call attention to both the presence and potential of technology in today's early childhood classrooms. However, many teachers may not be using technology in the delivery of the early childhood curriculum, and they may not understand that its use is indeed DAP (Parette, Quesenberry, & Blum, 2010). It is well known that instruction in early childhood education settings is characterized by activities that require children to do certain things to participate in those activities. It is also well known that technology is a tool that helps people to do something they could not do using human ability alone—either more effectively (completing a task) or more efficiently (completing a task faster or in greater quantity). For example, pencil and paper are traditional tools used by young children for writing and a book is a traditional tool for reading. However, they are not the only ways to accomplish the specific tasks of transcription (i.e., creating text) and reading. A word processing program provides an alternative to using a pencil to create text. Interactive books and iPad applications may use voice components in which works are highlighted from left to right while being pronounced, which provide powerful and engaging alternatives to reading print. Such technology alternatives are not only used at home by many young children, but they are increasingly preferred by young learners in instructional settings because they are more engaging and minimize errors made in reading, writing, and communicating with others. Most children can learn using traditional approaches to instructional delivery, so using technology to support learning in the classroom is not necessarily a better approach. However, if technology is part of a young child's culture and is a preferred method of learning, consideration must be given to its use to support instruction. Thus, its use is DAP!

BARRIERS TO TECHNOLOGY USE: THE DISCONNECT BETWEEN WHAT YOUNG CHILDREN PREFER AND WHAT EARLY CHILDHOOD EDUCATION PROFESSIONALS DO

Teachers regularly use technologies in their daily lives outside of the classroom, so it is surprising that there is often hesitation about or resistance to using technology with young children. Admittedly, numerous issues may present barriers to the use of technology in the classroom, including cultural influences, generational differences, classroom budget limitations, attitudes about technology, and lack of knowledge and/or training.

Cultural Influences

Public schools and early childhood education programs are distinct cultural groups with varying values, behaviors, and characteristics. These programs mirror the communities within which they reside, and it is not uncommon to encounter resistance to technology use (International Society for Technology in Education, 2009). This is particularly true if the community has values that have led to a recognized tradition of delivering the curriculum in ways that are not supported by technology. Sometimes these strongly held values among education professionals are different from the technological skills valued in mainstream culture. For example, early childhood education professionals who work in schools that have yet to embrace the use of technology may cling strongly to more traditional approaches to learning and see little value in the use of technology. To the extent that a teacher identifies with such cultural values, varying degrees of unwillingness to accept a greater use of today's technologies may be anticipated. The NAEYC (1995) has provided recommendations for the preparation of early childhood education professionals to develop skill sets related to culture, language, and diversity. Further, the NAEYC (2009) expanded understanding of DAP by emphasizing three challenges to the discipline: 1) increasing achievement and reducing children's learning gaps, 2) enhancing educational connections for preschool- and elementary-age children, and 3) emphasizing teacher knowledge and decision making as critical to the effectiveness of education. Specific guidance regarding culturally sensitive strategies for education professionals have been offered in the literature (e.g., Parette & Angelo, 1998; Parette, Huer, & VanBiervliet, 2005; Parette & McMahan, 2002).

Generational Differences

Generational differences among early childhood education professionals may impose barriers to technology use with young children, especially for teachers who developed technology knowledge and skills later in life. Younger teachers from the Millennial generation (born after 1976; Howe & Strauss, 2000) grew up in a world in which they were surrounded by technologies and are typically comfortable using them. A particular challenge for the field is to understand what technologies and features are used and preferred by today's families (Parette, Meadan, Doubet, & Hess, 2010), as well as how these technologies may be effectively integrated into classroom practices (Schomberg & Donohue, 2012).

Budget Limitations

Typically, teachers have limited classroom budgets for the purchase of consumables and technologies to support their curricula (Judge, 2006). With limited fiscal resources, programs and schools may tend to purchase only materials that have been traditionally used in classroom settings or materials that the teacher became familiar with in his or her preservice preparation. This problem is compounded by the dynamic and ever-changing array of technology that may be considered by early childhood programs; if the acquisition of technologies must be delayed until funds are available, they may become obsolete by the time the purchase can be made! Therefore, today's teachers need to be prepared to use a toolkit of free and inexpensive technologies that can support the curriculum (Hourcade, Parette, Boeckmann, & Blum, 2010).

Attitudes about Technology

Teachers' attitudes may also impose barriers to the use of technologies in early childhood education. Some early childhood education professionals may simply feel that teaching and delivering the curriculum in traditional ways is preferable to new ways of doing things. For example, showing and reading aloud from a book may be preferred to an interactive e-book that has built-in speech. Writing on a blackboard may be preferred to use of an interactive whiteboard. There may also be the reality of differences among teachers in their ability to adopt technology-supported educational practices. Parette and Stoner (2008) observed both early adopters and late adopters among early childhood education professionals. Early adopters are interested in using technology, developing new knowledge and skills regarding its use, and integrating it readily into their classroom practices. Late adopters tend to be more hesitant about technology use; they may be slow in developing knowledge and skills about new technology and integrating it into their classroom practices. It is encouraging that many of today's teachers have grown up with technology and are therefore likely to be more receptive to its integration into the classroom. Additionally, the NAEYC and Fred Rogers Center (2012) position statement on technology and interactive media as DAP should provide guidance to teachers and facilitate attitudinal change within the discipline.

Lack of Knowledge and/or Training

Preservice preparation of teachers has traditionally been woefully remiss in developing competencies related to the integration of technology in the early childhood curriculum. Most programs rely on a single course, or a module within a course in the undergraduate curriculum, to develop technology skills (Gronseth et al., 2010). Often, these skills are not integrated across the curriculum and early childhood education professionals may enter the field with little or no understanding of how to use technology in their classrooms. Fortunately, greater interest in the role of technology in early childhood settings is now present, as reflected in the revised NAEYC and Fred Rogers Center (2012) position statement on technology and media. In addition, specific pedagogical recommendations for effectively integrating technology into early childhood education preservice programs are available (e.g., Blum, Parette, & Travers, 2011; Parette, 2011; Peurling, 2012). However, until most teachers actually develop knowledge and skills related to technology integration in classroom settings, they will continue to rely on the expertise of consultants and/or technology specialists and professional development after obtaining their teaching degrees. For professionals who are already teaching, specific approaches for developing knowledge and skills include user groups (Parette & Stoner, 2008), summer institutes (Keengwe & Onchwari, 2009), and webinars (Schomberg & Donohue, 2012).

This book is designed to address the need for increased knowledge and skills among all early childhood education professionals. Such skills can ensure more effective use of technology to support the learning of young children in today's classrooms.

MOVING TOWARD AN UNDERSTANDING OF INSTRUCTIONAL TECHNOLOGY

Considerable literature advocates the use of instructional technology (IT) to develop important skills to support young children's learning, particularly in emergent literacy areas. However, there is also emerging evidence for the use of IT to support the learning of young children in the areas of writing, communication, social behavior, and play.

What the Research Says

In early childhood classrooms where IT has been used, gains in children's developmental progress have been reported. In a large-scale study by Penuel et al. (2009), preschool children who participated in a media-rich curriculum incorporating public television, video, and games into classroom instruction developed early literacy skills (letter recognition, letter/sound association, concepts about stories), and print increased among the 4- and 5-year-olds from economically disadvantaged communities. Similarly, Pasnik, Strother, Schindel, Penuel, and Llorente (2007) reported the positive effects of media on young children's learning across numerous studies. In the area of literacy skill development, progress was demonstrated in letter knowledge, phonological awareness, word recognition, and aural story comprehension. The use of media supported improved recognition of letters, blending and segmenting of phonemes, recognition of the onset and rhymes in words, and recognition of nonwords. Pasnik et al. also found that the use of media in instructional settings increased children's abilities to recognize printed words. Finally, studies examined in the report indicated that young children were able to recall and understand elements of stories better with the help of media.

Although an evidence base exists to support the developmental gains that can be made by children with the use of technology, much research remains to be conducted regarding the impact of instructional technologies in classroom settings. From our perspective, the issue is not whether to use instructional technologies to support instruction. Rather, the key challenge for today's teachers is how to use technologies effectively and efficiently to support learning experiences for young children in the early childhood classroom.

So just what is IT? For the learner, IT can support increased instructional effectiveness, efficiency, and appeal (Newby, Stepich, Lehman, & Russell, 2006). As previously noted, technologies are tools that help children do things either more effectively or more efficiently. With IT, children may learn more effectively or do something better than they would without the help of technology. The previous example of using a word processing program to create text is an effective way to transcribe—that is, it allows a child to generate text that the child might have difficulty creating with a pencil and paper. Other technologies result in greater efficiency, allowing the same amount of (or more) learning or task completion in a shorter amount of time. In the example of the word processing program, more text might be created in a shorter period of time using the word processing program, particularly for young children who may be developing skills in writing and thus require more time for handwriting.

Many technologies are simply more appealing and engaging than traditional materials, which increases the possibility that young children will devote more time and energy to learning or doing something. For example, interactive web sites such as Sesame Street (http://www.sesamestreet.org), PBS Kids (http://pbskids .org), and Starfall (http://www.starfall.com) have activities that include animation, voices, vivid colors, and other attributes that are far more engaging for most young children than more traditional educational activities, such as a worksheet. Similarly, a digital whiteboard and a digital projector allow children to see these web-based activities in a large-screen format, which is interesting for young learners, especially those who tend to learn through visual representations.

The use of IT by the early childhood teacher also assumes that careful planning occurs to connect the curriculum being used to learning standards, instructional strategies, and assessment of child performance. Thus, IT tools are used to plan instruction, which includes 1) making decisions about relevant technologies to be used to support classroom lessons; 2) deciding how the technologies will be used with specific instructional strategies (e.g., direct instruction, modeling, scaffolding); and 3) determining how child learning will be assessed when the technologies are used (Newby et al., 2006). Other technologies used specifically for productivity are referred to as *information and communication technology* (see Table 1.1). However, for purposes of clarity, the term IT will be used throughout this book to refer to *any* technology used to plan and deliver the curriculum to young children. The primary goal of this book—and the task that confronts all teachers—is to make good decisions regarding specific IT tools to be used to support learning.

Table 1.1. Technologies used to support the early childhood curriculum

Technology category	Examples
Instructional technology	Media technologies, such as computers, digital projector, SMART Board, iPad, iPod, digital audio and video recording devices
	Instructional process technologies, such as direct instruction, exploratory play and guided discovery, modeling, prompting, scaffolding
Information and communication technology	E-mail, computers, copiers, word processing and graphics software, Microsoft PowerPoint, mobile phones, text messaging, blogs, wikis, Internet
Assistive technology	Foam pencil grips, visual schedules, graphic organizers, electronic communication systems, wheelchairs, hearing devices, text-to-speech software, talking word processors, seating and positioning systems

From Parette, H.P., & Peterson-Karlan, G.R. (2010). Assistive technology and educational practice. In P. Peterson, E. Baker, & B. McGaw (Eds.), International encyclopedia of education (3rd ed., Vol. 2, pp. 537–543). Oxford, England: Elsevier. Copyright 2010, adapted by permission from Elsevier.

The process of making decisions about how to use IT evolves as the array of available technologies becomes increasingly versatile, requiring more thoughtful decisions about their use in the curriculum. IT is typically used in large- and small-group settings in the early childhood classroom; however, there may be instances when IT is used for individual children (e.g., if a single child has access to a computer game or activity during free play) or in a small-group activity. Most children will derive some benefit from the use of IT because it may help them to learn more effectively or efficiently. It is true that traditional learning approaches still result in learning; however, such traditional activities may not be as interesting and engaging.

Assistive Technology

Although most typically developing young children can learn more effectively or efficiently using IT in classroom settings, children with disabilities need additional supports to participate in activities. Some children may have difficulty hearing, seeing, moving and manipulating objects, following routines, adhering to social rules, and/or communicating with others. Children with these disabilities may not have access to the learning opportunities of typically developing children and therefore need additional assistive technology supports. For example, Mrs. Hearns presents a Microsoft PowerPoint lesson on beginning sounds to her preschool class during opening circle time. Students are shown a picture of a ball and asked what the beginning sound is. When the children raise their hands, Mrs. Hearns calls on Tiffiny, who says /b/. She presents another slide, on which the children see a picture of a cat. She calls on Trevor, who is nonverbal and uses a four-message communication device. Trevor presses a button on his device, which pronounces the sound /k/.

Mr. Bivens uses his SMART Board routinely for Clicker 6 lessons presented in his kindergarten classroom. Children come to the SMART Board and touch buttons that are presented in learning grids to make selections. When it is Shanika's turn, she uses a powered wheelchair to come to the SMART Board. Because she has limited strength in her hands, Shanika grips a foam-wrapped stick that she uses to make contact with the SMART Board screen to make her selection.

In the earlier vignette regarding Ms. Steele's classroom, it was noted that there were certain expectations of children's performance in scheduled activities. Casey is very distractible and has difficulty with routines in the classroom, so Ms. Steele gives him a sheet of paper prior to his arrival in the literacy center. The paper has five Boardmaker symbols representing the steps in the routine—go to the literacy center, sit, listen, make a drawing, and put things away. This sheet provides structure so Casey knows exactly what sequence he is expected to follow. Ms. Steele uses similar sheets for other activities to help Casey.

Generally, assistive technology (AT) is "any tool that helps a child with a disability do things he or she could not do without the tool at some expected level of performance" (Parette, Peterson-Karlan, Wojcik, & Bardi, 2007, p. 22). Whether it is putting away learning materials, completing a painting, or identifying beginning sounds, performance is expected of children in completing any classroom task. Thus, when AT is provided to help a child do something that is expected, it becomes compensatory. AT is individually matched to and uniquely required for a child to participate in the curriculum or classroom and make educational progress. In the preceding examples, children with disabilities were expected to participate in planned classroom activities, and they needed AT to accomplish the expected tasks. Making decisions about children with disabilities is a problem-solving process that will be discussed in greater depth in Chapter 5.

Universal Design for Learning and Technology in the Early Childhood Classroom

IT integration hinges on several principles (NAEYC, 2008):

1. The technologies should align well with the curriculum.

2. The choice of technology should be based on how well each tool serves classroom learning and teaching needs.

3. Teachers must ensure opportunities for all children to participate and learn in the technology-rich environment.

To serve the needs of all young children in a technology-supported curriculum, a framework known as universal design for learning (UDL) can be helpful (Division for Early Childhood, 2009). Early childhood curricula that employ UDL principles are proactive and designed to provide young children with multiple means of engagement, action and expression, and representation (Rose & Meyer, 2006). With UDL, teachers use an array of strategies and materials that ensure active participation of all children. Varying strategies and materials are used in assessments, goals, curricula content, the classroom environment, instructional methods and materials, and interactions with children (Division for Early Childhood, 2007). Technology use affords teachers the opportunity to create accessible classroom settings.

A UDL framework can also help teachers understand why today's technologies are preferable to traditional educational approaches. Before technology became a central part of everyday life, educators primarily used traditional materials to develop and deliver content, with little flexibility for change. For example, reading materials were in print format only. Teachers read the text to children and showed pictures in books, followed by oral questioning to assess children's understanding, regardless of whether the children were auditory or visual learners. Children frequently used consumables such as worksheets and line drawings (for coloring), which allowed for only a single use and little (if any) ability to make changes. Flexible adaptation was typically restricted to enlarging materials using a photocopier (and sometimes was restricted to black-and-white printing). Sharing materials among teachers, professionals, and families required a physical transfer of print materials.

Today's technologies present strikingly different learning opportunities. They are flexible, digital, shared, dynamic, and interactive, and the use of such technologies aligns with UDL principles. In today's classroom, reading materials are available both digitally and on paper. Print-based books now have digital audio components or companion materials that can be delivered via computer; other books are entirely electronic and can be delivered via laptops, tablets, or e-book readers. Young children can interact with the physical book and/or the virtual version. In the virtual form, children can have a word or a passage spoken by the device as they read along. Support materials can be created and delivered either in paper form, often using color printers; in digital file formats by teachers, using school networks or flash drives to install them on the students' desktops, laptops, or iPads; or via e-mail and web sites, which can also be used to share materials with children's families. Support materials can be shared among educational professionals on Internet activity sites (examples of these sites are discussed later in the chapter).

Finally, the computer-delivered media (unlike linear paper-based media) can react dynamically to a child's response, permitting branching or other nonlinear interactions. The use of UDL principles that incorporate technology enables teachers to provide multiple means of engagement (i.e., how the technology stimulates young children's interest and motivation for learning), representation (i.e., how the technology allows young children to present information and content), and expression (i.e., how the technology differentiates the manner in which young children can express what they know). Classroom activities designed using technology and these UDL principles support the developmental learning needs of young learners from a variety of cultural, linguistic, and economic backgrounds, as well as those who have disabilities.

Cultural Supports   Young children from varying cultural backgrounds may have preferences for individual or collaborative learning activities (Parette et al., 2005). Some ethnic groups come from collectivist cultures, in which conforming and contributing to the group may be a strongly held value by families of young children. Technologies that allow multiple children to participate, interact, contribute, and collaborate in classroom activities may be preferred for these children. For example, interactive whiteboards allow multiple users to participate in an activity. Many iPad applications can, by design, be both viewed and used by several children to create a product or play a game.

Linguistic Supports   Numerous technologies are now available that provide content and voice in various languages that allow UDL principles to be applied in learning activities. For example, the standard version of Clicker 6 enables education professionals and children to use French, Spanish, or English for activities created using the software. It also has numerous additional language editions (e.g., Russian, Farsi, Chinese) that may be purchased to provide voices in these languages. Inexpensive e-book apps developed for the iPad (e.g., Grimm's Red Riding Hood, Grimm's Rapunzel, Scott's Submarine) allow young learners from different linguistic backgrounds to interact with non-English text. TumbleBooks, which are popular animated books available on the Internet (http://www.tumble books.com), have a growing number of titles available in both Spanish and French. Publicly accessible software programs, such as VoiceThread, allow children to upload and engage with text, audio, and video in their native languages. Free and inexpensive iPad apps, such as Educreations and Doodlecast for Kids, allow children to record their own drawings and/or text, voices, and video.

Economic Background Supports   In many classrooms, young children from low socioeconomic backgrounds may be present. Although there may be limited technology available in these children's homes, the number of computers, smartphones, and other technologies has increased among lower income families recently. Also, the increased availability of computers in public libraries has resulted in greater access to free software and web-based games and activities that support learning.

READILY AVAILABLE TECHNOLOGY USE IN EARLY CHILDHOOD CLASSROOMS

Given that IT use in early childhood education classrooms is developmentally appropriate, the question arises regarding both the affordability and accessibility of these technologies. Budgets are tight in many early childhood settings, so ease of use and access are important factors for teachers who are considering whether or not to use technology in their classrooms.

One solution is the use of a technology toolkit, which is a collection of readily available technologies (both hardware and software) that can be easily accessed to provide meaningful classroom learning experiences. Certain core technologies in the toolkit must be present in order to employ other technologies. Two or more technologies working together create a system that allows students to realize a technology's potential. For example, a computer and software installed on the hard drive work together with a digital projector to deliver a presentation. A computer with Internet connectivity works with a web site containing learning activities to enable children to interact and participate.

School systems and programs must provide and support a toolkit of technologies needed for teachers to effectively use technology in classrooms (Blum, Parette, & Travers, 2011). For example, a software program may be free, low cost, or downloadable, but without a computer to support its use (because a computer was not provided to the classroom), the software program is not readily available. Similarly, if a computer is available, the teacher must be able to access external resources (e.g., free and downloadable software, web sites, activity exchanges) without the burden of administrative privileges being required (often controlled by school or program information technology personnel).

Key toolkit technologies that should be considered for the classroom are a computer, Internet access, child's mouse, digital projector and/or digital whiteboard

Figure 1.1. Internet sites provide access to readily available classroom activities and downloadable software, such as Tux Paint. (Image used by permission of Bill Kendrick.)

(e.g., SMART Board), printer, flatbed scanner, digital camera, iPad/iPod, and IntelliKeys® keyboard. At a minimum, a computer with connectivity to the Internet and some means of projection are essential.

Computers with Internet Access

Teachers generally recognize the importance of computers in today's classrooms. Of particular importance are computer models that have built-in touchscreen capability. Touchscreens enable a young child to make direct selections by reaching out and touching the screen (i.e., interactivity). Being able to interact with manipulatives or learning materials has long been recognized as DAP for young children, particularly for sensory-motor learners. Computers also have built in accessibility features designed to provide compensatory supports to young children with disabilities who may have difficulties such as tracking an onscreen cursor, perceiving print, or using a standard mouse.

Many web sites with readily accessible teacher-made and other high-quality child activities to support learning are accessible to classrooms that have computers with connectivity (see Appendix 1.A). Free and inexpensive software with specific educational applications can also be downloaded (e.g., Tux Paint; see Figure 1.1).

Child's Mouse

If direct access to a computer screen is not possible, many children will need to interface with the computer using a mouse (flexibility and interactivity). From a developmentally appropriate perspective, many young children will not be able to coordinate mouse movements with a pointer on the computer screen without repeated opportunities. Special types of mouse devices that have been developed for young children are preferable to a standard mouse because they allow easier grasping and manipulating of pointer movements.

Digital Projector and/or Digital Whiteboard

When connected to a computer, a digital projector and/or digital whiteboard (e.g., SMART Board, Promethean Board) enables the early childhood education professional to project anything seen on the computer monitor onto a large screen (see Figure 1.2). Text, pictures, videos, animations, web site activities, and other engaging information can be visually presented in an interactive and flexible format to small groups or an entire classroom. In the case of digital whiteboards, young children can physically interact with learning activities presented on a screen.

Printer

Printers have a variety of flexible and educationally relevant uses. In many classrooms, the printer is helpful in creating learning activity manipulatives and con-

Figure 1.2. Interactive whiteboards, such as the SMART Board, are increasingly popular in early childhood classrooms. They afford teachers access to an array of readily available technologies. (From SMART Technologies ULC; www.smarttech .com. SMART Board® and the SMART logo are trademarks of SMART Technologies ULC and may be registered in the European Union, Canada, the United States and other countries; used by permission.)

sumables, as well as permanent hard copies of lessons, data, and student work, which may be necessary for filing purposes or for reporting results.

Flatbed Scanner

Scanners are flexible input devices (essentially highly specialized cameras) designed to capture printed text or pictures, drawings, and children's work products and convert them into digital images/data. The resulting images can be embedded in other applications, such as Microsoft PowerPoint and Microsoft Word, or uploaded to various sites and applications on the Internet.

Digital Camera

Increasingly used in today's early childhood classrooms, digital cameras enable young children to capture images both inside and outside the classroom. Children can then download the images to a computer; embed the images in an array of other applications (e.g., Microsoft Word or PowerPoint documents); upload the images to web-based applications, such as tikatok.com to create personalized talking books; or share the images as student learning accomplishments with other students, parents, and community members. Camera features are also available on many handheld devices and tablets.

Figure 1.3. IntelliKeys® keyboard and overlays provide a larger surface area for young children to interact with the computer. (From Cambium Learning Tecnologies; reprinted by permission.)

iPads and iPods

Handheld devices such as the iPad and iPod Touch have gained great popularity in early childhood settings in a short period of time. Many learning applications have been developed for both the iPad and iPod. For example, the APPitic directory (http://www.appitic.com) lists more than 1,800 applications for education, organized by theme, preschool content area, disability, and other categories. When connected to a digital projector or digital whiteboard, these handheld devices can provide a big-screen presentation of the activity that all children can see.

IntelliKeys® Keyboard

For many young children participating in activities developed using special software applications, it is helpful to have an expanded keyboard, which provides a larger surface area to execute a keystroke (see Figure 1.3). The IntelliKeys® keyboard is an excellent alternative to a traditional QWERTY keyboard. It comes with a wide array of overlays, which change the visual presentation of the keyboard for the child and can be shared.

Key Software Programs

In addition to these key systems technologies, core software programs to support the curriculum should be considered as components of the early childhood education toolkit. Flexible software programs supported by a research base include Microsoft PowerPoint, Clicker 6 (Crick Software), Boardmaker with Speaking Dynamically Pro (Mayer-Johnson), and IntelliTools Classroom Suite (Cambium Learning Technologies). Each of these readily available technologies are digital and possess one or more UDL-related strengths that support the early childhood curriculum (dynamic, flexible, interactive, shared). Many activities also have been developed using these programs, which are archived at activity exchanges on the Internet. The activities can be easily downloaded and modified if needed, and they are ready for immediate use in the classroom (see Appendix 1.A).

Microsoft PowerPoint Microsoft PowerPoint, which is standard on most computers today, provides teachers with powerful features to create highly engaging instructional activities by manipulating varying types of pictures (static and animated); symbols/text; the type of voice or sound output (synthesized or digitized); the symbol size, shape, and position of different elements; and the choice between a color or black-and-white display. The animations and other features used to emphasize elements are particularly powerful and can be used to create similar effects in activities seen on web sites. Numerous reports regarding its uses have been published, and downloadable, ready-made presentations are available at Internet activity sites (see Appendix 1.A) (Parette, Hourcade, & Blum, 2011; Parette, Hourcade, Boeckmann, & Blum, 2008; Parette, Blum, Boeckmann, & Watts, 2009).

Clicker 6 Designed to incorporate the major recommendations of the National Institute of Child Health and Human Development (2000), Clicker 6 (Crick Software) allows teachers to easily create dynamic and flexible literacy activities (see Figure 1.4). Using the templates available (or teacher-made activities downloadable from the Learning Grids World web site), activities can be created which are visually and systematically represented with groups of words or iconic symbols. Students can also make and hear selections and physically interact with the activities using an interactive whiteboard. Research provides support for its usefulness in developing emergent literacy skills among young children (Karemaker, Pitchford, & O'Malley, 2008; Parette, Hourcade, Dinelli, & Boeckmann, 2009).

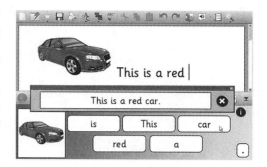

Figure 1.4. Clicker 6 is a grid writing program designed to support literacy activities in the classroom, and is supported by the Learning Grid World Activity Exchange (© Crick Software; used by permission.)

Boardmaker with Speaking Dynamically Pro   One of the most commonly used software programs in inclusive early childhood education classrooms is Boardmaker with Speaking Dynamically Pro (Mayer-Johnson), which allows teachers to create a range of customized visual supports (e.g., activity schedules, task charts, power cards) for young students using Picture Communication Symbols (PCS), including communication boards, picture schedules, and instruction sheets. Activity exchanges are also available (e.g., Boardmaker Share; see Figure 1.5), which enable early childhood education professionals to download activities created by other teachers (see Appendix 1.A).

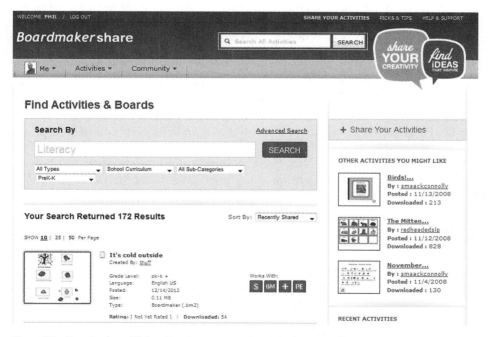

Figure 1.5.   Boardmaker with Speaking Dynamically Pro is widely used in today's education settings to create visual and communication supports for young children. It is complemented by readymade activities at the Boardmaker Share site (http://www.boardmakershare.com/default.aspx.) (The Picture Communication Symbols ©1981–2013 by DynaVox Mayer-Johnson LLC. All Rights Reserved Worldwide; used by permission.)

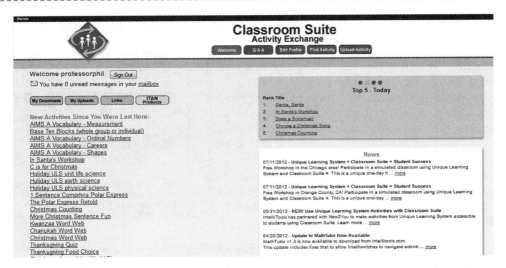

Figure 1.6. The IntelliTools Classroom Suite Activity Exchange site provides access to a large number of free and engaging activities created using the Classroom Suite 4 software (http://aex.intellitools.com.) (Used by permission of Cambium Learning Technologies.)

IntelliTools Classroom Suite IntelliTools Classroom Suite 4 (Cambium Learning) is a research-based, flexible, dynamic authoring software package. It includes activity templates that can be immediately used or customized to provide engaging planned activities related to reading, writing, and other skills using explicit direct instruction, constructive practice, and embedded assessments. The IntelliTools Classroom Suite Activity Exchange (see Figure 1.6) is also available for early childhood education professionals to download ready-made activities (see Appendix 1.A).

Once a computer with Internet access is in place in the classroom, other technologies become readily available to teachers, including free or inexpensive web tools and accessible web site resources and activities. Locally available technologies may be acquired from stores and used as part of a system to develop and deliver learning activities.

For example, Mrs. Hearns has become familiar with using Microsoft PowerPoint to develop classroom learning activities. The software is installed on her classroom computer, and its animation and emphasis features allow her to create engaging slides with many of the same characteristics as interactive web activities. She uses VoiceThread, a free web tool that allows children to record audio, video, and text to comment on materials that she has uploaded for the learning activities.

Mr. Bivens routinely downloads teacher-made activities from the SMART Activity Exchange, which can be used on his SMART Board. He can preview these activities in advance because he downloaded the free SMART Notebook software, which helps him to decide which activities will be most appealing to his kindergarten students. Mr. Bivens adds digital photos of his students and images of previous activities to enhance the SMART activity. He also uses a number of links to various technologies that are part of a UDL toolkit (see Figure 1.7).

Figure 1.7. Free universal design for learning literacy technology. (From http://udltechtoolkit.wikispaces.com. Licensed under a Creative Commons Attribution Share-Alike 3.0 License; http://creativecommons.org/licenses/by-sa/3.0/)

Ms. Steele went to her local Walmart and purchased a LeapFrog Tag reading system book for use in her literacy center. The book has a pen that, when touched to the text, activates a voice that reads the words to the students. She designs a Clicker 6 activity that focuses on comprehension questions associated with the Tag book. The children view the Clicker 6 activity on a SMART Board, which allows them to physically interact with the screen and make selections. She also routinely accesses a comprehensive free resource called *Exploring New Territories* (Florida Department of Education, 2010) to explore links to web sites with technologies that support young children both with and without disabilities.

In each of these instances, teachers used core classroom technologies to develop and deliver learning activities. Appendix A includes examples of readily available technologies that apply to the early childhood classroom. However, simply having readily available technologies for use with children is inadequate to ensure their successful integration in the curriculum. A thoughtful process is required to make decisions about the technologies used to support learning, the teaching strategies required, and how children's progress will be assessed. This process will be discussed at length in subsequent chapters.

OUTCOMES OF INTEGRATING TECHNOLOGY IN THE CLASSROOM

Teachers who integrate technology into curricula often observe moments where both anticipated and unexpected outcomes emerge. For example, one teacher who had been provided with an array of technologies to support children's emergent literacy development commented on what both she and her children had experienced (Parette, Stoner, & Watts, 2009, p. 265):

I just think that I strive for, "How can I put it into technology?" So, I'm constantly thinking, what will make this be a bigger picture? Like when they're laughing because they see a groundhog going through a tunnel. We talk about fast and slow or I bring in all the actions. It's real life to them on the computer and the animation that comes through instead of stick figures. I think I just see an increase in their desire to participate in the activities as students.

In this example, the teacher used a digital projector with her classroom computer and was constantly thinking of new ways to use available software and other technology supports to deliver the curriculum. She was particularly interested in the use of these supports in conjunction with research-based instructional strategies, such as direct instruction to teach specific emergent literacy skills.

Similarly, another teacher who worked with a nonverbal preschool student with autism spectrum disorder was troubled that the student could not participate in the curriculum by telling stories in the same way as other students during circle time. He had limited oral language skills coupled with deficits in social interactions. However, the teacher discovered that the child could type using the computer keyboard and a symbol-based software program to tell a story, as discussed in the following quote (Parette, Stoner, et al., 2009, p. 266):

Well, we had just talked to parents and asked if they heard him speak more than one word because we weren't hearing it. He came over to tell me a story and usually he doesn't, but he came this day. I was modeling for him, "Tell me what you really like." And I couldn't get anything out of him and I was typing and it was showing on the big screen and he was watching and then I typed, "I love..." and just waited. He reached for the keyboard and he typed d–i–n–o–s–r. Yes! The previous student's story had a picture, you know the picture popped up of a dinosaur and he saw that on the screen. So I went back and respelled it so the picture would come up and that was quite a moment with that child and then he read, he read, "I love dinosaurs." And he is hyperlexic but usually he just writes, he's not verbal.

Such experiences in which teachers try things in different ways using technology and the resulting outcomes support the importance of understanding what is required to use various technologies, as well as developing a level of comfort and expertise in using them effectively with children.

Blum, Parette, and Watts (2009) reported on a group comparison study that examined phonological awareness outcomes of a curriculum using direct instruction embedded in Microsoft PowerPoint and delivered using a digital projection system. Results were reported from an early childhood center of 55 preschool children who were at risk of disability. Findings indicated that students receiving the PowerPoint-based curriculum doubled their initial sound fluency progress over the comparison group (moderate effect size with Cohen's $f = .28$). Findings for alliteration and rhyming were inconclusive.

SUMMARY

Because young children have many experiences with and preferences for technologies prior to coming to any early childhood setting, the use of technology in classroom activities must be considered an important facet of DAP. Cultural influences, generational differences, classroom budget limitations, attitudes about technology, and teachers' lack of knowledge and/or training potentially present barriers to acceptance of technology in today's classrooms. Many of these technologies are, by design, instructional and result in increased instructional effectiveness, efficiency, and appeal. The real challenge in today's classrooms is how to use UDL principles with IT to provide multiple means of engagement, action and expression, and representation.

ADDITIONAL READINGS

Blanchard, J., & Moore, T. (2010). *The digital world of young children: Impact on emergent literacy.* New York, NY: Pearson Foundation. Retrieved September 22, 2012, from http://www.pearsonfoundation.org/downloads/EmergentLiteracy -WhitePaper.pdf

Burdett, C. (2010). Technology and literacy in early childhood educational settings: A review of research. *Journal of Early Childhood Literacy, 10,* 247–270.

Glaubke, C. (2007). *The effects of interactive media and preschoolers' learning: A review of the research and recommendations for the future.* Oakland, CA: Children Now. Retrieved January 4, 2013, from http://www.childrennow.org/uploads/ documents/prek_interactive_learning_2007.pdf

Li, X., Atkins, M., & Stanton, B. (2006). Effects of home and school computer use on school readiness and cognitive development among Head Start children: A randomized controlled pilot trial. *Merrill-Palmer Quarterly, 52,* 239–263.

McLuhan, M. (1964). *Understanding media: The extensions of man.* New York, NY: New American Library.

Papert, S. (1980). *Mindstorms: Children, computers and powerful ideas.* New York, NY: Basic Books.

Rideout, V., Vandewater, E., & Wartella, E. (2003). *Zero to six: Electronic media in the lives of infants, toddlers and preschoolers.* Menlo Park, CA: Kaiser Family Foundation.

REFERENCES

Blum, C., Parette, H.P., & Travers, J. (2011, April). *Future of instructional technology in early childhood special education.* Paper presented at the Council for Exceptional Children Convention and Expo, Washington, DC.

Blum, C., Parette, H.P., & Watts, E.H. (2009). Engaging young children in an emergent literacy curriculum using Microsoft PowerPoint: Development, considerations, and opportunities. In A.M. Vilas, A.S. Martin, J.M. González, & J.A. González (Eds.), *Research, reflections and innovations in integrating ICT in education* (Vol. 1, pp. 41–45). Badajoz, Spain: FORMATEX.

Division for Early Childhood. (2007). *Promoting positive outcomes for children with disabilities: Recommendations for curriculum, assessment, and program evaluation.* Missoula, MT: Author.

Division for Early Childhood & National Association for the Education of Young Children. (2009). *Early childhood inclusion.* Retrieved September 22, 2012, from http://www.naeyc .org/files/naeyc/file/positions/DEC_NAEYC_EC_updatedKS.pdf

Florida Department of Education. (2010). *Exploring new territories.* Retrieved September 22, 2012, from http://www.fdlrs.org/docs/ent2010web.pdf

Gronseth, S., Brush, T., Ottenbreit-Leftwich, A., Strycker, J., Abaci, S., Easterling, W., et al. (2010). Equipping the next generation of teachers: Technology preparation and practice. *Journal of Digital Learning in Teacher Education, 27*(1), 30–36.

Hourcade, J.J., Parette, Jr., H.P., Boeckmann, N.M., & Blum, C. (2010). Handy Manny and the emergent literacy toolkit. *Early Childhood Education Journal, 37,* 483–491.

Howe, N., & Strauss, W. (2000). *Millennials rising. The next great generation.* New York, NY: Vintage Books.

International Society for Technology in Education, Partnership for 21st Century Skills, & State Educational Technology Directors Association. (2009). *Maximizing the impact. The pivotal role of technology in a 21st century education system.* Retrieved September 22, 2012, fromhttp://www.setda.org/c/document_library/get_file?folderId=191&name=P21Book_complete.pdf

Judge, S. (2006). Constructing and assistive technology toolkit for young children: Views from the field. *Journal of Special Education Technology, 21*(4), 17–24.

Karemaker, A., Pitchford, N.J., & O'Malley, C. (2008). Using whole-word multimedia software to support literacy acquisition: A comparison with traditional books. *Educational and Child Psychology, 25,* 97–118.

Keengwe, J., & Onchwari, G. (2009). Technology and early childhood education: A technology integration professional development model for practicing teachers. *Early Childhood Education Journal, 37,* 209–218.

National Association for the Education of Young Children. (1995). *Responding to linguistic and cultural diversity. Recommendations for effective early childhood education.* Retrieved September 22, 2012, from http://www.naeyc.org/files/naeyc/file/positions/PSDIV98.PDF

National Association for the Education of Young Children. (1996). *Technology and young children: Ages 3 through 8. A position statement of the National Association for the Education of Young Children.*

National Association for the Education of Young Children. (2008). *Meaningful technology integration in early learning environments.* Retrieved September 22, 2012, from http://www.naeyc.org/files/yc/file/200809/OnOurMinds.pdf

National Association for the Education of Young Children. (2009). *Developmentally appropriate practice in early childhood programs serving children from birth through age 8. A position statement of the National Association for the Education of Young Children.* Retrieved September 22, 2012, from http://www.naeyc.org/files/naeyc/file/positions/PSDAP.pdf

National Association for the Education of Young Children & Fred Rogers Center for Early Learning and Children's Media. (2012). *Technology and interactive media as tools in early childhood programs serving children from birth through age 8.* Retrieved September 22, 2012, from http://www.naeyc.org/files/naeyc/file/positions/PS_technology_WEB2.pdf

National Institute of Child Health and Human Development. (2000). *Report of the National Reading Panel. Teaching children to read: an evidence-based assessment of the scientific research literature on reading and its implications for reading instruction: Reports of the subgroups.* Washington, DC: U.S. Government Printing Office.

Newby, T.J., Stepich, D.R., Lehman, J.D., & Russell, J.D. (2006). *Instructional technology for teaching and learning: Designing instruction, integrating computers, and using media* (3rd ed.). Upper Saddle River, NJ: Pearson Merrill Prentice Hall.

Parette, H.P. (2011, November). *Readily available technology integration in early childhood education: Lessons learned.* Paper presented at the annual meeting of the Assistive Technology Industry Association, Chicago, IL.

Parette, H.P., & Angelo, D.H. (1998). The impact of assistive technology devices on children and families. In S.L. Judge & H.P. Parette (Eds.), *Assistive technology for young children with disabilities: A guide to providing family-centered services* (pp. 148–183). Cambridge, MA: Brookline.

Parette, H.P., Blum, C., & Watts, E.H. (2009). Use of Microsoft® PowerPoint™ and direct instruction to support emergent literacy skill development among young at risk children. In A.M. Vilas, A.S. Martin, J.M. González, & J.A. González (Eds.), *Research, reflections and innovations in integrating ICT in education* Vol. 2 (pp. 864–868). Badajoz, Spain: FORMATEX

Parette, H.P., Hourcade, J.J., & Blum, C. (2011). Using animation in Microsoft® PowerPoint™ to enhance engagement and learning in young learners with developmental delay. *Teaching Exceptional Children, 48* (4), 58–67.

Parette, H.P., Hourcade, J.J., Boeckmann, N.M., & Blum C. (2008). Using Microsoft® Power-Point™ to support emergent literacy skill development for young children at-risk or who have disabilities. *Early Childhood Education Journal, 36,* 233–239. doi:10.1007/s10643-008-0275-y

Parette, H.P., Hourcade, J.J., Dinelli, J.M., & Boeckmann, N.M. (2009). Using *Clicker 5* to enhance emergent literacy in young learners. *Early Childhood Education Journal, 36,* 355–363.

Parette, H.P., Huer, M.B., & VanBiervliet, A. (2005). Cultural issues and assistive technology. In D.L. Edyburn, K. Higgins, & R. Boone (Eds.), *The handbook of special education technology research and practice* (pp. 81–103). Whitefish Bay, WI: Knowledge by Design.

Parette, P., & McMahan, G.A. (2002). What should we expect of assistive technology? Being sensitive to family goals. *Teaching Exceptional Children, 35*(1), 56–61.

Parette, H.P., Meadan, H., Doubet, S., & Hess, J. (2010). Supporting families of young children with disabilities using technology. *Education and Training in Autism and Developmental Disabilities, 45,* 552–565.

Parette, H.P., Peterson-Karlan, G.R., Wojcik, B.W., & Bardi, N. (2007). Monitor that progress! Interpreting data trends for AT decision-making. *Teaching Exceptional Children, 39*(7), 22–29.

Parette, H.P., Quesenberry, A.C., & Blum, C. (2010). Missing the boat with technology usage in early childhood settings: A 21st century view of developmentally appropriate practice. *Early Childhood Education Journal, 37,* 335–343.

Parette, H.P., & Stoner, J.B. (2008). Benefits of assistive technology user groups for early childhood education professionals. *Early Childhood Education Journal, 35,* 313–319.

Parette, H.P., Stoner, J.B., & Watts, E.H. (2009). Assistive technology user group perspectives of early childhood professionals. *Education and Training in Developmental Disabilities, 44,* 257–270.

Pasnik, S., Strother, S., Schindel, J., Penuel, W.R., & Llorente, C. (2007). *Review of research on media and young children's literacy.* Retrieved September 22, 2012, from http://cct.edc.org/rtl/pdf/RTLLiteratureReview.pdf

Penuel, W.R., Pasnik, S., Bates, L., Townsend, E., Gallagher, L.P., Llorente, C., et al. (2009). *Summative evaluation of the Ready to Learn initiative.* Newton, MA: Educational Development Center.

Peurling, B. (2012). *Teaching in the digital age: SMART tools for age 3 to grade 3.* St. Paul, MN: Redleaf Press.

Rose, D.H., & Meyer, A. (Eds.). (2006). *A practical reader in universal design for learning.* Cambridge, MA: Harvard University Press.

Schomberg, R., & Donohue, C. (2012, May 9). *Teaching with technology: Guidance from the NAEYC and Fred Rogers Center joint position statement.* Retrieved September 22, 2012, from http://www.earlychildhoodwebinars.org/presentations/teaching-with-technology-guidance-from-the-naeycfrc-position-statement/

Appendix 1.A Readily available resources for the early childhood education classroom

Category	URL	Description
Downloadable software		
Tux Paint	http://tuxpaint.org	An open source, easy-to-use drawing program designed for young children. It has sound effects and a cartoon guide to offer support as children use the program
ZAC Browser	http://www.zacbrowser.com/	Browser designed for the PC and specifically for children with autism spectrum disorders. Appropriate for all children
SMART Notebook Express	http://smarttech.com/us/Support/Browse+Support/Download+Software/Software/SMART+Notebook+Express/SMART+Notebook+Express/SMART+Notebook+Express	Software enables education professionals to open, edit, save and share SMART notebook files
Best Freeware Download	http://www.bestfreewaredownload.com/categories/download-education-kids-freeware-6-71-0-d.html	Provides links to free software to support varying aspects of the curriculum
Educational Freeware	http://www.educational-freeware.com/freeware/category-Toddlers.aspx	Presents a comprehensive listing of free, downloadable, Windows-compatible learning games designed for young children
Free Download Manager	http://www.freedownloadmanager.org/downloads/preschool_software/	Archive for a variety of art-related shareware programs
File Buzz Download	http://www.filebuzz.com/files/Preschool_Education/1.html	Site providing 60 downloadable low-cost programs that have relevance to activities in the preschool curriculum
Best Software Downloads	http://www.bestsoftware4download.com/s-faycfmse-preschool-software-25-d.html	Both freeware and shareware (ranging in price from $9.95–$19.95)
Downloadable activities		
Spectronics Activity Exchange	http://www.spectronicsinoz.com/activities	Collection of activities designed for use with a number of popular software programs, including Clicker 6, IntelliTools Classroom Suite, Boardmaker with Speaking Dynamically Pro, and the Communicate series
SMART Activity Exchange	http://exchange.smarttech.com/#tab=0	Resource for downloadable teacher-made SMART Board activities
Classroom Suite Activity Exchange	http://aex.intellitools.com/	Contains downloadable teacher-made activities designed specifically for use with the IntelliTools Classroom Suite
Boardmaker Share	http://www.boardmakershare.com	Resource site containing thousands of teacher-made Boardmaker activities searchable by activity area and grade level
Learning Grids World	https://www.learninggrids.com/us/WelcomePage.aspx	Free teacher-made activities designed for WriteOnline, Clicker 6, and ClosePro (Crick Software products)

Resource	URL	Description
Talking Book Library	http://www.talkingbooklibrary.net/Matrix.htm	Site containing primary-level talking books created both by teachers and students, which can be saved and modified
Accessible Books	http://www.setbc.org/setbc/accessiblebooks/freebooks foryou.html	The site presents a compilation of both teacher- and student-made PowerPoint Talking Books. Microsoft Word, Clicker 6, and IntelliTools books are also represented
Web-accessible learning activities and games		
Disney Junior	http://disney.go.com/disneyjunior	A Disney web site presenting animated and interactive games, music stories, and activities related to Disney characters such as Handy Manny and his friends; useful to support beginning reading skill development
Sesame Street	http://www.sesamestreet.org/home	Web site presenting high quality animated and interactive games, videos, and other supports for developing emergent literacy skills
Starfall	http://www.starfall.com	Web site presenting an array of animated and interactive activities designed to develop phonemic awareness; printable worksheets
Dove Whisper	http://dovewhisper.com	Curricula support links both within a computer center (math, science, literacy, and themes) and favorite links (science, math, social studies, language arts, reading, generic) pages
PBS Kids	http://pbskids.org	Site containing activities, games, and literacy supports related to Sesame Street, Curious George, Clifford the Big Red Dog, and other children's shows
VoiceThread	http://voicethread.com	A free online resource allowing teachers and students to create multimedia slide shows having images, text, audio, and video. Students can comment on the content using text, audio, and video, and work can be shared with others
Nick Jr.	http://nickjr.com	A free online resource for teachers or parents, providing activities connected to popular Nickelodeon television shows (e.g., *Dora the Explorer*). Includes parenting tips that pop up on the web site
Up to Ten	http://www.uptoten.com	This site provides access to multimedia activities, games, and stories, some of which are appropriate for preschool and kindergarten students, as well as apps for the iPad and iPhone

(continued)

23

Appendix 1.A *(continued)*

Category	URL	Description
Printable worksheets		
Education.com	http://www.education.com/worksheets/preschool	Printable preschool worksheets covering a wide range of subjects
tlsbooks.com	http://www.tlsbooks.com/	Free worksheets organized by grade level and content area
Kids Learning Station	http://www.kidslearningstation.com	Free printable worksheets, especially for writing printable games are available, as well as links to other sites that have free printable worksheets
Comprehensive resource documents		
Exploring New Territories	http://www.fdlrs.org/docs/ent2010web.pdf	Compiled by the Florida Instructional Technology Training Resource Unit, this resource book contains a wealth of resources by content area to support children's participation in the curriculum
EZ AT 2	http://www.pacer.org/stc/pubs/EZ-AT-book-2011-final.pdf	Resource document regarding simple assistive technologies used with children from birth to 3 years old
Free technology toolkit for universal design for learning in all classrooms	http://udltechtoolkit.wikispaces.com/	This wiki has links to technologies designed to support writing, literacy, study skills, and math. Other pages provide links to audio book sites, research tools, graphic organizers, multimedia and digital storytelling tools, text-to-speech, collaborative tools, universal design for learning, and additional tools
Off-the-shelf products		
LeapPad Learning System	http://shop.leapfrog.com/leapfrog/index.jsp	An array of curricula support toys designed to support literacy; found in many stores
iPad Touch	http://www.apple.com/ipad/	iPad is the first tablet computer developed by Apple Inc. and is part of a device category between a smartphone and a laptop computer
iPod	http://www.apple.com/ipod/	This palm-sized electronic device was primarily created to play music, although it can serve as a backup device, a basic organizer, and an alarm clock
iPhone	http://www.apple.com/iphone/	An Internet-enabled smartphone that combines features of a mobile phone, wireless Internet device, and iPod into one device
VTech	http://www.vtechkids.com/	An array of curricula support toys designed to support literacy; found in many stores. Vtech tablets are more durable than typical tablet computers

Widely available programs

Microsoft PowerPoint	http://office.microsoft.com/en-gb/powerpoint/	Presentation software having an array of features to enhance the delivery of content, including animation
Microsoft Word	http://office.microsoft.com/en-us/word/	Word processing program having numerous features enabling manipulation of text and contrast, embedding sounds and web links, and other features to support delivery of curricula

Mobile applications

Best Apps for Kids	http://bestappsforkids.com/category/apps-for-education/early-learning-apps/	An array of free apps, selected by parents, that hold potential for facilitating learning
APPitic	http://appitic.com/	Compilation of more than 1,300 apps that have been vetted by Apple Distinguished Educators; categorized by preschool, special education, themes, multiple intelligences, Bloom's Taxonomy, and National Education Technology Standards
Moms with Apps	http://momswithapps.com/	A collaborative group of family-friendly developers seeking to promote quality apps for kids and families. Links to a wide array of apps are provided
Touch Screen Preschool Games	http://www.touchscreenpreschoolgames.com/games	Provides links to a compilation of apps for the iPhone, iPod, and iPod Touch
SNApps4kids	http://snapps4kids.com/	Categorized listing of apps designed for use with children having disabilities
Apps in Education	http://appsineducation.blogspot.com/2011/12/more-kindergarten-ipad-resources.html	Blog providing apps and web site links to supports for both preschool and kindergarten children
Free and Low-Cost Preschool/Kindergarten Apps for iPad Instruction and Curriculum Integration	http://www.danking.net/iPad/docs/Free%20and%20Low%20Cost%20PreK%20and%20Kindergarten%20Apps%20for%20iPad%20Master%20List%205-25%282%29.pdf	Listing of iPad resources and iPad communities having links and other resources
Apps 4 Children with Special Needs	http://www.livebinders.com/play/present?id=170107	Variety of resources related to apps for children with disabilities
SpedApps2	http://spedapps2.wikispaces.com/	Wiki site maintained by therapists with recommendations regarding apps used with children with disabilities for communication and language, reading, writing, math, science/social studies, art/creativity, music, motor, and cortical vision impairments

(continued)

Appendix 1.A *(continued)*

Category	URL	Description
Apps4Stages	http://apps4stages.wikispaces.com/	Wiki site dedicated to stages of child characteristics and recommendations for features to consider in computer software for learning, along with teaching strategies that match and scaffold student need
TCEA-Recommended iPod Apps	https://docs.google.com/spreadsheet/ccc?key=0At6rnmB5cDEPdDFkcmhoTUpQNUZzMlZMNXc3SEvyRmc#gid=0	Google document created by the Texas Computer Education Association containing recommended e-book apps

Instructional materials development

Category	URL	Description
Kerpoof	http://www.kerpoof.com/#	Provides an array of tools enabling young children spell pictures; make movies, cards, drawings, and pictures; and tell stories. All products are printable
Story Bird	http://storybird.com/	Enables children to create high-quality books, play them like games and send them as cards
Bubblejoy	http://www.bubblejoy.com/create.php	The application allows children to create a video greeting card using their own videos; they can choose from different card designs that will support a curriculum topic
Moshi Monster	http://www.moshimonsters.com/	Young children can adapt their own monsters, give them a name, and design their color schemes. The monster makes new friends, chats with others, plays games, and develops its own personality through its growth
Shidonni	http://www2.shidonni.com/v2/LandingPage.aspx	Children can create their own animals and watch them come to life, providing opportunities for discussion or show-and-tell activities
Volki	http://www.voki.com/	Children can create animated and speaking avatars using their voices or using a text-to speech application. They can fully customize their characters, which move their heads and eyes with the movement of the mouse
Talking Pets	http://www.talkingpets.org/	Similar to Voki, the characters on this site are limited to animals and the child can use the text-to-speech application (e.g., children might be surprised by making a cat talk and hearing the cat ask questions to them)
Fotobabble	http://www.fotobabble.com/	This site presents a way to make photos talk. The child uploads pictures, records his or her voice, and publishes it—providing a way to motivate children to speak

Resource sites		
National Association for the Education of Young Children (NAEYC) Technology and Young Children Interest Forum	http://www.techandyoungchildren.org/	Links and resources for technology applications provided by members of NAEYC
Tots 'n Tech	http://tnt.asu.edu/	This web site, maintained by a federally funded project, provides links to resource sites, low-tech solutions for infants and toddlers, resource briefs on assistive technology, and other supports
ELE: Fred Rogers Center Early Learning Environment	http://ele.fredrogerscenter.org/	Library and "playroom" with an online community that has professional development activities for educators of young children up to 5 years; includes high-quality resources for parents and teachers; video, multimedia, and interactive resources
Other common technologies		
Clicker 6	http://www.cricksoft.com/uk/products/tools/clicker/home.aspx	Authoring software providing reading and writing supports
IntelliTools Classroom Suite	http://store.cambiumlearning.com	Authoring software providing reading, writing, and math supports; contains embedded assessments to monitor progress
Boardmaker Plus	http://www.mayer-johnson.com/boardmaker-plus-v-6/	Software used to create visual strategies, including communication boards
Assistive technology		
Family Center on Technology and Disability	http://www.fctd.info/	Comprehensive technology site providing information and resources to families and service providers. Links to fact sheets, PowerPoint presentations, resource guides, member organizations, and reviews of instructional and assistive technologies
Assistivetech.net	http://assistivetech.net/webresources/stateTechActProjects.php	Provides links to State Tech Act projects that may have equipment loan programs and other classroom supports

(continued)

27

Appendix 1.A *(continued)*

Category	URL	Description
Universal design for learning		
OS X Accessibility Features	http://www.apple.com/accessibility/macosx/vision .html	Description of various accessibility features on the Apple OS X including voiceover, screen magnification, cursor magnification, high contrast and reverse video, Safari reader, finder views, view options, dock magnification, talking alerts, talking calculator, talking clock, converting text to speech, and cascading style sheets
Windows Accessibility	http://windows.microsoft.com/en-us/windows/help/ accessibility	Description of various accessibility features on the Windows operating system, including display and readability, sounds and speech, and keyboard and mouse options
Accessibility in Windows 7	http://www.microsoft.com/windows/windows-7/ features/accessibility.aspx	Description of accessibility features on Windows 7, including speech, magnifier, on-screen keyboard, narrator, and visual notifications
Subtitling Add-In for Microsoft PowerPoint	http://sourceforge.net/projects/stamp-addin/	Adds closed captioning to a PowerPoint presentation in embedded videos (Windows)
Text-to-speech for Microsoft Office 2010	http://office.microsoft.com/en-us/onenote-help/ using-the-speak-text-to-speech-feature -HA102066711.aspx#_Toc282684835	Allows highlighted text to be read by the built-in computer voice when displayed on the screen. Compatible with Word 2010, Outlook 2010, PowerPoint 2010, and OneNote 2010
Read Please	http://www.readplease.com/english/readplease.php	Free online reader allowing digital text to be read to a child; has adjustable voice speed and low-vision color option
Mozilla Firefox add-ins	https://addons.mozilla.org/en-US/firefox/	Provides an array of Mozilla Firefox add-ins to make the Internet more accessible
Digital text		
Project Gutenberg	http://www.gutenberg.org/catalog/	Archive for thousands of books available in digital format
Bookshare	http://www.bookshare.org/	Free site providing access to digital books for children with disabilities

28

2

Integrating Technology in Early Childhood Classrooms

Howard P. Parette, Jr., George R. Peterson-Karlan, and Craig Blum

After reading this chapter, you should be able to

- Describe the role of curriculum modifications and adaptations
- Define embedded learning opportunities and understand their relationship to the curriculum
- Identify key activities in which technologies can be used across preschool and kindergarten settings
- Discuss elements of a technology integration framework

PLANNING AND IMPLEMENTING TECHNOLOGY-SUPPORTED INSTRUCTION

Early childhood classrooms vary markedly across the country. However, certain characteristics distinguish developmentally appropriate programs that integrate technology into their curricula. Such programs include technology-supported learning experiences and activities that are high quality, have curriculum modifications and adaptations, include embedded learning opportunities, and use explicit, child-focused instructional strategies (Sandall & Schwartz, 2008). In creating a developmentally appropriate, technology-supported learning environment, teachers assume roles as primary decision makers and problem solvers. They are the day-to-day designers and implementers of planned learning activities for all children, as well as the primary problem solvers and assessors of children's performance. These roles are particularly important in the process of thoughtfully integrating technology into the early childhood classroom.

Curriculum Modifications and Adaptations

Given that all young children should benefit from educational experiences provided in today's inclusive classrooms, early childhood teachers must sometimes plan and deliver activities in different ways to meet the diverse learning needs of children. Modifications and adaptations can be used to enhance participation for all young children. When using universal design for learning (UDL; see Chapter 1) as a framework for creating and delivering classroom learning experiences, the needs of all young children are considered in developing instruction that is supported by technology. However, even when UDL principles are considered, there may be additional curriculum modifications or technology additions that are sometimes warranted to support a particular child.

Sandall and Schwartz (2008, p. 14) defined curriculum modifications as a "change made to the ongoing classroom activity or materials in order to achieve or maximize the child's participation." These modifications are planned and may include making alterations to the physical, social, temporal environment; simplifying an activity; building on a child's preferences; providing adult or peer support; and/or adapting materials in a way that increases or enhances participation for a child. When children are more actively engaged with an activity or in interactions with peers and adults, they tend to develop and learn at a faster pace. Consider the following examples.

At the start of circle time, Choo has difficulty remembering which carpet square is his. Mrs. Hearns has taken a digital picture of Choo and attached it to his carpet square to provide a visual cue to help him select the proper square. Katie has trouble remembering the sequence of activities in the morning. She carries a laminated activity schedule containing Boardmaker symbols paired with text to help her remember the sequence of activities. Tyrone enjoys his scheduled activities in Mr. Bivens's kindergarten classroom but often forgets to do certain things in preparation for snack time. Before the class is prompted to get ready for snack time, Mr. Bivens gives Tyrone an iPad that presents a video illustrating the steps for getting ready for the activity.

In each of these instances, children have been provided with technology supports that help them complete tasks in classroom activities. This support ensures their participation in certain elements of the early childhood curriculum.

Embedded Learning Opportunities

In any early childhood classroom where both UDL principles and developmentally appropriate practices are applied, daily schedules and routines will allow for a mix of both unstructured child-directed activities and more structured teacher-directed activities. Allowing for both structured and unstructured activities supports more effective implementation of the curriculum while also supporting young children's learning. In large-group and small-group activities, embedded learning opportunities (Sandall & Schwartz, 2008) can ensure that curriculum standards and goals are addressed. Such opportunities can be supported by technology so that objectives from any particular child's individual service plan are effectively addressed.

In modern classrooms, a technology-supported embedded learning opportunity is created when a specific activity or part of an activity is used to teach a specific individualized education program (IEP) goal or objective using planned, systematic instructional procedures supported by relevant instructional technology. In a typical inclusive early childhood classroom, planned learning opportunities are interspersed, or embedded, throughout daily activities. Embedding provides young children with opportunities to practice individual service plan goals and objectives that are included within an activity or classroom event. Embedding "expands, modifies, or adapts the activity/event while remaining meaningful and interesting to children" (Bricker, Pretti-Frontczak, & McComas, 1998, p. 13). The following examples demonstrate the use of embedding.

Roberta goes to the literacy center with her typically developing peers who know they must select a printed book to read. Rather than selecting a book, Roberta is given an iPad by her teacher, Mr. Bivens. She clicks on an inexpensive app, Read Me Stories, and chooses from among eight stories that present colorful pictures paired with text that is read in a child's voice. Because Roberta's service plan has a goal to increase her sight word vocabulary, Mr. Bivens sits beside her as she progresses through each screen of her selected story and points to targeted sight words on the screen. Mr. Bivens pronounces a word and then asks Roberta to say the word as it is repeatedly presented across screens. This activity is helpful for Roberta because she is just developing word recognition skills.

Colin sits on the classroom floor with his peers as Mrs. Hearns opens circle time with a PowerPoint calendar activity. Mrs. Hearns has designed a calendar slide that shows the days of the week in a grid, applying an animation feature to each day so that it will ripple when she clicks her mouse. As the activity unfolds, the students are asked to identify the day of the week that their class is in session. When the appropriate day is identified, Mrs. Hearns clicks her mouse, the word ripples, and she verbally reinforces the children's response. Then she asks students to name family or community events and activities that take place on that day of the week. As she listens to their responses, she writes each word down on her whiteboard.

Because Colin has a service plan objective that addresses beginning sound recognition and Mrs. Hearns knows what his target beginning sounds are for the week, she pauses when certain words are called out that begin with targeted instructional beginning sounds relevant to Colin. She says, "Colin, listen to the word, and tell me what the beginning sound is." She pronounces the word, and then waits for a response. If he hesitates, she draws a line under the word and says "Ball begins with /b/. Say /b/." She then orally reinforces his response and continues with the lesson.

Because embedding is both systematic and individualized, it has been shown to be effective for both typically developing children and those with special needs in early childhood settings. The fact that embedded activities enable teachers to follow children's interests and preferences is particularly important. It also allows teachers to present multiple and varied practice opportunities to children in the classroom. Finally, the use of embedded learning ensures timely and logical feedback regarding children's performance (Grisham-Brown, Pretti-Frontczak, Hawkins, & Winchell, 2009).

Technologies should always be an important consideration in the structure and presentation of embedded activities for all children. Young children now develop in a culture of technology in which digital approaches can engage their interests and attention. For other young children with disabilities, technology is a way to support and scaffold their success in engaging in developmentally appropriate activities.

For example, Mrs. Hearns greets the children in her classroom enthusiastically as they seat themselves on their carpet squares for the morning circle time activity. She wants to apply new strategies that she recently learned in a user group that she attended in which several teachers shared their technology experiences and learning. The children, though giggling and touching one another while making this transition, have their attention focused on the interactive whiteboard. Music is playing as a Handy Manny story (http://tv.disney.go.com/playhouse/handymanny/stories/index.html) is awaiting their engagement and participation. The story begins with vivid screen presentations of the characters, and text appears at the bottom of the screen. As the text is spoken, words are highlighted from left to right. After several screen presentations, the narrator challenges the students to make a choice about what happens next in the story by selecting from various options. Mrs. Hearns calls upon students to come forward and make a selection on the whiteboard. When the students are asked to arrange four fishing poles in order by height during the Handy Manny story, Mrs. Hearns asks the class which pole should come next and reinforces their correct responses.

Chanda, a child with physical disabilities who uses a wheelchair, is unable to make a prediction, but one of her IEP goals is to identify common objects and curriculum materials. Because Handy Manny and his friends are frequently used in her curriculum, Mrs. Hearns integrates direct instruction with Chanda during the large-group activity in which the children identify several characters. She says, "Chanda, who is this on the screen?" while pointing to Handy Manny. Chanda has a four-message communication device with pictures of the four characters on the screen. Mrs. Hearns waits for a response; when none is forthcoming, she points to the correct picture on Chanda's communication device. Chanda presses that button, prompting a prerecorded message, "That's Handy Manny!" She continues moving through the story with the class, affording students opportunities to interact with the interactive whiteboard while posing individual questions to Chanda. Prompts and reinforcement are routinely provided to include her in the large-group activity while addressing her service plan goal.

Contemporary early childhood classrooms are also increasingly blended, meaning that early childhood education professionals must identify children who require intensive instruction, as well as make decisions about connecting individual children's needs with particular learning standards (Grisham-Brown, Hemmeter, & Pretti-Frontczak, 2005). This is accomplished using specific, child-focused instructional strategies and assistive technology that help children who need more intensive levels of support and instruction to develop the skills needed to take advantage of embedded learning opportunities. Specific instructional strategies used when integrating technology in early childhood classrooms are described in Chapter 3; assistive technology is specifically addressed in Chapter 5 and subsequent chapters.

THE IMPORTANCE OF PLANNED
ACTIVITIES ACROSS INSTRUCTIONAL SETTINGS

In this book, a distinction is made between activity areas, routine activities, and planned activities. Activity areas represent all the typical events or blocks of time that occur in a day in the curriculum. For example, arrival at the preschool program is the first activity area, which may then be followed by circle time, choice time, snack time, small group, outdoor play, lunch, and departure. At the kindergarten level, there may be an arrival routine, followed by morning circle/attendance, reading/literacy, writing/language arts, math, lunch, recess, art/music, social studies/science, and a dismissal routine.

In some activity areas, children engage in routine activities that may or may not be connected to the curriculum and specific learning objectives. For example, children arrive at school and put their things away, wash their hands and engage in toileting, participate in snack and lunchtime activities, engage in free play that may involve choices regarding play manipulatives and materials, and transition out of the program or school at the end of the day. When used in a developmentally appropriate way, technology can be of great benefit to children's learning in planned activities in many activity areas (Clements & Sarama, 2003).

Within each of these activity areas, opportunities for child participation and use of instructional technology include the whole class (i.e., large group), partial class (i.e., small group), and individual instructional arrangements. In each of these areas, a child will be participating at differing levels of interaction with adults and peers. Opportunities for embedded activities and the use of technology for the delivery of instruction exist at each level. For example, some activities such as arrival, circle time, meal time (snack or lunch), and departure may lend themselves to the use of a computer and digital projection system or interactive whiteboard in which software or web-based activities are presented to an entire class. During arrival, a teacher could have the students go to the whiteboard to mark their lunch preference, which is then emailed to the office once everyone has checked in for the day. Other activities, such as a literacy center (small group) or choice time (where children choose from available exploratory activities and materials), may be best presented in a small-group setting. For example, if there is only one computer in the classroom, a group of three to four students might sit with the teacher and interact with a Starfall.com or Sesame Street literacy activity. Similarly, if the teacher uses a handheld technology (e.g., iPad, IntelliKeys® keyboard) that enables an individual child to make selections and interact with others, it might be more appropriate for use in a smaller group so that all children can use the technology and observe others using it—an outcome that might not be possible in a large-group setting. During choice time, bookmarked web sites with games, ready-made activities, and iPad apps could be potential technology supports.

Because individual appropriateness is a component of DAP (Kostelnik, Soderman, & Whiren, 2011), consideration must also be given to instructional technologies that complement the learning experiences, characteristics, and preferences of each child. For example, some children may need simple iPad apps that require a single tap of the finger to control what happens on each screen, whereas other children who may be more proficient or familiar with the features of apps can be presented with more complex activities that require multiple selections to be made on any given screen. Children who may be distracted by too much visual or auditory information may prefer simple web-based activities with minimal stimuli present.

Of particular importance, however, are those activity areas in which planned activities with specific learning outcomes occur. From this point forward, the focus will be on such planned activities for small and large groups of children and the role of instructional technology in the classrooms. Although the importance of discovery and incidental learning, child-directed learning, or other developmentally appropriate experiences are noted, the following section will focus on planned instructional activities for groups of children as compared with individual instruction.

ORGANIZATION OF PLANNED ACTIVITIES

The nature of instructional settings affects how technology is integrated into early childhood education programs. All classrooms serving young children provide instruction using a combination of four different organizational approaches: whole class, learning centers, small group, and one-to-one instruction. Whole class activity areas in which all children are involved include opening circle, snack time, lunch, recess, and closing circle. Smaller groups of children participate in learning centers, which may either be theme-based (e.g., dinosaurs, community helpers), subject-based (e.g., literacy/language, math, social studies), or activity-based (e.g., blocks, water play, manipulatives; Morrison, 2010). Teachers also guide learning or engage in direct instruction (e.g., discussion of theme topics, teaching concepts, special art projects) with small groups of children. Finally, individualized instruction may be provided within activity areas for those children who require more intensive instruction or remediation (Wortham, 2012).

In each of the activity areas, there are generally behaviors or tasks that are expected of young children (see Figure 2.1). For example, arrival may require children to follow a routine such as putting personal articles of clothing in a bin of their own, placing a checkmark by their names on a whiteboard or attendance chart, and taking items from their backpacks to the teacher or to their desks. In circle time, young children must select carpet squares, follow instructions, sing a song, answer questions posed by the teacher, point to pictures to demonstrate understanding of stories, and talk about their home experiences. During choice time, children may select picture books from a shelf, read the books, and complete worksheets regarding the story.

In all activity areas, children are expected to do some unplanned tasks that are not directly connected to the curriculum, such as helping others, reporting needs for assistance from the teacher, calling attention to a spill using art materials, or expressing classroom distress requiring intervention. Other tasks, however, are addressed in planning by the teacher, and it is through those planned activities that most learning takes place. Table 2.1 presents activity areas found in both preschool and kindergarten programs.

On examining the diverse array of activity areas in Table 2.1 and considering the number of tasks expected from children, the question then arises as to how technologies—particularly those that are readily available—can be used to develop planned activities throughout the day. To do this, educators can follow a three-phase framework for technology integration presented in Figure 2.2: EXPECT IT-PLAN IT-TEACH IT. This framework is based on best practices in the field of early childhood education and current understanding of curriculum standards, instructional practices with young children, UDL principles, assessment strategies used to document instructional effectiveness, and an understanding of the emerging role of technology in today's classroom settings. The framework has

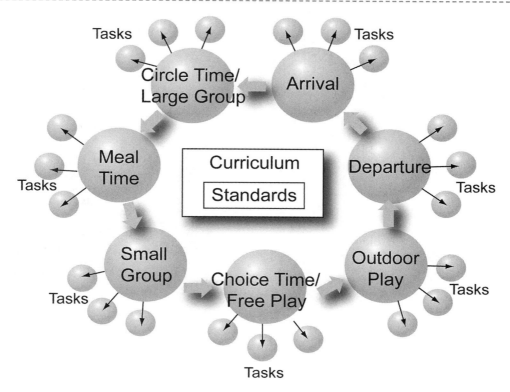

Figure 2.1. Relationship of standards to the curriculum, classroom activities, and embedded tasks. (© 2013 H.P. Parette, G.R. Peterson-Karlan, & C. Blum.)

been tested in preservice coursework designed specifically for early childhood education majors, with successful outcomes identified (Blum & Parette, 2011; Parette, 2011).

 EXPECT IT: Connecting to Standards and Learning Objectives

Before any instructional activity can even be considered, a connection must be made with the learning standards associated with a curriculum (Blum & Parette, 2011; Smaldino, Lowther, & Russell, 2012). Standards are designed to address what children are expected to know and do, and they provide roadmaps for early childhood education professionals to ensure children's participation in the early childhood curriculum (Kostelnik et al., 2011). Curriculum standards and their related learning objectives (often called benchmarks or indicators) provide the starting point for integrating technology into classroom instructional activities (Copple & Bredekamp, 2009; Division for Early Childhood, 2007; Sandall, Hemmeter, Smith, & McLean, 2005).

Many opportunities to address learning standards are present in typical early childhood education classrooms. Although learning standards are typically printed in published curricula used by early childhood programs, they are also accessible on web sites maintained by states' departments of education. Teachers must understand these standards and the associated learning objectives in the

Table 2.1. Preschool and kindergarten activity areas and typical planned activity tasks.

Activity area	Typical planned activity tasks			
	Prereading	Writing	Social behavior and communication	Play
Preschool				
Arrival	Identifying where to hang up coats or personal items in cubby or hook by picture or name Making snack and/or drink choices using pictures or words Coloring at seat (writing)	Sign-in on the attendance sheet using a pencil/marker/crayon or name stamp	Greeting teachers and/or peers by name as they enter the classroom	Identifying and interacting with toys, activities, or classroom centers as other children arrive
Circle time/large group	Singing songs (phonemes that rhyme; alphabet awareness) Listening to stories Participating in calendar tasks (reading words, dates, symbols, pictures) Participating in group discussions (interactive discussion about stories)	Write name (scribble, mock letters, or actual letter (s) in name) on artwork Write name (scribble, mock letters, or actual letter(s) in name on label) for locker/cubbie	Selecting who they sit by to encourage peer interactions Playing games and singing songs that encourage peer interactions Selecting a friend to play with during choice time Deciding (with a friend) where to play first Following directions given by the teacher Actively participating in cooperative activities	

Choice time/free play	Creating art (writing, name writing) Looking at/reading books (left to right orientation, awareness of plot, themes) Listening to stories Engaging in dramatic play (expression of characters and plot elements, language development) Constructing projects (e.g., diorama of story) Writing	Write a grocery list (scribble, mock letters, or actual letters) on a note pad in the kitchen play area Draw with markers and colored pencils in the writing center Use stencils for tracing In the block area write an order for construction of a building	Sharing materials and toys Turn-taking on computer and when playing games Problem solving Resolving conflicts Complimenting Being helpful	Making choices about play items Observing play of others Initiating activities with peers Dressing up Stacking blocks Playing at water table Manipulating cars/trucks Putting together puzzles Moulding Play-Doh Using art materials to create products (e.g., drawing, painting) Writing with pencil and crayons
Snack time			Working with others to pass out napkins and snack/mealtime materials to others Passing food and drinks to one another Using social etiquette (e.g., saying "please" and "thank you") Participating in teacher-initiated discussions	
Small group	Listening to stories Participating in flannel story boards Engaging in science experiments (following visual steps) Cooking (following visual steps)	Sign-up on sheet for computer use Write or draw an individual page for a class book using mock words and sign name Trace numbers given a model Create a birthday, holiday or thank you card for family member or friends	Taking turns using play equipment Using equipment cooperatively (i.e., wagons, balls, long jump rope)	Matching and instructional games Art activities Singing songs that include with actions

(continued)

Table 2.1 (continued)

Activity area	Typical planned activity tasks			
	Prereading	Writing	Social behavior and communication	Play
Outdoor play			Taking turns using play equipment Using equipment cooperatively (i.e., wagons, balls, long jump rope)	Making choices about play items Observing play of others Initiating activities with peers Swinging on the swing set Climbing the monkey bars Sliding down the slide Creating and playing games with peers Kicking/tossing a ball Playing in the sand Riding a tricycle Riding in a wagon Playing with a parachute Jumping on a trampoline
Lunch			Participating in cooperative projects having shared materials Using board games that require sharing, turn-taking (i.e., Candyland, Don't Spill the Beans)	
Departure	Selecting materials for cleanup based on pictures or words Gathering home materials (following steps based on pictures)	Write a check mark to sign out	Saying nice things about peers (e.g., using a compliment-stuffed animal that is passed around at closing circle) Saying "goodbye" to peers	Singing songs that include actions Participating in free play activities while waiting for parents/transportation

Kindergarten				
Arrival routine	Identifying where to hang up coats or personal items in cubby or hook by picture or name Coloring at seat (writing)	Sign-in on the attendance sheet using a pencil	Interacting with "bus buddies" while walking together to and from bus pick-up/drop-off Helping peers hang up coats, bags, etc.	
Morning circle/attendance	Making snack and/or drink choices using pictures or words Communicating news to teacher and classmates (use of symbols and communication, words) Participating in Show and Tell (communication related to self, description of objects)	Take turns writing on the daily message board	Passing out materials needed for an activity Sharing information about themselves (show and tell) and calling on friends who have questions about what they brought	Participation in calendar activities including "Days of the Week" song Chanting ABC's and familiar poems and songs with rhythmic patterns and expressive movement (e.g., "Itsy Bitsy Spider"; "Row, Row, Row, Your Boat")
Reading/literacy	Communicating news to teacher and classmates (use of symbols and words for communication) Listening to stories (attending, plot, characters, left to right orientation) Engaging in dramatic play (expression of characters and plot elements, language development) Reading stories and other peers' logs	Selects a book to "read" then writes and draws about it using mock or real words Writes a mock title and the beginning of a "story" given a stem idea	Reading and discussing stories about friendships	Choosing books from bookcase during free choice Clicking on computer menu of free online read-aloud books and listening using a headset Watching puppet play based on book of the week

(continued)

Table 2.1 *(continued)*

Activity area	Prereading	Writing	Social behavior and communication	Play
		Typical planned activity tasks		
Writing/language arts	Communicating news to teacher and classmates (use of symbols and communication, words) Tracing shapes and letters Writing name, words, and sentences Participating in dramatic play (expression of characters and plot elements, language development) Documenting science experiences (writing) Journaling	Write entry in their daily journal Retell orally and write story using mock or real words about a recent field trip Participates orally in a "shared writing" chart with early childhood education professional Write labels for various centers or bulletin board displays	Writing and illustrating a story on a topic that two children agree on (encourages peer interaction, problem solving, etc.)	
Math	Counting manipulatives (communication about math concepts) Using a cash register and/or calculator (number recognition) Engaging in dramatic play (measuring, communication about relative size of objects etc.) Counting the days of attendance (communication about a math concept) Using base 10-blocks at calendar time (communication about a math concept)	Uses individual write-on board with marker/eraser to write numbers from a model given by early childhood education professional	Teachers purposely provide too few manipulatives for a small group of children so they have to share in order to solve math problems	

Lunch			Using social etiquette (e.g., saying "please" and "thank you") Participating in teacher-initiated discussions about the food they are eating	
Art/PE/movement/music/	Reading labels for art supplies Reading task charts for cleaning up drawing areas Singing songs about remembering counting and letters	Write labels using words for describing details of artwork	Teacher encouraging peer interaction and problem solving through games and activities (red rover, duck, duck goose, etc.) **Art**—Sharing materials Helping one another (i.e., help their friend put on art smock) **PE**—Playing cooperative games that promote turn-taking **Music**—Singing songs about friendship, singing songs with movements that encourage peer interaction, musical chairs	Using different art materials (e.g., sponges, glue sticks, paint brushes) at easels or with work trays and sharing with peers Modeling clay figures Rolling and bouncing squishy balls Navigating scooter boards in relays Playing with a hula-hoop to music Tossing and catching scarves Participating in unison to repeat rhythmic patterns or games of claps and snaps Using rhythm instruments (e.g., bells, shakers, wood blocks with sticks) Singing songs Participating in fingerplays

(continued)

Table 2.1 *(continued)*

Activity area	Typical planned activity tasks			
	Prereading	Writing	Social behavior and communication	Play
Recess				Making choices about play activities
				Observing play of others
				Initiating activities with peers
				Swinging on the swing set
				Climbing ladders and monkey bars
				Sliding down the slide
				Creating and playing games with peers
				Kicking/tossing a ball
				Playing on a teeter-totter
				Engaging in pretend play when in a playhouse
Social studies/science	Writing and communicating observations about the class garden	Draws picture of display objects from nature and labels them using directionality and letters	**Social Studies**—Discussing and voting on classroom rules	Using math manipulatives and puzzles
	Writing (documentation) and communicating height or changes throughout science concepts (e.g., seedling sprouting or chicks hatching)		Complimenting one another when they see a peer following the rules	Sorting and counting small objects
	Participation in community projects		**Science**—Working in small groups and using problem solving skills to complete a science experiment	Exploring patterns and shapes
	Communication and writing about participation in community projects			

Writing to grandparents and parents

Observing community leaders in their role and writing thank you notes (e.g., firefighter, police officer, principal)

Dismissal routine

Reading and writing lists to collect belongings

Reading and writing letters, words, symbols for personal organization (e.g., information in correct folder, items to keep at home, items to bring back, put items in pack on back of wheel chair, finding the right bus or car line)

Sign-out on the attendance sheet using a pencil

Singing songs that include actions

Participating in free play activities while waiting for parents/transportation

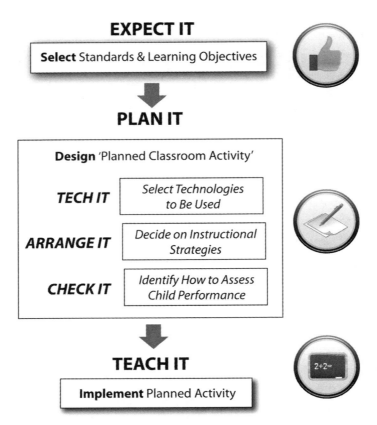

Figure 2.2. The EXPECT IT-PLAN IT-TEACH IT technology integration framework. (© 2013 H.P. Parette, G.R. Peterson-Karlan, & C. Blum.)

curriculum being used before they develop and implement any planned classroom activity. Consider the following example.

Mrs. Hearns, a preschool teacher in Illinois, examines her curriculum guide to plan prereading activities that will be part of circle time (large-group instruction) for the week. Because it is the beginning of the school year, the students are just beginning to develop emergent literacy skills, and Mrs. Hearns knows that the language arts section of her curriculum guide emphasizes development of early reading skills. The first standard in the language arts section of her curriculum focuses on application of word analysis and vocabulary skills. She also notes that five benchmarks, or learning objectives, are listed beneath the standard. Knowing that she must choose from among these learning objectives before designing her planned reading activity for circle time, Mrs. Hearns decides that she will focus on two learning objectives: 1) Identify some letters, including those in own name, and 2) Make some letter–sound matches. Now that this decision has been made, Mrs. Hearns can move forward with the next phase of technology integration.

After Mr. Bivens examines the language arts curriculum guide for his kindergarten class, he selects two learning objectives that require his students to listen to a recorded story, recount the elements of the story, and then answer questions about it. Mr. Bivens can now make other decisions to plan his technology-supported classroom activity.

PLAN IT: Developing Engaging Learning Activities Supported by Technology

Once a decision has been made regarding a specific standard to be addressed and the related learning objectives, the teacher can then plan the learning activity (Blum & Parette, 2011; Smaldino et al., 2012). In this PLAN IT phase, there are three steps: TECH IT, ARRANGE IT, and CHECK IT (see Figure 2.2).

TECH IT: *Selecting Technologies*   The first step in PLAN IT is to make a decision about the technologies that will be used in the planned activity (TECH IT). In this aspect of planning, it is assumed that educators have a level of operational and functional competence appropriate for the technology they will be using and some understanding of children's interests. Just as one would not go and buy tools that were unfamiliar to build a house, a teacher should not arbitrarily choose technologies with which he or she is unfamiliar when planning an instructional activity, nor which he or she believes would not be engaging for young children.

Because her learning objectives focus on letter identification and letter-sound matches, Mrs. Hearns decides that she will use a Starfall.com activity to address recognition of letters and sounds associated with four phonemes: /b/, /p/, /k/, and /d/. These activities engage the children as the animation and sounds prompt them to follow along, pronouncing the names of letters and sounds along with the recording (see Figure 2.3). She also wants to use PowerPoint slides that would allow her to use animation, recorded sounds, and Boardmaker symbols in her planned activity (see Figure 2.4). Mrs. Hearns can use her computer and digital projector to show them on her wall-mounted screen. She will also use a word processing program to create response cards with the letters *b, p, c,* and *d.* The cards will be laminated, and each student in the class will have a set.

Mr. Bivens wants to read *The Very Hungry Caterpillar* to his class during opening circle, and he knows that several versions of the book are available on YouTube in engaging video formats. He also searches the SMART Activity Exchange, which has many teacher-developed activities categorized by standards, content, and grade level. He finds numerous SMART Notebook lessons for this story, which he can simply download and use with his SMART Board. He chooses one that includes recounting and comprehension questions that will allow students to physically manipulate pictures on the SMART Board screen to demonstrate their understanding of the elements and sequences in the story.

Both Mrs. Hearns and Mr. Bivens chose several familiar technologies to support their planned activities. They relied both on available software and other instructional technol-

Figure 2.3.   ABC Letter Activity at Starfall.com. (Used by permission of Starfall Education.)

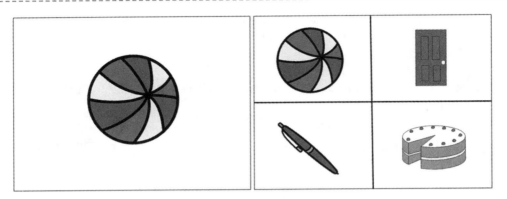

Figure 2.4. Sample PowerPoint slides created using Boardmaker symbols in phonemic awareness activities complemented by direct instruction. (From Blum, C., & Watts, E.H. [2008]. *Ready-to-go curriculum.* Normal: Illinois State University. The Picture Communication Symbols ©1981–2013 by DynaVox Mayer-Johnson LLC. All Rights Reserved Worldwide. Used by permission.)

ogies in their classrooms, as well as already-developed materials available on the Internet.

 ARRANGE IT: Deciding on Instructional Strategies   Once decisions have been made regarding specific technologies that will be used in a planned activity, the teacher must decide how the technologies will be used in conjunction with strategies—both instructional arrangements and specific instructional strategies (Blum & Parette, 2011; Smaldino et al., 2012). Instructional arrangements may include large groups, small groups, learning and activity centers, or (in some instances) individual settings. A decision must also be made regarding specific instructional strategies that will be used to deliver the content of the planned lesson. This may include one or more specific evidence-based practices widely used in education, such as direct instruction, exploratory play and guided discovery, modeling/hand-modeling, prompting, and scaffolding. These instructional strategies are described in Chapter 3.

Because Mrs. Hearns has identified four clusters of sounds (/b/, /p/, /k/, /d/) that will be presented, she decides that the Starfall.com activities will be used to introduce the four letters and their sounds using hand-modeling during circle time. For example, as each of the four activities is introduced on screen, all children will see and hear it pronounced as they are seated on the floor viewing the screen. An animal or object representing the sound will appear. Mrs. Hearns will provide a mand by asking, "What is the letter?" and then saying the letter. The class will then be asked to repeat the sound, and Mrs. Hearns will use positive reinforcement by saying, "Good, the letter is *b*." Mrs. Hearns will present several screens for the four letters, in which each will be introduced with its name and sound. In the screens that follow, the letters will be highlighted and appear next to pictures with short captions that feature objects whose names begin with the target letter. She decides that she will then transition into a more systematic instructional presentation using Boardmaker, PowerPoint, and direct instruction (see Chapter 3 for a discussion of this strategy).

Mrs. Hearns will script her slides so that she uses sequential language, modeling, prompts, opportunities to participate, and feedback with each sequence of instructional slides. She decides that she will use Microsoft Word to create sets of four cards for each student. Each of the four cards has one of the four letters presented in the slides. Throughout the presentation, children will see the pictures (e.g., ball, pen, cat, door), which will fade in and out using the animation features in PowerPoint. Mrs. Hearns decides that as she moves from one instructional slide to the next, she will ask, "What sound does *b* begin with? Use your cards!" Children will select from their letter cards and hold up their respective responses. The next slide will prompt the students to repeat the beginning sound four times as a picture appears each time in animation. Social praise will be given to the students for chorally responding after the last picture appears. This progression of slides will be repeated for all four beginning sounds in the lesson.

Mrs. Hearns appreciates the fact that the instructional approach used in her PowerPoint slides has a series of evaluation slides at the end of the presentation. These slides will allow her to assess all children in the class regarding their understanding of the four beginning sounds. Each beginning sound assessment will be followed by an animation slide offering visual and animated positive reinforcement for the students' correct responses. If students do not perform the review skill correctly, Mrs. Hearns will give them corrective feedback using scripted instructions in the curriculum.

Mr. Bivens decides that during the planned lesson he will open a short YouTube video of *The Very Hungry Caterpillar*. The animated story will be projected onto his screen while a recording will narrate the story for the children, and he can stop it periodically to ask children to make predictions. The SMART Notebook activity that he has downloaded will allow children to come to the SMART Board as called upon, place their hands on pictures representing elements of the story, and move them into a sequence. Mr. Bivens will remember to mark the initials of any student having difficulty on the SMART Board page, which will become a permanent product for those having difficulty with the learning objective.

Both Mrs. Hearns and Mr. Bivens have embedded relatively easy assessment strategies that enable them to identify children having difficulty with learning objectives in the planned lesson.

CHECK IT: Choosing Assessment Strategies   Finally, the early childhood teacher must assess children's performance on the learning objectives, which may include checks for understanding (e.g., questioning children as learning content is sequentially presented), classroom-based assessment (e.g., checklists or regular anecdotal records of a child's progress or classwork), and curriculum assessment (e.g., specific assessments developed around a specific curriculum). Specific assessment strategies are discussed in Chapter 4.

Mrs. Hearns will pose a question about beginning sounds during the PowerPoint presentation. Each student will be expected to select from among four cards, then hold up the card denoting the letter that represents the beginning sound of the object in the Boardmaker picture. Mrs. Hearns will be able to quickly scan the cards and make a checkmark on her CHECK IT sheet by the names of students who have selected a card with the incorrect sound. (Note: Teachers can design their own assessment sheets for any activity using CHECK IT strategies described in Chapter 4.) A slide with an animated picture will prompt the students to repeat the beginning sound four times. Mrs. Hearns will praise the students for responding after the last graphic appears. She will then check children's understanding by showing slides where they must choose a picture that begins with one of the four beginning sounds requested by Mrs. Hearns. This allows her to assess whether children have learned the sounds presented in the planned activity, as well as to provide corrective feedback to any children that demonstrate difficulty.

TEACH IT: Implementing Engaging Learning Activities Supported by Technology

Once decisions have been made in both the EXPECT IT and ARRANGE IT phases, the teacher should have a clearly planned lesson that integrates technology. All that remains is to TEACH IT.

During circle time, Mrs. Hearns tells her children that they are going to explore four sounds. She turns on her digital projector and the screen opens up to Starfall's ABCs Letter Activities. She clicks on B, causing an animated slide to appear in which a letter (both uppercase and lowercase) moves and is pronounced. Mrs. Hearns asks the children, "What letter is this?" She calls attention to the animated bee on the slide and asks the students, "What is resting on the letter B?" Students respond, "It's a bee," and she reinforces their response by saying, "That's right, it is a bee." Mrs. Hearns clicks the arrow navigation key and the slide changes. The word *ball* is presented, with the first letter B appearing in a different color than the other letters. When she clicks on the B, the /b/ sound is pronounced, and the word changes colors as several additional words float into view, each with the same beginning sound (e.g., bouncing ball). She returns to ABCs Letter Activities and clicks on P, C, and D, presenting two slides each in the same way that she did with B. Mrs. Hearns has prepared questions to elicit student participation, and then she moves directly into a more structured instructional format using her PowerPoint presentation. Through direct instruction, she is able to quickly sequence the four targeted sounds using PowerPoint slides, modeling sounds and corresponding letters. Mrs. Hearns allows the children to practice saying the sounds and holds up the proper response cards while she provides feedback.

Mr. Bivens tells his students during circle time that they are going to listen to the story of a very special caterpillar. He asks the children if they know what a caterpillar is, whether they have seen one before, and where caterpillars live. He turns on his SMART Board, and the children see the YouTube video screen. Mr. Bivens clicks the play button and the animated narration begins. He stops the narration periodically to ask questions about the story and ask students to predict what might happen next. He also calls attention to what the caterpillar eats on each successive day of the week. At the conclusion of the story, he promptly clicks on his SMART Notebook activity and moves to a slide in which children can come to the SMART Board, place their finger on a picture of food eaten by the caterpillar, and drag it to the day of the week (presented as text). He calls children in sequence, asking them to find food and place it by the proper day of the week. If a child makes an error, Mr. Bivens says, "What day of the week did the caterpillar eat apples?" He relies on the class to provide corrective feedback. Mr. Bivens also writes children's initials by the day of the week when errors are made and saves the slide to review later for assessment purposes.

In the preceding instances, CHECK IT was integrated into the teaching process. Both Mrs. Hearns and Mr. Bivens use differing assessment strategies that allow them to observe a child's performance. Mrs. Hearns uses a strategy that allows her to know if all the children have acquired a certain skill during the instructional session before moving on to additional instruction. In this instance, if she observes that any children fail to perform a desired skill in the lesson on beginning sounds, she can quickly provide remediation and additional practice to ensure that learning occurs. For Mr. Bivens, a permanent product is created using the SMART Board, which he can review later.

WHAT THE RESEARCH SAYS

In 2012, the National Association for the Education of Young Children revised its position statement regarding the role of technology in today's early childhood classrooms. Of particular importance in this position statement—grounded in research, theory, and observations from the field—is that "technology and interactive media are tools that must be used appropriately and intentionally" (p. 3). Further, it noted the importance of teachers having the knowledge, skills, and experience to select and integrate technology in developmentally appropriate ways; exemplars of technology integration designed to enhance children's learning; and guidelines for effective integration of technology.

SUMMARY

Three major steps in an instructional design and implementation process have been identified in this chapter: EXPECT IT-PLAN IT-TEACH IT. In the EXPECT IT phase, the teacher connects curriculum standards and benchmarks to the planned instructional activity. During PLAN IT, the teacher outlines a process for selecting appropriate technologies, instructional arrangements, and strategies and integrating them into planned instructional activities. PLAN IT also yields assessment strategies to determine a child's progress in attaining the selected instructional benchmarks. Finally, TEACH IT brings all of these planning elements together during the instruction that occurs within the target activity.

ADDITIONAL READINGS

International Society for Technology in Education. (2007). *National educational technology standards (NETS) and performance indicators for students.* Eugene, OR: Author.

Neuman, S.B., & Roskos, K. (2005). The state of state pre-kindergarten standards. *Early Childhood Research Quarterly, 20,* 125–145.

Office of Head Start. (2010). *The Head Start child development and early learning framework: Promoting positive outcomes in early childhood programs serving children 3–5 years old.* Washington, DC: Administration for Children and Families.

Pasnik, S., Penuel, W.R., Llorente, C., Strother, S., & Schindel, J. (2007). *Review of research on media and young children's literacy: Report to the Ready to Learn Initiative.*

Retrieved September 25, 2012, from http://cct.edc.org/rtl/pdf/RTLLiterature Review.pdf

PBS and Grunwald Associates. (2010). *Digitally inclined. Teachers increasingly value media and technology.* Retrieved September 25, 2012, from http://www.pbs.org/teachers/_files/pdf/annual-pbs-survey-report.pdf

Scott-Little, C., Kagan, S.L., & Frelow, V.S. (2005). *Inside the content: The breadth and depth of early learning standards.* Greensboro, NC: University of North Carolina.

Technology and Young Children Interest Forum Members. (2008). *Meaningful technology integration in early learning environments.* Retrieved from http://www.naeyc.org/files/yc/file/200809/OnOurMinds.pdf

Wang, X.C., & Hoot, J.L. (2006). Information and communication technology in early childhood education. *Early Education & Development, 17,* 317–322.

REFERENCES

Blum, C., & Parette, H. (2011, November). *Readily available technology and problem solving in early childhood settings.* Paper presented at the Assistive Technology Industry Association (ATIA)-Chicago Annual Meeting, Chicago, IL.

Bricker, D., Pretti-Frontczak, K., & McComas, N. (1998). *An activity-based approach to early intervention* (2nd ed.). Baltimore, MD: Paul H. Brookes Publishing Co.

Clements, D., & Sarama, J. (2003). *Strip mining for gold: Research and policy in educational technology: A response to "Fool's Gold." AACE Journal, 11*(1), 7–69.

Copple, C., & Bredekamp, S. (2009). *Developmentally appropriate practice in early childhood programs serving children from birth through age 8* (3rd ed.). Washington, DC: National Association for the Education of Young Children.

Division for Early Childhood. (2007). *Promoting positive outcomes for children with disabilities: Recommendations for curriculum, assessment, and program evaluation.* Missoula, MT: Author.

Grisham-Brown, J., Hemmeter, M.L., & Pretti-Frontczak, K. (2005). *Blended practices for teaching young children in inclusive settings.* Baltimore, MD: Paul H. Brookes Publishing Co.

Grisham-Brown, J., Pretti-Frontczak, K., Hawkins, S., & Winchell, B. (2009). Early learning standards: An examination of how to teach in blended preschool classrooms. *Topics in Early Childhood Special Education, 29*(3), 131–142.

Kostelnik, M.J., Soderman, A.K., & Whiren, A.P. (2011). *Developmentally appropriate curriculum. Best practices in early childhood education* (5th ed.). Upper Saddle River, NJ: Pearson.

Morrison, G.S. (2010). *Fundamentals of early childhood education* (6th ed.). Upper Saddle River, NJ: Merrill.

National Association for the Education of Young Children & Fred Rogers Center for Early Learning and Children's Media. (2012). *Technology and interactive media as tools in early childhood programs serving children from birth through age 8.* Retrieved September 22, 2012, from http://www.naeyc.org/files/naeyc/file/positions/PS_technology_WEB2.pdf

Parette, H.P. (2011, November). *Readily available technology integration in early childhood education: Lessons learned.* Paper presented at the annual meeting of the Assistive Technology Industry Association, Chicago, IL.

Sandall, S., Hemmeter, M.L., Smith, B.J., & McLean, M.E. (2005). *DEC recommended practices. A comprehensive guide for practical application in early intervention/early childhood special education.* Missoula, MT: Division for Early Childhood.

Sandall, S.R., & Schwartz, I.S. (2008). *Building blocks for teaching preschoolers with special needs* (2nd ed.). Baltimore, MD: Paul H. Brookes Publishing Co.

Smaldino, S., Lowther, D., & Russell, J. (2012). *Instructional technology and media for learning.* Upper Saddle River, NJ: Pearson.

Wortham, S.C. (2012). *Assessment in early childhood education* (6th ed.). Upper Saddle River, NJ: Merrill.

3

Using Instructional Strategies in Early Childhood Classrooms

Craig Blum and Howard P. Parette, Jr.

After reading this chapter, you should be able to

- Describe different approaches to curricular sequences and their relationship to technology integration
- Identify how to consider available technologies for integration into the curriculum and instructional strategies during the TECH IT and ARRANGE IT planning process
- Become familiar with an array of instructional strategies and how they are used with technology integration in an early childhood classroom
- Become aware of assistive technology and its relationship to instructional strategies
- Identify how to collaborate with families on the use of instructional strategies and technology

---

CURRICULAR SKILL SEQUENCES

Instructional strategies and instructional technology choices are among the most important decisions a teacher makes. Although there are numerous choices to make about instructional technology when planning classroom activities, a number of effective instructional strategies also may be considered. This book is organized around effective teaching practices rather than technology applications because technology is not an end but rather a means by which teachers can support learning for young children. In other words, technology integration is simply a part of good teaching.

In the EXPECT IT-PLAN IT-TEACH IT model of technology integration, the teacher should always begin with the EXPECT IT phase—that is, selecting the standards and learning objectives for teaching (see Figure 2.2). This chapter discusses the decision-making process that happens during the PLAN IT phase, when teachers are considering what instructional technology and instructional strategies fit the standard and learning objective identified for a planned activity.

Sequence	Description	Sequence Example		

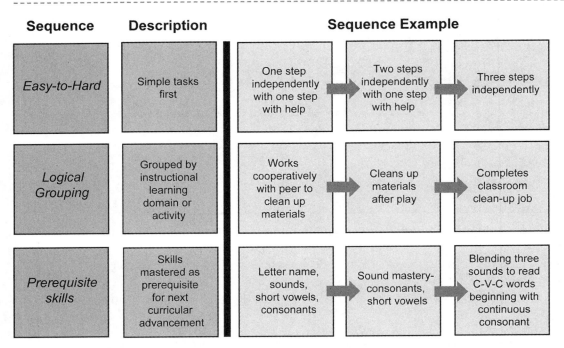

Figure 3.1. Curricular sequences with examples. (© 2013 H.P. Parette & C. Blum.)

The decision about what instructional strategy and instructional technology to use in a planned classroom activity is connected to the curriculum itself. Curriculum design can assume three major sequences: easy-to-hard, logical groupings, and prerequisite skills (Blum, Parette, & Watts, 2009; see Figure 3.1). Most teachers today follow some predeveloped curriculum. However, it is sometimes necessary to specially design the curriculum for children with disabilities or provide a supplemental curriculum using one of the sequences previously noted. Additionally, it is helpful to have knowledge of these sequences to better understand how young children progress through the curriculum and how the curriculum relates to technology integration (Blum et al.).

Easy-to-Hard Curricula Sequence

The first type of curricula sequence is easy-to-hard—that is, the easiest skill for the child to learn is taught first. As learning activities become more complex, increased demands are placed on learners. Hence, one approach is to teach simpler skills first, which provides a foundation for more complex skills. With young children, it is essential to ensure that the child is not overloaded with activities that are too complex when integrating technology into the curriculum.

Several research-based principles should be considered when integrating technology into the curriculum and instructional strategies to ensure that the activities are appropriate (Blum et al., 2009; Mayer, 2001):

- *Multimedia principle*: Young children learn better from words and pictures than from words alone.

- *Coherence principle*: Young children learn better when extraneous words, pictures, and sounds are excluded.

- *Signaling principle*: Young children learn better when the target words or letters include cues (e.g., highlights, animation flashes, pictures cuing what comes next) about the organization of the presentation.

- *Redundancy principle*: Young children learn better from animation and narration than from animation, narration, and on-screen text.

- *Spatial contiguity principle* (space on a screen): Young children learn better when corresponding target words or letters and pictures are presented close to each other rather than far apart on the page or screen.

- *Temporal contiguity principle* (order of presentation): Young children learn better when corresponding target words or letters and pictures are presented simultaneously rather than successively.

If teachers fail to consider these research-based principles when using multimedia as part of curricular design and technology integration, they can overload young children and decrease their abilities to learn from media; the term for this is *extraneous overload*. Therefore, teachers can start with simple visual materials and gradually increase complexity (easy-to-hard sequence). However, the complexity of multimedia should never exceed developmentally appropriate levels and should always consider the complexity of the learning task (in addition to the multimedia). Cluttered visuals with too much information are never good.

Logical Grouping Curricula Sequence

A second type of curricula sequence is *logical grouping* (also called clusters). These sequences do not fall in an easy-to-hard order and are often taught more naturalistically or logically. Typically, logical grouping is used for life skills instruction or when it is desired for the curriculum to follow a natural order. This type of sequence may be taught concurrently. The logical grouping sequence shown in Figure 3.1 is one in which the child 1) works cooperatively to clean up with peers, 2) cleans up materials after play, and 3) completes a classroom cleanup job.

For example, Mrs. Hearns uses technology integration to support a logical concurrent sequence. Mrs. Hearns has a step-by-step job list on her iPad, which is set up with different icons to show reminders of when to clean up, as well as the steps of taking turns when cleaning up toys or other classroom jobs at the end of the day. Using this technology, Mrs. Hearns is supporting the children in learning skills concurrently and naturalistically regardless of their complexity.

Prerequisite Skill Curricula Sequence

A common curricula sequence for academic skills is the prerequisite skill sequence. In this approach, there are foundational skills that must be mastered before any advanced skill can be learned. These prerequisite skills should be learned first so that children are able to accomplish the next step in the curricular sequence. Figure 3.1 depicts a prerequisite skill sequence for emergent readers to master consonant-vowel-consonant (C-V-C) words, in which there is a mastery curricular step of letter-sound correspondence before sound blending begins. Often, the prerequisite skill sequence is similar to the easy-to-hard sequence because the easiest skills typically come first.

Mrs. Hearns uses Clicker 6 to follow the prerequisite curriculum by having children select letters and hear the sounds in a Clicker 6 activity on her SMART Board. The activity features a voice that pronounces sounds paired with pictures of words and letters. As the children progress through the instructional sequence of the activity, they say the sounds *without* speech support and then hear the answer. Finally, whole C-V-C words can be blended together in Clicker 6, and pictures of words automatically appear. Sentences then can be constructed from words created and read back to the children using the speech support. Each use of the Clicker 6 activity follows prerequisite skills outlined by her curriculum.

Some children will not be able to master prerequisite skills at the same pace as the rest of the class or at the pace set by the curriculum. Frequently, these children are at risk, have disabilities, or are learning English as a second language. For children with disabilities, special problem-solving and assistive technology may be required (see Chapter 5). Other children may require special instructional strategies, often used in small groups, to assist them in maintaining the pace of instruction. Response to intervention (RTI) is an approach to delivering instruction that addresses the needs of young children who are unable to respond to the general curriculum. (Note that the term *multitiered system of support* is now being used by some states instead of the more popular term RTI, but the meaning is the same; Greenwood et al., 2011).

In an RTI model of support, children are monitored through valid benchmarking assessments using curricular-based measures, such as individual growth and development indicators (see Chapter 4). If children do not respond to instruction as indicated by curricular-based measures, then specialized interventions are delivered. In RTI, if a child does not respond to one tier of instruction, he or she moves to a more intensive tier of support. Typically, there are three tiers in a RTI program in an early childhood setting (Cates, Blum, & Swerdlik, 2011; see Figure 3.2). Tier 1 is the core curriculum, or the general curriculum that the school/program uses to meet all children's needs. Typically, most children will respond to that curriculum (also called a tier of support).

Children who do not meet their benchmarks in Tier 1 are considered to be at risk. In Tier 2, these children might receive a specialized intervention in a small group tailored to help them overcome their common challenge. For example, Ahn Tuan, a Vietnamese child, has been identified through screening as having a vocabulary that is at risk for his age. Ahn Tuan's parents speak English as

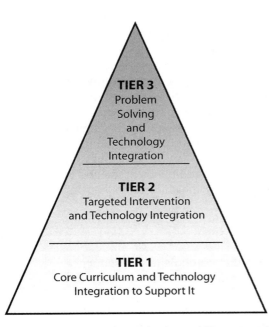

Figure 3.2. Technology integration in a multitier system of support. (© 2013 H.P. Parette & C. Blum.)

their first language and do not speak Vietnamese, so it has been ruled out that he is an English-language learner. Because Ahn Tuan is not responding to the language-rich curriculum that is standard in his preschool classroom, his teachers decided to enhance both his program and that of a few other children having similar challenges, using a small-group approach and iPads. The Puppet Pals app was identified as being potentially useful to allow vocabulary expansion. The teachers use explicit modeling of vocabulary usage while children create their own puppet shows as extensions of stories read to them during the day. Because of the explicit instruction and the focus on specific vocabulary matched to the children's needs, this is a Tier 2 intervention. Only children with these unique needs were targeted.

By providing more targeted interventions to children with specific learning challenges, a teacher is providing early intervention that may prevent learning difficulties in the future. If a student fails to respond to this Tier 2 intervention, he or she moves to Tier 3, in which the child receives more individualized support. This tier may require specialized problem solving, as discussed in Chapter 5.

TECH IT AND ARRANGE IT: MAKING TECHNOLOGY INTEGRATION DECISIONS DURING THE PLANNING PROCESS

Several key considerations influence technology integration in classrooms during the PLAN IT phase of the EXPECT IT-PLAN IT-TEACH IT technology integration model. Defining the learning objective and connecting it to a targeted standard is always the starting point for the teacher. Without knowing what needs to be taught to young children, it would be difficult to plan for it.

In addition, teachers must understand the curriculum and the existing system of support to implement the curriculum. Different schools or programs have different approaches to curricula and tiers of support. Some programs may not even have multiple tiers of support yet, whereas others may have a very informal curriculum. However, states are raising the bar for what is expected in the early childhood classroom, and educational standards and practices are becoming more consistent across the states. Further, it is important to recognize that there are standards of practice in early childhood education that are beyond the scope of this book. Teachers must be proficient in these standards of practice, and they will influence how technology integration occurs in the classroom.

When deciding on instructional strategies, some of the key features that should be considered are not under the teacher's control. For example, state standards may be mandated. The early childhood program may have already made a decision about the curriculum and how many computers and other technology infrastructure supports (e.g., digital projector, scanner, software) are available in the classroom. The program may even prescribe a particular set of instructional strategies. The degree to which a program has implemented a multitier system of support is something that is typically decided by a program or school district, not the teacher. Therefore, it is essential to have an understanding of the program and its underlying instructional strategies, curriculum and tiers of support, and available instructional technology.

In the PLAN IT phase, decisions about arranging for instructional strategies (ARRANGE IT phase) and making technology choices (TECH IT phase) concern

PLAN IT

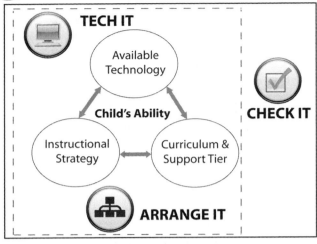

Figure 3.3. Relationship of TECH IT to instructional strategies and curriculum and support tier (ARRANGE IT). (© 2013 H.P. Parette & C. Blum.)

the interrelated options available in the classroom. Figure 3.3 depicts how instructional strategies, curriculum and tier of support, and available technology are three interrelated considerations that influence choices of technology. The double arrows between circles represent how each element of technology integration is interconnected and can potentially influence other elements. All of these decisions revolve around a child's ability given his or her level of development; thus, from the perspective of developmental appropriateness, technology cannot be identified without this essential consideration during the PLAN IT phase. Young children do not experience curriculum, technology, or instructional strategies as separate components. Rather, they see learning experiences, including their experiences with technology in the classroom, as part of an environment marked by a strong relationship with their peers and adults. For young children, much of their learning is an extension of play activity. However, teachers have the power to plan a learning activity using instructional technology to help children learn a particular objective connected to a given standard.

In the following vignette, Mrs. Hearns considers technology, curriculum and level of support, and instructional strategy. Only the EXPECT IT-PLAN IT-TECH IT-ARRANGE IT phases are included because that is where the selection of instructional strategies occurs; therefore, these phases are relevant to the planning process. Other aspects of technology integration, such as the CHECK IT-TEACH IT-SOLVE IT phases (discussed in Chapter 5), are essential but have no bearing on instructional strategy selection.

 EXPECT IT

Mrs. Hearns identified recognition of C-V-C words for the standard rhyming words (i.e., word families) in response to seeing the letter with an oral prompt. The learning objective is to orally respond to -*at* words (e.g., *bat, cat, sat, rat, mat, hat*) and -*ig* words (e.g., *big, fig, dig, wig*), recognizing that they are rhyming and have a V-C ending in common. Within the next few weeks, she wishes to accomplish a set of predetermined activities and learning objectives that are part of the core curriculum.

PLAN IT

The words selected are in a set of predetermined activities and learning objectives that are part of the core curriculum for all children. The teacher's manual explains that the *-at* and *-ig* words are necessary for the class to learn prior to moving on to more advanced sounds and blending activities. Mrs. Hearns realizes that her curriculum is using a prerequisite sequence and she thinks to herself, "Because the children need to master this before moving on, I could consider using a technology tool to help ensure mastery." Although the curriculum did not call specifically for this, Mrs. Hearns considers what her instructional technology options might be. She wants to follow a prescribed curriculum lesson that involves puppets.

TECH IT

Mrs. Hearns believes that an appropriate extension of this prescribed lesson would be to use some PowerPoint templates to practice the C-V-C words in the curriculum. She has a computer set up as a center, so she plans to have the children practice during center time. The PowerPoint activity has key C-V-C words used in a silly story she created. If the user clicks on a target word in the story, silly rhymes using target words will appear and are pronounced. If the child clicks again, pictures matching the silly rhyme will appear and a highlight of the blended letters (i.e., *-at, -ig*) will also appear. Children can insert their new rhyming words into the story to see if they make sense.

ARRANGE IT

Mrs. Hearns uses modeling and shared PowerPoint reading as an instructional strategy. She likes this additional element because it helps her children begin to build emergent skills related to comprehension and listening—and it is fun for the children. Notice how Mrs. Hearns considered each of the elements as she planned her activity. The learning objective, standard curriculum sequence, tier of support (core curriculum), and instructional strategy are prescribed by the curriculum, which led Mrs. Hearns to carefully consider the TECH IT phase. She realized that the curriculum and learning objective had a unique and important purpose. She then decided that the TECH IT step would include an extension activity that would help her children achieve the learning objective. She used PowerPoint to create a short book that emphasized the C-V-C words used in the curriculum.

For teachers who are new to technology integration, it may seem that there are many factors to consider and that decision-making is a daunting task. However, as one gains more experience with the EXPECT IT-PLAN IT-TEACH IT technology integration model in practice, technology integration decisions become more obvious as both the technology and available instructional strategy choices present themselves.

One common misconception about technology integration is that there is a single technology solution that will meet the needs of a given student or group of students. For children with disabilities, a specialized problem-solving process has been developed and is explained in Chapter 5. This process will narrow technology possibilities and help teachers to make decisions that match a child's needs with technology solutions. However, there may be several assistive technology (AT) options available for a child with a disability that require individual and family preferences as part of the decision making process (Sadao & Robinson, 2011). Often, teachers obtain AT on a trial basis to determine if it is the most effective and efficient technology. Although problem solving helps to identify the needs of the student, final technology decisions are often not made until a child has had some experience with the technology.

For typically developing students, there are an even wider array of technology options that may be considered during the PLAN IT process. Because educational technology is evolving so quickly, new apps, software, and new educational applications of existing software and hardware are frequently available. Hence, the purpose of technology integration in early childhood education is not to dictate the absolute best solution. It is to understand the technology integration planning process that will allow an early childhood educator to make the best possible technology integration decisions. The EXPECT IT-PLAN IT-TEACH IT technology integration model is designed to help teachers make the best possible decisions and integrate them into daily instruction.

Although it is important to understand that technology integration is part of the instructional planning process and that there may be multiple technology options that will help the children obtain their particular learning goals, that does not mean that all technology solutions are equally effective. Some technologies may be completely ineffective. As will be discussed throughout this book, using evidence-based practice and collecting data on the effectiveness of technology integration in the classroom are essential parts of determining the usefulness of a given solution.

Day-to-day planning is one of the most important activities for the early childhood education professional because it lays the foundation for strong practice. Actively planning activities that include technology integration is important for all classrooms. Although it may seem overwhelming at times, teachers do become more comfortable with integrating a variety of technologies, and they develop new skills permitting them to adopt more technology in their classroom.

OPTIONS FOR TECHNOLOGY INTEGRATION

Several technology integration options are available to early childhood education professionals. An array of these options may be used at any time and include the following:

- *Integrating technology to supplement the existing curriculum:* As one of the most common approaches, Mrs. Hearns would identify her standard and objective in the existing curriculum and then select technology to support the use of technologies such as PowerPoint or web-based materials on Starfall.com.

- *Using a stand-alone, predeveloped curriculum that uses technology:* Mrs. Hearns uses Clicker 6, which has built-in curriculum activity templates. Software packages with such predeveloped learning activities can be costly, although schools and programs often purchase them. In this example, the teacher does not develop the programs or the instructional strategies associated with them; instead, the teacher uses them to meet specific curricular goals aligned with standards.

- *Using a curriculum that comes with existing technology applications:* Curriculum developers are increasingly including resources as part of the standard curricular package. For example, Mrs. Hearns has an interactive DVD that has big books on it for shared reading. Although these materials are directly connected to the curriculum and include predeveloped learning activities, they offer Mrs. Hearns limited flexibility.

- *Using digital technology to enhance learning:* Another option is for Mrs. Hearns to consider products generated by digital devices, such as pictures from a digital camera, images printed from the Internet, or Boardmaker software icons that support emergent literacy and students with disabilities. By using this digitally generated technology, Mrs. Hearns will have to use her knowledge of instructional methods to ensure that the application is used in a way that enables the students to accomplish the learning objective (EXPECT IT).

All of these options should be a part of any teacher's technology integration toolkit. Often, these options may be combined, depending on the circumstances and resources available in the classroom. Teachers who only have a computer with Internet access and use a curriculum that is traditional and does not include technology will need to focus on integration through readily available applications that are part of classroom infrastructure (e.g., digital camera, scanner). Although this is not a comprehensive toolkit, there are a substantial number of readily available applications online. Similarly, many simple learning activities can be created using a digital camera. When teachers use these technology integration options, they will need to carefully select instructional strategies and align them with the curriculum.

In other instances, the curriculum prescribes instructional strategies. This is often true of stand-alone technology packages and especially true of curricula marketed with technology resources. For example, Clicker Phonics follows an instructional sequence and uses strategies unique to Clicker 6 features. Other technology packages, such as Kidware, have different literacy levels but allow exploration within the levels. Even in more structured programs, teachers may be able to select parts of the program that fit the needs of a particular learner.

Regardless of whether instructional strategies or methods are fixed or flexible in the curriculum, teachers need to have a working knowledge of these various options and the impact they can have on young children. They must also understand the curriculum and methods employed to ensure their correct use (Morrison, 2012; National Association for the Education of Young Children, 2009). Table 3.1 lists common instructional methods and strategies that demonstrate the integration of technology in an early childhood classroom.

Finally, it is important to understand that technology of any kind is a medium by which instruction is provided to students; it is not the instructional method itself. Instructional methods are based on how young children learn best. Instructional technologies use instructional methods with various media (including web-based, computer-based, or digitally-based components) to accomplish learning objectives.

In another example, Mrs. Hearns uses scaffolding (providing assistance so a young child can accomplish a task) with digital photos on an iPad. Mrs. Hearns noticed that some children were having difficulty following multiple-step directions

Table 3.1. Common instructional strategies and methods

Instructional strategy/method	What is it?	Technology integration example
Exploratory play	Children discover things through the course of natural and self-directed play.Teachers set an activity up enabling children to discover experiences consistent with standards (EXPECT IT).	Mrs. Hearns permits small groups of children to use a Sesame Street game, *ELMO's Song: Food,* that permits exploration. She allows students to talk about the game and interact with it.
Guided discovery	Children are engaging in play activities but with more guidance. Modeling (see below) and other instructional strategies may be introduced to accomplish learning objectives (EXPECT IT).	Rather than simply letting the children explore, Mrs. Hearns becomes more directive in the lesson, connecting the food items that appear in a lesson on types of food and asking children questions about what foods are and which ones are healthy.
Demonstration/ modeling	Demonstration involves one person showing another how to do something. To demonstrate, one must 1) gain joint attention or the child's common focus on what is being demonstrated, 2) show or model the activity, and 3) provide prompts for the child to respond to the demonstration or modeling.	Using a SMART Board, Mrs. Hearns uploads brief digital video steps of how to walk to the gym. The video shows how to line up and how to know who is the line leader. It focuses on the key expected behaviors when walking in the hall. By touching the SMART Board, children can stop and start the video at key parts to discuss classroom expectations. They can even move the different video clips around after being asked to sequence the clips in the correct order.
Embedded learning opportunities	These planned learning experiences occur within natural routines and activities. They are important for typically developing children and children with disabilities.	Mrs. Hearns has Shanika, a child with Down syndrome, included in her class. Using Boardmaker symbols she created for the steps of playing a game during center time, Shanika used the symbols to keep from getting lost and know when to take turns and clean up. Embedded within the learning center are skills such as taking turns. The Boardmaker symbols are assistive technology support.
Interactive discussions	A reciprocal verbal discussion takes place between teacher and child, child and child, or child and teacher. Interactive discussions typically take place in large or small groups.	Mrs. Hearns brought her digital camera on a community walk. She let children take pictures of various landmarks in the community. She embedded the pictures on slides in PowerPoint and projected them on a screen. During a brief large group lesson (10 minutes), children had an interactive discussion about the walk. Mrs. Hearns typed one sentence per slide based on the children's discussion. It became a book that they shared (printed) and it was posted on the class web site for families. Families then could review it at home.

Table 3.1   *(continued)*

Instructional strategy/method	What is it?	Technology integration example
Problem solving	Children are taught problem-solving skills that typically involve planned activities to support children's thinking, analyzing, and reasoning. Teachers typically set up learning activities where there are multiple solutions or elements of scientific method for exploration (i.e., observation, hypothesizing, prediction, experimentation, conclusion, and sharing of ideas about the experiment).	Children make predictions and the teacher keeps track if something sinks or floats. Children then categorize the digital pictures of these objects in a PowerPoint template of sinking and floating. Using the digital pictures, the children keep track of their observations during the sink and float experiment. They then compare them to their initial categorizations on PowerPoint slides. The children have an interactive discussion about why they think objects sank or floated.
Direct instruction/ child-focused instructional strategies (CFIS)	Direct instruction or CFIS is a set of very specific teacher-directed instructional procedures designed to teach specific skills or concepts. Often young children who have are at risk of disabilities benefit a great deal from this type of explicit instruction, although all children can benefit. Obtaining joint attention first, explicit modeling, guided practice, reinforcement, and explicit and systematic prompting approaches are typical of this instructional method.	Mrs. Hearns uses IntelliTools Classroom Suite, a multimedia and authoring tool. It permits her to compose simple sentences, have students hear them, and use icons for visual support. Using direct instruction principles, Mrs. Hearn writes a simple sentence about an activity during center time. She uses visual icons to match the words in the sentence, then shows the students how to play it back aloud (modeling). She then asks the children in the small group to write a sentence together (guided practice). Children then compose their own sentences with the teacher typing. Icons are found to match the sentence. Children are prompted as needed to write sentences with subject and verbs reinforced with praise. Additionally, each child prints his or her completed sentence and posts it on the writing wall with the child's name and picture on it.
Prompting	Prompting is verbal, visual, auditory, or tactile cues most often delivered by the teacher to remind the student to complete a step or part of an activity. Sometimes young children can learn to self-prompt to complete a simple task. For some children with disabilities, specialized prompting methods are frequently used to assist them in becoming more independent.	Mrs. Hearns has developed some PowerPoint slide templates to help students identify the letters beginning the names of different animals. She wants to add a prompting feature to help her students who struggle with the answer. Using the animation features of PowerPoint, if the student does not click on the correct answer within 5 seconds, two question marks appear next to two of the three possible answers. This narrows the answers to two; the eliminated answer is crossed out. The student has been prompted, with a slight delay allowing the student an opportunity to respond independently.

(continued)

Table 3.1   *(continued)*

Instructional strategy/method	What is it?	Technology integration example
Signals	Signals are also prompts, but they happen before the teacher has permitted the child to have an opportunity to respond. Signals can be helpful to students because they cut down or eliminate errors before they happen. Signals can be especially useful in assisting children in transitions or preventing other undesired behavior (e.g., the teacher signals the student to walk single file in the hall before he or she is in the hall walking).	Using Boardmaker icons, Mrs. Hearns posts signals of expected behaviors during circle time. There are icons are posted in the classroom to represent looking at the teacher, listening when others talk, and keeping hands to oneself. The teacher points to these icons before the circle activity begins so it can signal the children on what is expected.

in various art activities. To assist the students in understanding what to do next, she provided step-by-step photos so that each child can tap an iPad screen and move to the next step. This method is helpful because students can see the step concretely; also, it allows them to control the pace in the small group planned activity. Mrs. Hearns is aware that this approach is scaffolding, as well as that the iPad provides unique features to make this instructional strategy more effective.

Further scaffolding uses a learning principle called the *zone of proximal development* (Vygotzky, 1978), which is a task that can be performed by a child with the assistance of a more competent person (e.g., teacher, parent). Tasks that are below the zone of proximal development can be accomplished independently by young children; tasks that are above this zone are developmentally inappropriate because children are not ready to learn them yet. For example, a child may be learning to write her name and using an iPad app, Educreations, to practice writing her name. Although the child can write the first letter in her name without assistance (below the zone of proximal development), she is still learning the spacing of letters and how to form the other letters in her name. The zone of proximal development is how much of her name the child can write when supported with prompting, cues, or scaffolding. In this instance, the teacher might draw guidelines within the app or provide verbal prompting about how to form the letters. However, expecting the child to write her name independently and without error is above the zone of proximal development. Because the child cannot achieve this goal even with support, it should not be attempted. If a teacher begins instruction above the zone of proximal development for a child, the child may be discouraged from wanting to learn the activity.

In early childhood education, the zone of proximal development is an important principle because young children may accomplish much more when they are supported with adult assistance. Vygotzky (1978) emphasized the importance of social interactions in establishing this zone. For example, in an art activity with which a young child has difficulty, the child will naturally ask for help. The teacher then provides guidance, often through example, and the child can complete the activity. Although oral interaction with adults and peers remains an extremely important part of her classroom, Mrs. Hearns realizes that the interactive nature of the iPad technology enables her to scaffold instruction. Instead of being dependent on social interaction alone, the child can be more independent using the iPad and pictures. The technology allows for self-pacing and encourages the child to be more independent. The pictures presented on the iPad are also more concrete than social interaction, which is preferable for young children learning a new task (Morrison, 2012).

INSTRUCTIONAL STRATEGIES AND TECHNOLOGY INTEGRATION FOR AT-RISK CHILDREN AND CHILDREN WITH DISABILITIES

Thus far, numerous instructional strategies have been described—most of which can be applied to all children in the classroom. However, it is very common to have children with disabilities included with typically developing children in the early childhood classroom. Therefore, it is necessary to call attention to core instructional strategies that are useful with this diverse group of young children. Many children with learning disabilities are not identified until after their early childhood years because their learning challenges may not be apparent until they are introduced to more advanced learning skills (e.g., reading to gain knowledge, math computation, writing to demonstrate knowledge). Sometimes these students have early benchmark indicators (e.g., individual growth and development indicators, dynamic indictors of basic early literacy skills) that place them at risk of being identified as having a disability. Multitiered interventions (e.g., RTI) can help teachers identify children early and possibly prevent these children from needing special education services. This is not always possible, but early intervention can frequently help these children make substantial gains, thereby limiting the need for intensive education supports and permitting children to become more independent over a long period.

Role of Direct Instruction

Direct instruction can be used to assist young children who have or are at risk of disabilities in making gains in the curriculum. Although this approach is highly teacher-directed, it is focused on a young child's needs. Ensuring that instruction is developmentally appropriate, naturalistic, and meaningful for a child needs to be a part of direct instruction or any other instructional approach. Admittedly, there is some criticism of systematic approaches to instruction (Khon, 1999); if these approaches are not used properly, they may lack developmental relevance. There is evidence that when systematic or direct instruction is designed appropriately using more naturalistic approaches and meaningful instructional strategies, it is very helpful to young children (Keaton, Palmer, Nicholas, & Lake, 2007; Klahr & Nigam, 2004; Magliaro, Lockee, & Burton, 2005; Moustafa & Maldonado-Colon, 1999; Parette, Blum, Boeckmann, & Watts, 2009).

For example, Yesinia, a child with Down syndrome, is having difficulty putting her pack on and remembering the steps of transition to home. Mr. Bivens uses the systematic instruction process during the naturally occurring time Yesinia needs to put her backpack on. He chooses to instruct this way because it makes the instruction more meaningful, helps Yesinia learn to do it during natural occurring times of the day, and helps promote generalization to other situations that are similar. Using an iPad enables Yesinia to see a picture of what to do prior to completing the step. She also receives planned systematic prompts if she is unable to accomplish the task and reinforcement when she is successful at even small steps. The process of explicit modeling, expecting a clear response for each step, prompting in using a planned prompt if Yesinia was not successful, and reinforcing success are illustrations of key elements of systematic instruction. Although typically developing children learn to do these tasks simply by watching others model them once or twice and with a little practice and help, this approach is not explicit enough for Yesinia. Because of her disability, Yesinia does not recognize cues or the details of the steps as easily as her typically developing peers. The systematic approach to instruction directly addresses that need.

Direct instruction is important for many children who have or are at risk of disabilities because it is more explicit than exploratory approaches to instruction. For example, Hamid has been identified through screening at his preschool as being at risk for future learning problems. Although his teachers expose Hamid to language-rich activities that introduce him to the sounds of letters, ongoing progress monitoring is demonstrating that Hamid is failing to improve. Hamid's teacher now realizes that although the language arts curriculum is high quality for typically developing children, it does not provide any features to support children who do not respond to this method of instruction. To be more inclusive and child centered in her instruction, Hamid's teacher creates opportunities within the language center that are more explicit and use direct instruction. Purposefully, the language center is next to the SMART Board. Although there are plenty of exploratory language activities that can be initiated by students at the center, Hamid along with other students who were identified as being at risk for the same type of learning problem, have the opportunity to work in a more directed lesson by the teacher when using the SMART Board.

Using a teacher-assisted model of direct instruction, Hamid's teacher provides ample scaffolding in addition to the modeling, practice, and feedback on the SMART Board. Pictures connected to classroom literature are embedded in SMART Notebook activities. Sounds are made and recorded with appropriate images; when Hamid touches an image, he hears the model of the sound. For example, when the class is reading *The Three Little Pigs,* the teacher has scanned, uploaded, and linked a picture of a pig to a sound file in the SMART Notebook activity. When Hamid touches the picture, he hears, "Pig begins with /p/." The teacher then asks Hamid to repeat the sound, dialogs with him about the pig, remodels the sound, and provides feedback to help Hamid better approximate the /p/ sound. This approach is more directive than the teaching strategies that Hamid's teacher typically uses. However, because of Hamid's individual learning needs, it is far more child centered to be explicit and directive in her instruction than it would be to use the less directive and explicit approaches used with typical peers, which ultimately might not be successful. Additionally, the direct instruction format can be useful for typically developing students (Kostelnik, Soderman, & Whirem, 2011). Key features of direct instruction that have been described by others (Carnine, Sibert, Kame'enui, Tarver, & Jungjohann, 2006; Magliaro et al., 2005; Parette et al., 2009) include the following:

- Explicit communication is provided regarding how to perform a skill.

- Modeling is clear and distinct.

- Teachers guide children in making initial responses while providing scaffolding as needed.

- Curriculum is sequenced and focuses on mastery.

- Children are to use skills independently and in meaningful learning activities.

- Systematic prompting is provided in learning activities.

- Data collection is used to evaluate progress and analyze student errors, prompting teaching adjustments as needed.

- Direct instruction is used in small- and whole-group activities or with individual children.

- Direct instruction is connected to meaningful, naturalistic, and developmentally appropriate activities for young children.

Typically developing young children can learn a range of skills very efficiently. Because children with disabilities may have difficulty acquiring many of these skills, less explicit teaching methods can slow down their learning. For typically developing children, the direct instructional approach can bring clarity where confusion can exist.

Not all lessons in the early childhood classroom should be in a direct instruction format. Exploratory play, guided discovery, and other instructional methods that are driven by a child's own curiosity and permit incidental learning to occur are necessary and important components of early childhood educational programs. However, brief and direct instruction lessons are very useful in helping young children make significant gains. As noted in Chapter 1, Blum et al. (2009) found significant gains among at-risk preschool children who were provided with direct instruction paired with PowerPoint templates to teach initial sounds of words.

The following vignette illustrates how Mrs. Hearns considers direct instruction as a strategy during the EXPECT IT-PLAN IT-TECH IT-ARRANGE IT phases, in relation to curriculum, tier of support, and technology.

EXPECT IT

The standard is for all children to be able to identify initial sounds in words. As part of a program-wide screening strategy, a few children were identified using the individual growth and development indicators (see Chapter 4) as falling behind the rest of class. Mrs. Hearns uses this information to develop a targeted lesson during center time for children who are at risk. The learning objective is for the children to identify the initial sound of letters orally.

TECH IT

Mrs. Hearns is already using PowerPoint with the core curriculum to help the children in class learn rhymes and alliteration. Despite this, the children are not responding to the instruction. Mrs. Hearns knows that using Clicker 6 as a supplement to her core curriculum might provide these students with some extra practice in this area. Her students can use the unique features of Clicker 6 to practice letter substitution to create new words and have them pronounced orally by the program, allowing them to hear the sounds. This will help draw distinctions between the initial part of the word and the rest of the word. Clicker 6 also highlights text as it is being read to the child. To add context to the activity, Mrs. Hearns uses Alphabet Animals, a program that allows children to read books that emphasize alliteration of sounds. Alphabet Animals, which can be used on classroom computers with Clicker 5 or Clicker 6, provides engaging books that use animals to help teach phonics concepts such as alliteration. Mrs. Hearns uses the Clicker 6 activity embedded as part of literacy center and the children rotate through the activity daily.

 ## ARRANGE IT

Because these students are struggling, a form of direct instruction was chosen. Mrs. Hearns makes sure that she or another staff member is present when the children are at the center. She works specifically with this group while other children are working on a different activity at other centers. Mrs. Hearns sets this up so the children do not feel any different from other children in class and it is part of the routine. Although Clicker 6 has built-in modeling and elements of signaling through highlights, Mrs. Hearns provides additional scaffolding by questioning and talking with the children about the stories and activity. When correct responses are provided, she ensures the students are reinforced for their success.

Mrs. Hearns identified the unique needs of some the children in her class and made sure there was an opportunity for the children to receive explicit instruction. She considered technology and how it matched to the needs of her students. Further, she provided explicit support rather relying on the Clicker 6 program alone. Direct instruction is typically more teacher directed than many of the usual early childhood instructional strategies. However, when children are not learning using those methods, becoming more explicit and directive does facilitate learning. When children have or are at risk of disability or other learning challenges, teacher-directed instruction is frequently more centered on the child's needs than exploratory instructional methods. However, this does not mean that children who have

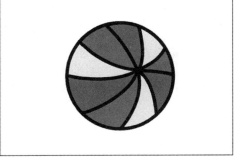

Figure 3.4. PowerPoint slides were used by Mrs. Hearns in tandem with direct instruction to teach awareness of the beginning sound /b/. (From Blum, C., & Watts, E.H. [2008]. *Ready-to-go curriculum*. Normal: Illinois State University. The Picture Communication Symbols ©1981–2013 by DynaVox Mayer-Johnson LLC. All Rights Reserved Worldwide. Used by permission.)

or are at risk of disability should only receive direct instruction. They also can benefit from exploratory methods; however, proper supports and/or skill levels must be in place for them to learn using this instructional format.

Child-Focused Instructional Strategies

To make progress in the early childhood curriculum, some children with disabilities will need even more specialized instructional strategies than direct instruction. Many of these children need individualized strategies that focus on their unique needs. These specially designed strategies have been referred to as *child-focused instructional strategies* because of their unique focus on the needs of an individual child (Sandall & Schwartz, 2008). It is important to break down planned activities into simple steps so that young children can learn to perform the most basic tasks in classroom activities. In Chapter 5, this will be discussed in more detail through an approach known as SOLVE IT. Breaking up activities into smaller steps and teaching the steps explicitly is a key child-focused instructional strategy. For example, Tanya, a child with Down syndrome, has difficulty when attempting to complete the steps of putting her coat on at the end of the day. To teach Tanya this activity, Mrs. Hearns breaks it down into simple steps for her. Before each step, Mrs. Hearns lists a natural cue—a naturally occurring signal that tells Tanya that she is to start a task or a step of a task. Most young children learn to respond to natural cues with ease; however, for Tanya and many young children with disabilities, learning when to respond with a step in planned activities may be difficult. Mrs. Hearns knows that child-focused instructional strategies help young children learn natural cues and the steps of the task systematically, so she has broken down the transitional activity of putting one's coat on into four basic steps.

Figure 3.5 illustrates how Mrs. Hearns identified natural cues for each instructional step to help Tanya. Note that they begin with transitioning from the previous activity and end with lining up. This is part of the natural routine in the class, so the goal is to teach Tanya to complete the routine during naturally occurring times. This approach creates the most realistic conditions for Tanya, increasing the likelihood that she will learn to put on her coat and zip it up if it is embedded in the natural routine. Mrs. Hearns uses an activity book created with digital camera pictures of each of the steps. Therefore, Tanya can see visual pictures of the steps using the activity picture book, with the pictures serving as models and signals for Tanya to perform the steps. Over time, Tanya will learn to perform the task like her peers without the book and in response to the natural cues, with Mrs. Hearns present-

Natural cue	Instructional step
Teacher says, "Line up and get your coats" (other children start to walk to coat rack).	Tanya walks to the coat rack to get her coat.
Tanya sees her coat hanging.	Tanya takes down her coat and puts it on.
Tanya sees that her coat panels come together once it is on.	Tanya zips up her coat.
Tanya sees other children start to line up.	Tanya walks to the line and stands in a single file line.

Figure 3.5. Mrs. Hearns breaks down the activity into natural cues with simple instructional steps so she can teach Tanya each step using child-focused instructional strategies.

ing these cues if Tanya does not respond to them. Mrs. Hearns provides praise for each step performed accurately, prompting for each step not performed, or corrections for incorrect or incomplete steps (e.g., runs to get coat instead of walks, does not zip coat).

Prompting and Child-Focused Instructional Strategies   *Prompts* are reminders to complete a task or step in planned activity or behave in accordance with rules. Prompts can assume many forms. They can be verbal, digital recordings, pictures of visual images, flashing animation, sounds, highlighted text, or even something tactile (e.g., a physical object might be used with a child who has a vision impairment).

There are many ways to approach prompting in systematic instruction using child-focused instructional strategies. However, many of those strategies are beyond the scope of this book and require significant explanation (see Additional Readings). Because the focus of this book is instructional technology, emphasis is placed on simple and useful prompting strategies and the use of technology.

Signals   One important prompting strategy for young children who have disabilities is the use of *signals*—prompts that remind children to do what is expected of them. A signal might be as simple as ringing a bell to remind children to be quiet, or it might involve multistep picture books created using digital camera images or Boardmaker icons to remind children what to do. Signals are always given prior to what the child is expected to do. They are often highly effective because the child receives the reminder prior to starting a step or a task in a planned activity. In other types of prompting, the teacher might wait to see if the child does what is expected and correct or prevent the child from making errors with a prompt to remind him or her what to do. If a child learns to respond to a signal and does not make the error in the first place, then the prompt has succeeded. When children complete a classroom task expected of them, they are more likely to acquire the curricular skill associated with that particular task.

Time Delay   A second specialized prompting method is *time delay*. Unlike a signal, which is provided before the expected behavior occurs, time delay requires that the child have an opportunity to respond, typically with a wait time of 5 seconds. This strategy helps children with disabilities (who often need considerable systematic prompting) to become more independent. Rather than providing prompts immediately, it allows a child to have some time to respond spontaneously.

Teachers can use timed animation features in PowerPoint to create wait time for prompts (Parette, Hourcade, & Blum, 2011). For example, the teacher can delay the appearance of an arrow or flashing hand prompt on a PowerPoint slide using the built-in timing features (see http://office.microsoft.com/en-us/powerpoint-help/). Using these animation features can be very useful: When delivering instruction in a planned activity using time delay, the teacher is likely to guess when a specific number of seconds has passed. Using the PowerPoint features results in instruction that is more precise.

Reinforcement During Child-Focused Strategy Instruction   Most young children benefit from encouragement, typically in the form of praise when tasks are completed correctly. When using instructional technology, it is important to encourage children using praise, but there are often circumstances when children need extra *reinforcement*. Special reinforcement systems may need to be created to help particular students to complete a task in a planned activity. These special reinforcement systems are not meant to become permanent supports; in fact, they should be faded over time in favor of naturalistic reinforcement. Naturalistic reinforcers occur naturally in the classroom or other environments and increase the likelihood that a desired behavior will occur in a planned activity.

Behavior includes not only compliance behaviors but also the steps of an activity or a task. For example, a compliance behavior could be lining up quietly in a single file line or selecting carpet squares and placing them in a circle for literacy center. A targeted learning objective step might be to identify the correct letter-sound in a Clicker 6 activity. Both of these behaviors—the compliance and the step—need some kind of reinforcement so that students will continue to perform them, and natural reinforcers are often present within technology. For example, a child who completes a task while working on a computer application might be reinforced by hearing or seeing "Good job!" or "You did it!" The Sesame Street web site and other games and activities provide reinforcement when students make appropriate on-screen choices. Some games provide printouts of completed learning activities. They are all naturally reinforcing to the child, and they can occur naturally during the activity.

A schedule of reinforcement details how frequently a teacher must deliver the reinforcer. Although some reinforcers occur naturally in classroom settings, others lie outside of a planned activity and thus are referred to as *specialized reinforcers*. For example, to praise a child at every step of an activity to get him or her to accomplish the activity is a specialized reinforcement strategy because typically a teacher would not need to provide reinforcement at this frequency. However, children with disabilities may need this type of instructional support. These children may also benefit from obtaining a reward for performing a task, which thus becomes another special reinforcement strategy.

For something to be a reinforcer, it must increase or maintain a target behavior. In other words, if the teacher is giving praise to a young child who does perceive praise to be rewarding and it does not increase the target behavior (e.g., lining up for lunch), then praise is not a reinforcer. To use specialized reinforcers correctly, the teacher must be child centered and identify reinforcers valued by the child. Although Mrs. Hearns typically expects the children in her classroom to line up and zip their jackets, providing a simple "good job" at the end, that is inadequate reinforcement for Tanya. The task is difficult for her, so Mrs. Hearns uses two specialized strategies. First, she praises Tanya after every step and adds a small star to her activity book each day the activity is completed correctly. Second, every time Tanya acquires three stars, Mrs. Hearns rewards her with 5 extra minutes on the computer or an iPad with a friend.

Some teachers believe that using reinforcers is bribery or that they ruin children's behavior. Research has indicated that this is not true, and reinforcement can promote new skills and independence if used correctly (Scheuermann & Hall, 2012). However, overuse, incorrect reinforcement procedures, or failing to fade specialized reinforcement can be problematic. Like all instructional strategies, reinforcement needs to be applied correctly. Technology may or may not be part of specialized or natural reinforcement strategies. However, it is an important facet of effective instruction and needs to be considered as an essential part of developing any technology integration approach.

TYPES OF TECHNOLOGY INTEGRATION AND INSTRUCTIONAL STRATEGIES

When integrating technology into the classroom, two options are available. First, instructional technology may be integrated solely to help all children meet an instructional objective in a planned activity. An example of this would be the Power-Point activity previously used by Mrs. Hearns to teach phonological awareness. Second, AT can provide a support for a particular child with a disability to meet a learning objective. An example of this would be the use of a voice-output device for a child who is nonverbal. In this instance, the AT is speaking for the child, thereby allowing access to planned activities that may use varying instructional technologies intended to help all children.

To make decisions about AT, a problem-solving process is required, as explained in more detail in Chapter 5. Instructional strategies and curricular considerations are essential for both types of technology integration. Typically, teachers use direct instruction and the other instructional strategies that integrate technology, as previously mentioned. For children with disabilities, child-focused instructional strategies are used with AT in combination with more general instructional strategies.

FAMILIES AND COMMUNITY SUPPORTS

Families play a key role in the life and education of young children. For this reason, using instructional strategies at home can be a powerful tool to complement children's learning. Teachers cannot expect families to have the same knowledge and skills in delivering instruction as education professionals. However, family members are experts in their own right and typically understand their children in ways that teachers cannot. Most families want to be involved in the education of their young children and may want to extend classroom instruction into the home environment. This may be especially true of families who are relatively proficient in technology and frequently use it at home, enabling them to seek out web-based resources and activity sites.

Chapters 6–9 discuss how families can support prereading, writing, social and communication behavior, and play in more detail. However, educators working with parents to supplement their child's education with technology at home should consider the following general guidelines:

- Avoid jargon and explain in simple language what the family can do using available technologies.

- Avoid using or recommending technology beyond that which the family has access to or is comfortable using.

- Simplify instructional strategies for use at home (e.g., provide easy-to-follow step-by-step instructions, omit steps that are overly complicated and are not feasible in a home environment).

- Provide examples of online resources (e.g., create a series of VoiceThreads regarding classroom activities and strategies that can be viewed at home, share links to Tots 'n Tech newsletters or Family Center on Technology and Disability resources).

- Share activity sites used in the classroom that have parent recommendations (e.g., Sesame Street, Starfall.com, pbskids.org).

- Create user groups that families may join to learn from each other by chatting about strategies used at home.

- Ask families what they would like more of and try to provide it.

- Provide resources at the start the year, and continue to update them as the curriculum progresses.

The ability of teachers to implement these recommendations, either individually or in combination, will vary markedly across schools. Resource constraints, time, degree of comfort in working with families, and other factors can affect the extent to which linkages are formed between classroom instruction, technology, and families. Even when barriers exist, the extent to which family connections are made and maintained can be expanded greatly by creativity and commitment to best practices of involving families in the education of their young children.

SUMMARY

In this chapter, two integral components of the PLAN IT process and their relationship to one another were described: making decisions about instructional technology (TECH IT) and instructional practices (ARRANGE IT). To effectively connect instructional technology and instructional practices, teachers must have an understanding of the instructional practices discussed in this chapter, especially direct instruction and child-directed tasks. Understanding curricular skill sequences is also critical in early childhood education classrooms. Although other instructional practices may also be developmentally appropriate in early childhood settings, direct instruction and child-directed tasks have been shown to support children in reaching learning objectives in their curricula.

ADDITIONAL READING

Gargiulo, R.M., & Kilgo, J.L. (2011). *An introduction to young children with special needs. Birth through age eight* (3rd ed.). Belmont, CA: Wadsworth.

REFERENCES

Blum, C., Parette, H.P., & Watts, E.H. (2009). Engaging young children in an emergent literacy curriculum using of Microsoft PowerPoint: Development, considerations, and opportunities. In A.M. Vilas, A.S. Martin, J.M. González, & J.A. González (Eds.), *Research, reflections and innovations in integrating ICT in education* (Vol. 1, pp. 41–45). Badajoz, Spain: FORMATEX.
Carnine, D.W., Sibert, J., Kame'enui, E.J., Tarver, S.G., & Jungjohann, K. (2006). *Teaching struggling and at-risk readers: A direct instruction approach.* Columbus, OH: Pearson.

Cates, G.L., Blum, C., & Swerdlik, M.E. (2011). *Effective RTI training and practices: Helping school and district teams improve academic performance and social behavior.* Champaign, IL: Research Press.

Greenwood, C.R, Bradfield, T., Kaminski, R., Linas, M.W., Carta, J.J., & Nylander, D. (2011). The response to intervention (RTI) approach in early childhood. *Focus on Exceptional Children, 43*(9), 1–22.

Keaton, J.M., Palmer, B.C., Nicholas, K.R., & Lake, V.E. (2007). Direct instruction with playful skill extensions: Action research in emergent literacy development. *Reading Horizons, 47,* 229–250.

Khon, A. (1999). *The schools our children deserve.* Boston, MA: Houghton Mifflin.

Klahr, D., & Nigam, M. (2004). The equivalence of learning paths in early science instruction: The effects of direct instruction and discovery learning. *Psychological Science, 15,* 661–667.

Kostelnik, M.J., Soderman, A.K., & Whirem, A.P. (2011). *Developmentally appropriate curriculum. Best practices in early childhood education* (5th ed.). Boston, MA: Pearson.

Magliaro, S.G., Lockee, B.B., & Burton, J.K. (2005). Direct instruction revisited: A key model for instructional technology. *Educational Technology Research & Development, 4,* 41–55.

Mayer, R. E. (2001). *Multimedia learning.* New York: Cambridge University Press.

Morrison, G. S. (2012). *Early childhood education today* (12th ed.). Boston: Pearson.

National Association for the Education of Young Children. (2009). *Developmentally appropriate practice in early childhood programs serving children from birth through age 8. A position statement of the National Association for the Education of Young Children.* Retrieved September 22, 2012, from http://www.naeyc.org/files/naeyc/file/positions/PSDAP.pdf

Moustafa, M., & Maldonado-Colon, E. (1999). Whole-to-parts phonics instruction: Building on what children know to help them know more. *The Reading Teacher, 52,* 448–458.

Parette, H.P., Blum, C., Boeckmann, N.M., & Watts, E.H. (2009). Teaching word recognition to young children using Microsoft PowerPoint coupled with direct instruction. *Early Childhood Education Journal, 36,* 393–401.

Parette, H.P., Hourcade, J.J., & Blum, C. (2011). Using animation in Microsoft PowerPoint to enhance engagement and learning in young learners with developmental delay. *Teaching Exceptional Children, 43*(4), 58–67.

Sadao, K.C., & Robinson, N.B. (2011). *Assistive technology for young children: Creating inclusive learning environments.* Baltimore, MD: Paul H. Brookes Publishing Co.

Sandall, S.R., & Schwartz, I.S. (2008). *Building blocks for teaching preschoolers with special needs* (2nd ed.). Baltimore, MD: Paul H. Brookes Publishing Co.

Scheuerman, B.K., & Hall, J. (2012). *Positive behavioral supports for the classroom.* Upper Saddle River, NJ: Pearson Education Inc.

Vygotsky, L.S. (1978). *Mind in society.* Cambridge, MA: Harvard University Press.

4

CHECK IT:
Assessment and Evaluation in Technology-Supported Early Childhood Classrooms

Hedda Meadan, Craig Blum, and Howard P. Parette, Jr.

After reading this chapter, you should be able to

- Describe the role of the CHECK IT phase in the EXPECT IT-PLAN IT-TEACH IT technology integration approach
- Describe the CHECK IT process
- Identify six CHECK IT data tools used to assess outcomes, evaluate outcomes, and solve problems in technology integration
- Describe the role of curriculum-based measures in the CHECK IT process
- Describe the meaning and application of instructional integrity.

ASSESSMENT IN EARLY CHILDHOOD CLASSROOMS

Today's early childhood education professionals are aware of the importance of documenting children's classroom progress (Kostelnik, Soderman, & Whiren, 2011; National Association for the Education of Young Children [NAEYC] and the National Association of Early Childhood Specialists in State Departments of Education [NAECSSDE], 2003; Nilson, 2010; Sandall & Schwartz, 2008). Passage of the No Child Left Behind Act of 2001 (NCLB; PL 107-110) placed greater responsibility on all education professionals to rely on scientifically based research to develop and implement instructional approaches. Given that there is an emerging evidence base that supports the use of technology with young children to develop important skills (see Chapter 1), there is also an expectation that assessment be an important facet of planned classroom activities.

NCLB also requires teachers to systematically monitor children's progress when teaching. Echoing this legal mandate, national early childhood professional organizations have emphasized that effective assessment should be an important part of every early childhood program, school, and individual teaching practices. In a joint position statement on assessment from the NAECSSDE and the NAEYC (2003), they set the following goals:

1. Make ethical, appropriate, valid, and reliable assessment a central part of all early childhood programs to measure young children's strengths, progress, and needs.

2. Use assessment methods that are developmentally appropriate, culturally and linguistically responsive, tied to children's daily activities, supported by professional development, inclusive of families, and connected to specific, beneficial purposes.

The principles embodied in this statement must also apply to effective integration of technology into early childhood settings using the EXPECT IT-PLAN IT-TEACH IT model. The NAEYC and NAECSSDE's summary statement also describes three purposes of assessment in early childhood programs. Assessment is used to

*   Make informed decisions about teaching and learning

*   Identify significant learning concerns that may require focused intervention for individual children

*   Help programs improve their educational and developmental interventions

Entire textbooks have been devoted to documenting young children's progress in today's classrooms (e.g., Nilson, 2010; Wortham, 2012). This chapter focuses on data collection strategies used for classroom-based evaluation and problem solving for children with special needs.

WHAT IS THE CHECK IT PROCESS IN THE TECHNOLOGY-SUPPORTED EARLY CHILDHOOD CLASSROOM?

As discussed in Chapter 2, effective integration of technology assumes that assessment (CHECK IT) is considered in *both* the PLAN IT and TEACH IT phases. In other words, it is necessary for teachers to plan for assessment based on the learning objective(s) for a specific instructional activity connected to the standards of his or her respective state or professional organization. Then it is necessary to implement the assessment as part of the planned instructional activity (TEACH IT) to evaluate its benefits to the child.

Assessment and its role in early childhood settings have been described in various ways. Kostelnik et al. (2011, p. 189) observed that it is "a systematic procedure for obtaining information from observation, interviews, portfolios, projects, tests, and other sources to make judgments about characteristics of children or programs." Most curricula used in early childhood classrooms include assessment strategies, data collection forms, and other materials and recommendations regarding how children's performance may be assessed. In the technology integration process discussed thus far, assessment of a child's performance in planned activities allows early childhood education professionals to make informed teaching decisions.

What Questions Need to Be Asked in the CHECK IT Phase?

Before specific assessment tools can be selected for use in a planned activity supported by instructional technology, the teacher should consider the purpose of the assessment. In the CHECK IT process, identifying an instructional question helps lead to selection of specific assessment tools and data collection strategies that are integral to the PLAN IT and TEACH IT stages. The nature of the question and its relationship to the CHECK IT process are described in the following sections.

The Instructional Question The CHECK IT process, which includes use of assessment tools and data collection strategies, can play several important roles in the delivery of instruction to young children using instructional technology. Assessment tools and data collection strategies can be used for the purpose of 1) screening to identify students at risk of delays or with disabilities, 2) conducting assessments to diagnose specific learning challenges, and 3) monitoring a child's progress so that the teacher can evaluate his or her effectiveness in the classroom. Most importantly, young children today are assessed because there is an instructional question that needs to be answered. Examples of instructional questions include the following:

- Does the student belong in a special education program?

- What kind of placement does a student need?

- Did my student learn what was expected?

- What effect did instructional technology have on my student's ability to learn an objective?

- What is the difference between how a student with disabilities in my class performs on an activity compared to a typically developing peer?

If answered to the best of one's ability, these important questions will increase the likelihood that a young child in the classroom will be successful. It is assumed and standard practice in the field of early childhood education that the only way to effectively answer such questions is by collecting data (NAEYC & NAECSSDE, 2003).

One cannot answer instructional questions from casual observations alone. The CHECK IT tools and data collection strategies presented in this chapter are part of a systematic approach to observation and data collection. Such a systematic approach will increase the probability that a teacher has the best chance of answering the instructional questions asked about his or her class as a whole or as individuals in a planned activity. Although there are many instructional questions that could be asked about children in any planned activity, two particularly important questions relate specifically to instructional technology integration: Did the child learn in my planned activity, and what does the child need to benefit from the planned activity?

Question 1: Did the Child Learn in My Planned Activity? The first question leads to choosing assessment tools and data collection strategies that help a teacher to understand whether instruction was effective. (Early childhood education professionals refer to this type of data collection as *evaluation*.) CHECK IT assessment tools and data collection strategies that have been chosen for this purpose will answer such questions as the following:

- How well did the child respond to instruction in the planned activity?

- Was the instruction in the planned activity effective?

- What was the impact of instructional technology used in the planned activity on the child's performance on targeted learning objectives?

Although answers to these questions can be complex, teachers can gain an understanding of their students' progress using the CHECK IT assessment tools and data collection strategies described in this chapter. Answering these questions helps teachers to make ongoing decisions about technology integration and instruction.

Question 2: What Does the Child Need to Benefit from the Planned Activity?   A second type of instructional question that must be answered addresses the nuts and bolts of the PLAN IT and TEACH IT phases. Specific questions about the child, the instruction to be provided, and the instructional technologies that might be needed should be considered, including such questions as the following:

- What are the child's strengths and weaknesses?

- What kind of program does the child need?

- What educational supports are needed to solve the child's learning problem(s)?

- What technology can support a child who is demonstrating an instructional deficit (e.g., he or she is not verbalizing with peers)?

These types of questions provide direction for the development of meaningful, engaging, planned instructional activities in which all children can both participate and learn.

 THE CHECK IT PROCESS

Educators need to follow four key steps for successful evaluation during the PLAN IT and TEACH IT phases. The steps are embedded within instructional planning and make up the CHECK IT process (see Figure 4.1).

During the PLAN IT phase, the teacher is preparing for technology integration in a planned classroom activity. In this phase, three interrelated activities occur: TECH IT, ARRANGE IT, and CHECK IT. To assess or evaluate young children during instruction, the first two steps of the CHECK IT process involve asking the instructional question and choosing a strategy. The last two steps of the CHECK IT process involve implementing the tool and making decisions based on the data. The following sections examine each of the steps presented in Figure 4.1 and provide some examples to better understand what takes place.

Step 1: Ask

The first step involves asking a question—either an instructional evaluation or problem-solving question. Asking the initial question occurs during the early PLAN

Step 1: *Ask a question*
        Ask instructional evaluation question or problem solving question.
Step 2: *Choose a strategy*
        Choose CHECK IT data tool/s that best measure/s what the child or
        children are expected to learn.
Step 3: *Check*
        Use CHECK IT data tool/s in an authentic manner and as prescribed.
Step 4: *Decide*
        Make an instructional decision based on the data.

Figure 4.1.   Steps in the CHECK IT process. (© 2013 C. Blum & H.P. Parette.)

IT process and is connected to the EXPECT IT learning objective linked to state standards or benchmark indicators. The evaluation question(s) should be asked so that when the teacher answers the questions, he or she can see if the child is progressing with regard to expectation of the standard(s). Asking the instructional question focuses on the problem identified in the context of a planned activity. For example, Mrs. Hearns asks the instructional question, "Did my students learn the initial consonant sounds?"

Step 2: Choose

In this second step, the early childhood education professional chooses the CHECK IT assessment tool(s) and data collection strategies that best measure what the child is expected to learn. Once instructional evaluation or assessment questions are asked in Step 1, specific tools and strategies (described in following sections, as well as Chapter 5) may be selected. Mrs. Hearns decided on the curriculum-based measure (CBM) for individual growth and development indicators (IGDI) for preschool because it can give her benchmarks on how her students are progressing in the language arts curriculum designed to improve letter-sound recognition.

During TEACH IT, the planned activity is being implemented, and it is at this point that the second part of the CHECK IT process is completed. As part of the instruction, two additional steps need to be completed.

Step 3: Check

In this step, the teacher uses a selected CHECK IT assessment tool or data collection strategy in an authentic manner and as prescribed. CHECK IT typically occurs in naturalistic environments during instruction or immediately after instruction. Some CHECK IT tools and strategies have specific instructions, or protocols, that must be followed. As discussed in Chapter 5, it is important that the assessment for problem solving be based on natural instructional environments.

Mrs. Hearns follows the instructions for using the IGDI for preschool during the school day. It has very specific instructions (protocols), and failure to follow them may make the results of the evaluation inaccurate.

Step 4: Decide

In this final step, the teacher makes an instructional decision based on the data collected. When monitoring young children's progress in planned activities, decisions are typically made about whether to continue with the instructional or assistive technology in place or whether to make changes. In either instance, data is used to make such decisions based on the progress of the student. More discussion about making data-based decisions will be presented in Chapter 5 as a component of problem solving.

What is critical in this last step of CHECK IT is that teachers are using data, based on the instructional questions they have asked, to make decisions about technology and students' progress or problem solving. Decisions based on data may lead to new instructional questions or changes in lesson planning. A different technology may be chosen based on the data, or a different instructional strategy with the technology might be selected.

Mrs. Hearns uses the results on the IGDI to monitor her students' progress. She started without any instructional technology and saw some improvement in her students' scores on the IGDI. She sees that since she incorporated Starfall.com into the curriculum, scores have improved and students are learning letter sounds at a faster rate. She decides to continue its use based on her data.

CHECK IT DATA TOOLS: STRATEGIES FOR THE EVALUATION OF YOUNG CHILDREN'S PERFORMANCE

A number of data tools may be used as part of the CHECK IT phase, and they all lend themselves to assessing whether children are learning in technology-supported planned activities. This chapter focuses on assessment tools that may be especially useful in technology-supported early childhood settings as part of the CHECK IT process. These tools, which can immediately be implemented using the EXPECT IT-PLAN IT-TEACH IT approach, include the following:

- Permanent products
- Systematic observation strategies
- CBMs and curriculum-based evaluation
- Family-reported data

Each of these assessment tools is discussed in the following sections.

Permanent Products

In all early childhood classrooms, children create things during the course of instructional activities. They draw, color, paint, paste materials, work with clay, construct things, and engage in other productive endeavors. The things that they make can be permanent products if captured and stored during the CHECK IT phase. This allows for comparisons of an outcome/product to a specific acceptable outcome that would typically be guided by the standard and learning objectives targeted in the EXPECT IT stage. Permanent products might also include such things as transcribed work of a child, completion of a worksheet, computer-generated art work, or product of a specific activity (e.g., cutting paper or building a tower from blocks).

With the use of technology in early childhood classrooms, teachers have an array of options for creating permanent products. From a universal design for learning perspective (see Chapter 1), it is desirable to have young children create permanent products that allow multiple means of engagement, representation, and action and expression to all children.

Printable, Web-Accessible Worksheets Sometimes it is advantageous for children to have worksheets that allow them to hold a pencil or crayon and trace, draw, connect dots, or other tasks. Several sites (e.g., education.com; starfall.com; tlsbooks.com) provide printable worksheets for use in planned activities. See Figure 4.2 for an example of a free, printable worksheet available for download to be completed and stored in children's folders.

Audio and Video Recordings Audio recordings can be used as a CHECK IT permanent product to gather speech and language samples (Blagojevic & Gathwait, 2001). These samples can then be used to assess young children's learning,

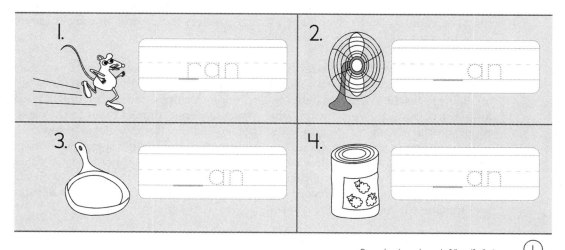

Figure 4.2. Downloadable printouts are available at Starfall.com and can be used to complement planned classroom activities. (Used by permission of Starfall Education.)

Figure 4.3. Audio can easily be inserted onto PowerPoint slides to enhance the presentation of content. (From J. Parette; used by permission.)

thinking, and/or social skills. For example, in PowerPoint, children may record sounds directly onto slides (see Figure 4.3; see http://office.microsoft.com/en-us/powerpoint-help/ for instructions). Children can create their own presentations with audio features to reflect their knowledge and understanding of instructional content. They can also record comments on a particular slide and connect the audio to embedded photos of or icons representing themselves. Free web technologies, such as VoiceThread, allow teachers and children to upload content (e.g., photos, drawings, text, web links, video) and make comments using text, audio, and/or video. Teachers will be limited only by their imaginations with regard to the many ways that audio and video can be incorporated into planned lessons and used for the CHECK IT process.

Mrs. Hearns presents a lesson using her SMART Board that focuses on the seasons. She has created a PowerPoint presentation that has digital camera pictures of her students' artwork. She has also uploaded these photos to VoiceThread. During Literacy Center time, children work in small groups at the computer to comment on the photos—both their own and those of others—providing audio narration and a product regarding their thoughts about the photo (see Figure 4.4).

Mr. Bivens has sent an e-mail invitation to all the parents of students in his kindergarten class to join his VoiceThread. Parents have responded and photos of their children have been added so that the images of the children appear around screens within the VoiceThread. Mr. Bivens knows that this gives his children a presence and allows him to periodically create VoiceThreads that are associated with class activities. Children are also able to participate outside of class by making text, audio, or video comments, which engages the parents in the classroom experiences.

Video Recorders   Live recordings of children can also be used to create a permanent product for data collection. A variety of recording alternatives are available to teachers who are delivering technology-supported instruction. For example, webcams are very inexpensive; when teachers connect them to the classroom computer, they can capture video footage of their students that explains their understanding of concepts, documents their reading comprehension, allows them to tell a story, and records other meaningful classroom tasks in planned activities. Webcams also allow young children to create and add their own videos to web site activities. Teachers can also record student participation with most mobile devices and transfer the footage to the computer.

Digital Cameras   Digital cameras provide yet another means of capturing video and photographs, which can be easily transferred to the computer and archived as permanent products. Photographs taken with a digital camera allow children and teachers to observe and record children's activities, special occasions,

Figure 4.4. VoiceThread screenshot presenting features that allow children to upload and comment on content using text, audio, or video. (Used by permission of J. Parette and VoiceThread.)

and classroom products (e.g., art projects). Images can be easily downloaded to the computer and made available to children to create other products using such programs as PowerPoint, VoiceThread, Fotobabble, and Animoto.

Screenshots If students are working at a computer terminal and they create a product individually or collaboratively, a screenshot of web site pages may be captured and pasted into Microsoft Word or PowerPoint. On a PC, Windows allows a screenshot to be captured using the PrtScn (print screen) key. This captured image can be pasted into other applications and resized if needed. On a Mac computer, multiple strategies can be used to capture entire screens or portions of the screen. Windows also allows screen portions to be captured using the built-in Snipping Tool, which can then be pasted into other documents.

Interactive Whiteboards Activities created on an interactive whiteboard (e.g., SMART Board) have space for notations on each slide, which teachers can save in their files. Similarly, if children are drawing or making selections within a planned activity on the whiteboard, the teacher can annotate a child's work (e.g., with the child's name) and then save entire screens or areas of a screen, which may be printed as permanent products.

Systematic Observation Strategies

Systematic observation is typically one of the most commonly used data collection strategies in the CHECK IT phase. Such strategies occur in naturalistic settings while children are engaged in planned activities and allow the teacher to make decisions about the effectiveness of technology-supported instruction. Specific systematic observation strategies that have proven helpful include the following:

- Anecdotal observations

- Checklists and inventories

- Event recording

- Time sampling

Each of these strategies is discussed in the following sections.

Anecdotal Observations One systematic observation strategy is to simply make anecdotal notations regarding what is observed (i.e., what children do or say) in the process of teaching a planned activity (see Figure 4.5). Such anecdotal records are typically short; they may be conveniently located around a classroom on sticky notes or index cards, thus allowing the teacher to make notes and fill in the interpretation section at a convenient time.

Checklists and Inventories Frequently used CHECK IT data collection strategies also include checklists and inventories, ranging from formal criterion-

Child's Name: Shanika Terrell	**Observer:** S. Hearns
Date: 9/15/2012	**Setting:** Preschool classroom
Time: 8:30 a.m.	

Students were shown a PowerPoint letter recognition activity that used direct instruction to teach b, p, k, and d. Modeling and prompts were used during the instructional setting, and students held up response cards to indicate their understanding of beginning sounds when pictures were shown on the screen. Shanika was distractible during each slide presentation, and held up the wrong response card when students were asked, "What sound does ___ make?" She missed ball, pen, door, and cake.

Interpretation: Shanika may not have found the PowerPoint slides engaging given that she preferred to "socialize" with her peers during instruction. Perhaps pictures of things that she is familiar with should be used in the design of the PowerPoint slides. It may also be that she needs more intensive 1:1 instruction which would support her participation in the large group activity.

Figure 4.5. Sample anecdotal record that may be used for observations of a child's performance in planned activities. (Source: Kostelnik, Soderman, & Whiren, 2011.)

Children's Prereading Skills Checklist									
State Goal 1 Learning Standard: Reads with understanding and fluency	Shanika	Cody	James	Amanda	Cheri	Brock	Lydia	Tamara	Aaron
Understands that reading progresses from left to right and top to bottom.	√	√	√	√	√	√	√	√	√
Identifies labels and signs in the environment.	√		√	√	√	√	√		√
Identifies some letters, including those in own name.	√	√	√		√	√	√		√
Makes some letter-sound matches.	√	√		√		√	√		
Predicts what will happen next using pictures and content for guides.	√		√		√			√	√
Begins to develop phonological awareness by participating in rhyming activities.		√			√		√	√	
Demonstrates understanding of literal meaning of stories by making comments.	√	√	√	√		√		√	√

Figure 4.6.   Emergent literacy skill checklist based on Illinois Early Learning Standards.

referenced lists of developmental skills and behaviors to inventories designed by teachers that relate to specific skills and behaviors expected in planned activities (see Figure 4.6). These CHECK IT strategies lend themselves to multiple uses. Teachers could use varying notations over time on the same document (e.g., a checkmark for the first assessment in week 1; a plus sign for the second assessment in week 2; a minus sign for the third assessment in week 3; Kostelnik et al., 2011).

Event Recording   A direct observation strategy that is used to record the number of times a child's behavior occurs within a planned activity is known as *event recording* (see Figure 4.7). Event recording is used when behavior tends to occur in a particular setting or during a particular time period. This tool is used frequently when the goal is to increase or decrease a specific behavior in a planned

Child's Name: Shanika Terrell
Behavior: Off-task behavior
Where: Hearns Room
When: During Circle Time (8:30–9:00)
Observer: S. Hearn
Dates: 11/5–11/9

Days	Tally	Total
1	//////	6
2	////	4
3	//////	6
4	///////	7
5	/////	5

Figure 4.7.   Frequency count tally sheet for documenting off-task behavior during a planned activity. (Source: Kostelnik, Soderman, & Whiren, 2011. Figure courtesy of H.P. Parette.)

activity. For example, the teacher makes tally marks each time a behavior occurs (e.g., off-task behaviors during a PowerPoint presentation to the group).

Time Sampling Another data collection strategy for direct observation is *time sampling*. In time sampling, the teacher records the occurrence of a behavior at a specific time or time interval. In contrast to event recording, in which the observer records a behavior any time it occurs, in time sampling, the observer records behavior at specific times during a planned activity. For example, during circle time in which a PowerPoint presentation is being used, a coded notation of participating children's behavior (e.g., sitting quietly, raising hands to participate, interrupting; see Figure 4.8) is recorded.

Curriculum-Based Measures and Curriculum-Based Evaluation

Curriculum-based measures (CBMs) have become increasingly important in early childhood education. Although they have been used for many years with older children, developmentally appropriate CBMs are now available for use with young children. Curriculum-based measures are general outcome assessments used to monitor children's progress, which are helpful for in-class decision making. They differ from other curricular measures in that they are not teacher-made and have the distinct advantage of being tested for their *reliability* (i.e., the extent to which the same results may be expected with repeated assessments/observations) and *validity* (i.e., the extent to which the assessment assesses what it was designed to measure). Teacher-constructed data collection strategies typically have unknown reliability and validity. When using teacher-constructed data collection strategies to evaluate the progress of young children, it is possible to make errors in instructional decisions.

What the Research Says: Understanding Reliability and Validity When measuring student learning in relation to technology, reliability and validity concepts are essential to consider and help the teacher know how useful and accurate a CHECK IT assessment tool or data collection strategy is. A simple way of understanding why it is important to have reliable educational data tools is to think of one's bathroom scale. The scale is designed to measure one's weight. Obviously, accuracy would be important. If stepping on the scale one minute records one weight, and then five minutes later it records something different, the scale would be an unreliable measurement of weight.

Researchers have found ways to calculate the reliability of different educational assessment tools and data collection strategies. If the assessment does not measure a learning outcome consistently within a short period of time, it is said to be an unreliable educational measure. It is not useful because it may measure learning one way on a given assessment day and yield a different measure of learning on another day. If someone conducting an assessment cannot score the assessment consistently or make consistent observations, the rating (scoring/observations) is unreliable. If a teacher cannot consistently score or share the same observations with others conducting the assessment, that data collection method will also produce inaccurate assessment of student learning. Therefore, it is crucial to use assessment tools and data collection strategies that are reliable to accurately evaluate the impact of technology integration (McLean, Wolery, & Bailey, 2004).

Students	Monday					Tuesday					Wednesday					Thursday					Friday				
	8:15	8:30	8:45	9:00	9:15	8:15	8:30	8:45	9:00	9:15	8:15	8:30	8:45	9:00	9:15	8:15	8:30	8:45	9:00	9:15	8:15	8:30	8:45	9:00	9:15
Shanika	A	B	B	C	A	A	A	C	B	B	C	C	A	A	B	B	B	C	A	C	A	B	B	C	C
Cody	A	A	A	B	A	A	A	A	A	A	B	A	A	A	B	B	A	A	A	B	B	B	B	A	A
James	C	B	C	C	B	B	B	C	C	C	C	B	B	C	B	B	B	B	C	C	B	B	B	C	B
Amanda	A	A	A	A	A	A	A	A	A	A	A	A	A	A	A	A	A	A	A	A	A	A	A	A	A
Cheri	B	B	C	B	B	B	B	B	B	B	B	B	B	B	B	C	B	B	BC	B	B	B	B	B	B
Brock	B	B	B	B	B	C	C	C	B	B	BC	C	B	B	B	C	B	C	C	B	B	B	C	C	C

A = sitting quietly   B = Raising hand to participate   C = Interrupting

Figure 4.8. Excerpt from time sampling sheet used to record the occurrence of three behaviors during a planned activity. (Source: Kostelnik, Soderman, & Whiren, 2011. Figure courtesy of H.P. Parette.)

Validity of the assessment tool or data collection strategy is also important to evaluate technology integration. Any CHECK IT assessment tool or data collection strategy needs to be valid for its use. Although there are many different types of validity concepts related to data collection, the most important idea to understand is that evidence is needed to justify that the teacher's conclusions drawn from data collection are accurate and valid (Messick, 1980). For example, you may choose event recording as a data collection strategy during the CHECK IT process to evaluate the frequency of vocabulary usage when children record a story about a picture they drew in the Educreations app on the iPad. However, if different classroom observers do not record it accurately, it will make the conclusions drawn from collecting the data invalid. The teacher must have evidence that different observers are collecting data accurately and as intended.

In the absence of a valid measure, educators may come to false conclusions about how effective the technology integration was or results of an assessment may be misinterpreted, leading one to poor solutions in the problem-solving process (see Chapter 5). For example, to evaluate the impact of an iPod app downloaded to support math instruction in addition, the teacher might use a test that collects data on single-digit addition that was first determined to be reliable. The test would likely be a valid measure of whether a student is learning single-digit addition as a result of math instruction on the iPod. However, this assumption of validity may be flawed, as there may be unique interactive features in the math app that do not generalize well to a pencil-and-paper test. Thus, the test may not be valid for what the students actually learned using the math app.

Depending on what one's goals are in this situation, the test might be changed or technology integration might be altered to better match the test. If the teacher believes the test is a valid skill and consistent with an EXPECT IT phase learning objective (i.e., adding using pencil and paper), then the app alone is not a complete source of instruction; the students need some practice using pencil and paper with the math app. On the other hand, if addition using paper and pencil is not part of the curricular goal, it may be less important to test on paper, and consideration might be given to using a CBM of single-digit addition.

For professionally-made and teacher-made data collection strategies, it is essential to choose assessments that are both reliable *and* valid. There are specific strategies teachers can use to establish reliability and validity of teacher-made materials, but they are beyond the scope of this book (see e.g., McLean et al., 2004 for more detail).

An important part of using CBMs in the EXPECT IT-PLAN IT-TEACH IT technology integration model is that they should be used with curriculum-based evaluations. Use of these measures is a problem-solving process in which teachers make instructional decisions based on the data (Deno, 1987; Kelley, Hosp, & Howell, 2008). Although teachers can develop measures based on their own curriculum, they may also use CBM tools that have already been developed, including the Preschool Indicators of Individual Growth and Development (http://ggg.umn .edu/), which focuses on the developmental growth of children; Dynamic Indicators of Basic Early Literacy Skills (https://dibels.uoregon.edu/), which focuses on students' early literacy skills; and AIMSWeb Test of Early Numerac (http://www .aimsweb.com) and easyCBM Math Numbers and Operations (http://easycbm .com), which were developed for kindergarten math.

Family-Reported Data

Families are an important source of information about their children's behavior and skills and should be included in CHECK IT approaches whenever possible. Parents and extended family members are experts in many respects given that they have observed their children's growth and development over time. To varying degrees, they have also provided models for their children regarding technology use, thus helping shape their children's preferences for and uses of technology. Only recently have teachers begun to ask families about their technology preferences and the types of supports that they need from schools (Parette, Meadan, Doubet, & Hess, 2010).

For example, at the beginning of the school year, Mrs. Hearns meets with Cody's family and asks them to fill out a short questionnaire regarding their preferences for technology use (see Figure 4.9). The questions are designed to be checked either *yes* or *no,* and they help Mrs. Hearns understand both what technologies Cody has used in the past and whether the family would use certain curriculum-supported technologies with Cody.

Questionnaires such as that shown in Figure 4.9 provide valuable information both for instructional planning and assessment purposes. They can be sent home with children to be completed by family members and returned, or they can be e-mailed to families. Early in the year, questionnaires can provide initial understanding of what technologies children prefer and how they are using them at home. This, in turn, provides guidance in planning activities. Over time, such questionnaires can be used to assess whether skills taught in the classroom have been generalized and are performed using technology in home settings.

INSTRUCTIONAL INTEGRITY

Until this point, CHECK IT assessment tools and data collection strategies focused on learning outcomes for young children have been discussed. However, what the teacher does to get to those outcomes is extremely important. Imagine that Mrs. Hearns learns to use a SMART Board so that it can be integrated into a shared reading activity with her students. However, in implementing her instruction, she skips some of the essential steps in using the instructional technology to support the shared reading experience. The question then arises, "Will the use of the SMART Board in the shared reading experience help the students achieve their learning objective (EXPECT IT)?" Unfortunately for Mrs. Hearns, the answer in this scenario is, "Maybe yes, maybe no." The outcome (i.e., student learning) will depend on how many steps Mrs. Hearns missed and how crucial they were in the instructional experience. When integrating technology as part of a planned activity, it is important to follow all steps, including specific steps in using the technology, that were planned using the EXPECT IT-PLAN IT-TEACH IT model. For example, setting up the SMART Board activity prior to class so that an activity is easily accessible is an example of a critical step.

How well one follows the steps of a planned activity is referred to as *instructional integrity,* also known as fidelity or treatment integrity. The simplest method for monitoring one's adherence to steps in a planned activity is to create a teacher self-checklist. This checklist should include any steps related to the use of technol-

Child's name: _____

Child questions	Yes (√)	No (√)
Does your child use a computer at home?		
If so, can your child use a mouse with the computer?		
Does your child use an iPad or iPod Touch at home?		
If so, are there certain apps that are enjoyable for your child? Please list:		
Has your child used a digital camera before?		
Does your child play games on a home entertainment center at home?		
Has your child used (or currently use) a cell phone (e.g., take pictures, talk on the phone with assistance)?		
Has your child used (or currently use) email (e.g., with assistance, or verbally stated an email to send to a family member that you wrote)?		
Does your child play games or participate in activities on web sites?		
Does your child use any technology purchased locally at stores? (e.g., VTech devices, LeapFrog products)		

Family questions	Yes (√)	No (√)
Do you play games on the computer with your child?		
If so, what games? Please list:		
Would you consider playing computer-based games and activities with your child that we use in school?		
Do you play games on an iPad or iPod with your child?		
If so, what apps do you use? Please list:		
Would you consider using iPad or iPod apps with your child that we use in school?		
Would you like to receive email or a blog on a secure web site about your child's classroom activities and performance?		
Do you use your computer to seek out resources to help your child?		
If so, what resource sites do you use? Please list:		
Would you like support in how to appropriately use technology to promote your child's learning?		
If so, are their specific needs you, your child, or others in your family have? Please list:		

Figure 4.9. Sample family questionnaire regarding children's technology use and preferences at home.

ogy (see Figure 4.10) and space to record whether the planned step was adhered to on a particular day when the planned lesson was taught.

Most teachers should find such checklists helpful, especially when a new instructional technology is introduced into an instructional plan. The checklist should be simple and readily available in the classroom (e.g., hanging on a clipboard in a convenient spot). Another option is to embed the checklist into the instructional technology being used. For example, a word processing file of the checklist could be archived on the classroom computer or it could be created on an iPad. However, neither strategy—clipboard or digital file—is better than the other; each educator's preference and classroom management style should dictate what form the checklist takes. It is far more important to monitor the instructional integrity of one's plan.

When the teacher starts a new lesson or starts to use a new instructional technology, it is helpful to use the self-checklist after every lesson. However, once the

Instructional Step	1/7	1/8	1/9	1/10	1/11	Step Integrity (%)
1. SMART Board shared reading lesson using poem connected to EXPECT IT standard and learning objective.	✓	✓	✓	✓	✓	100
2. Read poem together on SMART Board using the highlighting feature to focus children's attention to rime (at).	✓	✓	✓	✓	✓	100
3. Students choose not to initial letters at the bottom of SMART Board and drag into place.	✓		✓	✓	✓	80
4. Reread the new poem together with the children.	✓	✓	✓	✓	✓	100
5. Point out the changes in meaning and sounds that have been manipulated.	✓	✓			✓	60
						Average
Total Instructional Integrity (%)	100	80	80	80	100	88

Figure 4.10.   Teacher self-checklist used to determine instructional integrity. (© 2013 C. Blum & H.P. Parette.)

Total Instructional Integrity

N Steps Completed /Total *N* Steps x 100

On 1/8 in Figure 4.12 her Total Instructional Integrity was 4/5 = .80 x 100 = 80%. She did this calculation for each day and put the numbers in the self-check table.

She then averaged all the days for the week she implemented the planned activity.

100 + 80 + 80 + 80 + 100/5 = 88

88% - Total Average Instructional Integrity for 1st week of teaching using SMART Board for shared reading.

Instructional Step Integrity

Total *N* of an Individual Step Completed/Total *N* of Opportunities to Complete the Step X 100

Steps 1, 2, & 4 were implemented 100% of the time.

Step 3 was complete 4 times/5 opportunities = .80 x 100 = 80%.

Step 5 was completed 3 times/5 opportunities = .60 x 100 = 60%

Figure 4.11. Computation of total instructional integrity and instructional step integrity. (© 2013 C. Blum & H.P. Parette.)

educator attains a level of comfort in implementing the procedures, the checklist can be used less frequently (e.g., once every 2 weeks). It is particularly important for educators to measure their instructional integrity on a regular basis. Cates, Blum, and Swerdlik (2011) described how instructional integrity can be simply calculated using two different methods: total instructional integrity and instructional step integrity (see Figure 4.11).

Calculating Total Instructional Integrity

The total instructional integrity of a planned lesson is calculated using the following formula:

Total Instructional Integrity (%) = *N* of Steps Completed / Total *N* Steps in a Lesson × 100

This formula provides a percentage of the steps completed by the teacher for the planned activity. It looks at the numbers in a column of the self-checklist table for a particular instructional session. Although this percentage is an interesting number, it does not provide information about the steps that are being missed, which is important given that teachers tend to make repeated errors in classroom instructional sessions. They may skip the same instructional steps or consistently forget procedures related to technology integration. Total instructional integrity does not identify these areas of difficulty for the teacher, which suggests a need for an additional instructional integrity measure that can be used to complement total instructional integrity.

Calculating Instructional Step Integrity

To derive a measure of one's integrity in adhering to instructional steps, the following formula is used:

Instructional Step Integrity (%) = Total N of an Individual Step Completed /
Total N of Opportunities to Complete the Step
× 100

Calculating instructional step integrity looks at numbers across a row in the self-checklist table. This number provides a percentage of a completed individual step in the planned activity across instructional sessions.

Mrs. Hearns uses the instructional integrity self-check to monitor her instructional integrity during the week she was using the SMART Board for shared reading (see Figure 4.9). She noticed immediately that she was not always following Step 5, and she needed to slow the pace of the planned activity at the end to make sure she completed the step. She calculated her instructional integrity two ways (see Figure 4.9).

After conducting the calculations (see Figure 4.11), Mrs. Hearns did not worry that her instructional integrity was somewhat off the first week of completing the planned activity. She realized she needed to practice a bit more to make sure her students were benefiting from all the possible learning opportunities in her lesson. Over time, she did improve, as did her students' performance during the shared reading using a SMART Board.

SUMMARY

As teachers use the EXPECT IT-PLAN IT-TEACH IT approach to integrate instructional technology into their classrooms, they must also ensure that CHECK IT assessment tools and data collection strategies discussed in this chapter are incorporated into planned activities. Readily available instructional technologies provide new and engaging means of delivering instruction to all young children. However, whether or not the planned activities that are supported by instructional technology are indeed effective can only be answered when effective assessment and evaluation practices are used.

Major professional organizations have established guidelines for assessment and evaluation in early childhood classrooms. Combined with the EXPECT IT-PLAN IT-TEACH IT technology integration framework, the CHECK IT process is useful in evaluating young children's outcomes and assessing special needs for the purpose of problem solving. In today's educational environments, accountability has become increasingly important for everyone. Teachers must be mindful of their instructional integrity and use assessment strategies to reach out to families and demonstrate their conscientiousness and accountability as practitioners. In reflecting on the use of assessment and evaluation in one's own practice, consider the question, "Would I take off in a large jet plane at night with a pilot who had no radio or instruments?" Probably not. You would be concerned for your safety because the pilot has no way of making a moment-to-moment assessment of the flight situation to keep you safe.

The trust placed in all early childhood education professionals by families is a tremendous responsibility, and it affords them the great privilege of teaching young children. More than ever, as technology is integrated into preschool and kindergarten classrooms, teachers need to make sure that they "have their instruments on." Teachers can use the CHECK IT process and an array of assessment tools and data collection strategies to guide their instruction.

ADDITIONAL READINGS

Alberto, P.A., & Troutman, A.C. (2008). *Applied behavior analysis for teachers* (8th ed.). Upper Saddle River, NJ: Pearson Education.

Bagnato, S.J., & Neisworth, J.T. (1991). *Assessment for early intervention: Best practices for professionals.* New York, NY: Guilford.

Barton, E.E., Reichow, B., & Wolery, M. (2007). Guidelines for graphing data with Microsoft PowerPoint. *Journal of Early Intervention, 29,* 320–336.

Blanchard, J., & Moore, T. (2010). *A white paper. The digital world of young children: Impact on emergent literacy.* New York, NY: Pearson Foundation.

Brassard, M.R., & Boehm, A.E. (2007). *Preschool assessment. Principles and practices.* New York, NY: Guilford Press.

Carnine, D., Grossen, B., & Silbert, J. (1995). Direct instruction to accelerate cognitive growth. In J. Block, S. Everson, & T. Guskey (Eds.), *Choosing research-based school improvement programs* (pp. 129–152). New York, NY: Scholastic.

Cohen, D., Stern, V., & Balaban, N. (1997). *Observing and recording the behavior of young children* (4th ed.). New York, NY: Teachers College Press.

Cook, R.E., Klein, M.D., & Tessier, A. (2008). *Adapting early childhood curricula for children in inclusive settings.* Upper Saddle River, NJ: Pearson Merrill Prentice Hall.

Copple, C., & Bredekamp, S. (2009). *Developmentally appropriate practice in early childhood programs serving children from birth through age 8* (3rd ed.). Washington, DC: National Association for the Education of Young Children.

Division for Early Childhood. (2007). *Promoting positive outcomes for children with disabilities: Recommendations for curriculum, assessment, and program evaluation.* Missoula, MT: Author.

Gillis, A., Luthin, K., Parette, H.P., & Blum, C. (2012). Using VoiceThread to create meaningful receptive and expressive learning activities for young children. *Early Childhood Education Journal, 40,* 203–211.

Glaubke, C. (2007). *The effects of interactive media and preschoolers' learning: A review of the research and recommendations for the future.* Oakland, CA: Children Now.

Grisham-Brown, J., Hemmeter, M.L., & Pretti-Frontczak, K. (2005). *Blended practices for teaching young children in inclusive settings.* Baltimore, MD: Paul H. Brookes Publishing Co.

Hall, T., & Mengel, M. (2002). *Curriculum-based evaluations.* Wakefield, MA: National Center on Accessing the General Curriculum. Retrieved September 30, 2012, from http://aim.cast.org/learn/historyarchive/backgroundpapers/curriculum-based_evaluations

Helm, J.H., Beneke, S., & Steinheimer, K. (2007). *Windows on learning: Documenting young children's work.* New York, NY: Teachers College Press.

Intellitools. (2007). *The research basis for Intellitools products.* Petaluma, CA: Cambium Learning.

Judge, S.L., & Parette, H.P. (Eds.). (1998). *Assistive technology for young children with disabilities: A guide to providing family-centered services.* Cambridge, MA: Brookline.

Mistrett, S.G., Lane, S.J., & Ruffino, A.G. (2005). Growing and learning through technology: Birth to five. In D. Edyburn, K. Higgins, & R. Boone (Eds.), *Handbook of special education technology research and practice* (pp. 273–308). Whitefish Bay, WI: Knowledge by Design.

Morrison, G.S. (2010). *Fundamentals of early childhood education* (6th ed.). Upper Saddle River, NJ: Merrill.

Parette, H.P., Blum, C., & Boeckmann, N.M. (2009). Evaluating assistive technology in early childhood education: The use of a concurrent time series probe approach. *Early Childhood Education Journal, 37,* 5–12.

Parette, H.P., Blum, C., Meadan, H., & Watts, E. (2008, November). *Implementing and monitoring assistive technology: How to use concurrent time series designs and interpret outcomes.* Poster presented at the National Association for the Education of Young Children 2008 Annual Conference and Expo, Dallas, TX.

Parette, H.P., Peterson-Karlan, G.R., Wojcik, B.W., & Bardi, N. (2007). Monitor that progress! Interpreting data trends for assistive technology decision-making. *Teaching Exceptional Children, 40,* 22–29.

Parette, H.P., Watts, E., Blum, C., & Wojcik, B. (2010, January). *Documenting AT effectiveness using a time series probe research approach.* Paper presented at the Assistive Technology Industry Association Annual Meeting, Orlando, FL.

Sandall, S., Hemmeter, M.L., Smith, B.J., & McLean, M.E. (2005). *DEC recommended practices. A comprehensive guide for practical application in early intervention/early childhood special education.* Missoula, MT: Division for Early Childhood.

Shinn, M.R. (1989). *Curriculum-based measurement: Assessing special children.* New York, NY: Guilford Press.

Watts, E.H., O'Brian, M., & Wojcik, B.W. (2004). Four models of assistive technology consideration: How do they compare to recommended educational assessment practices? *Journal of Special Education Technology, 19,* 43–56.

REFERENCES

Blagojevic, B., & Gathwait, A. (2001). Observing and recording growth and change: Using technology as an assessment tool. *Scholastic Early Childhood Today, 15*(8), 36–44.

Cates, G.L., Blum, C., & Swerdlik, M.E. (2011). *Effective RTI training and practices: Helping school and district teams improve academic performance and social behavior*. Champaign, IL: Research Press.

Deno, S.L. (1987). Curriculum-based measurement. *Teaching Exceptional Children, 20,* 41–42.

Kelley, B., Hosp, J., & Howell, K. (2008). Curriculum-based evaluation and math: An overview. *Assessment for Effective Intervention, 33,* 250–256.

Kostelnik, M.J., Soderman, A.K., & Whiren, A.P. (2011). *Developmentally appropriate curriculum. Best practices in early childhood education* (5th ed.). Upper Saddle River, NJ: Pearson.

McLean, M., Wolery, M., & Bailey, D.B. (Eds.). (2004). *Assessing infants and preschoolers with special needs*. Englewood Cliffs, NJ: Prentice-Hall.

Messick, S. (1980). Test validity and the ethics of assessment. *American Psychologist, 35,* 1012–1027.

National Association for the Education of Young Children and the National Association of Early Childhood Specialists in State Departments of Education. (2003). *Early childhood curriculum, assessment, and program evaluation. Building an effective, accountable system in programs for children birth through age 8*. Washington, DC: Author. Retrieved September 30, 2012, from http://www.naeyc.org/files/naeyc/file/positions/CAPEexpand.pdf

Nilson, B.A. (2010). *Week by week. Plans for documenting children's development* (5th ed.). Belmont, CA: Wadsworth.

No Child Left Behind Act of 2001, PL 107-110, 115 Stat. 1425, 20 U.S.C. §§ 6301 *et seq.* (2001).

Parette, H.P., Meadan, H., Doubet, S., & Hess, J. (2010). Supporting families of young children with disabilities using technology. *Education and Training in Autism and Developmental Disabilities, 45,* 552–565.

Sandall, S.R., & Schwartz, I.S. (2008). *Building blocks for teaching preschoolers with special needs* (2nd ed.). Baltimore, MD: Paul H. Brookes Publishing Co.

Wortham, S.C. (2012). *Assessment in early childhood education* (6th ed.). Upper Saddle River, NJ: Merrill.

5

Technology Problem Solving for Children with Disabilities

George R. Peterson-Karlan, Howard P. Parette, Jr., Craig Blum

After reading this chapter, you should be able to

- Describe the connection between the EXPECT IT-PLAN IT-TEACH IT framework and problem solving for children with disabilities
- Describe and be aware of the role of the individualized family service plan and individualized education program objectives in problem solving
- Describe what partial participation is and how it relates to problem solving for assistive technology
- Describe the Break It Down process and how it is used in SOLVE IT
- Describe how to use probes as part of CHECK IT to evaluate assistive technology solutions

In Chapter 2, the EXPECT IT-PLAN IT-TEACH IT framework was introduced to help early childhood education professionals understand the process of integrating instructional technology into classroom activities. The framework connects instructional technology to curriculum standards, day-to-day classroom activities, and teaching and assessing children's educational progress using technology. Many decisions about what to teach, what instructional technology to use, how to instruct, and how to assess are made during the EXPECT IT and PLAN IT phases before any instruction is attempted with young children in the classroom.

The EXPECT IT-PLAN IT-TEACH IT framework yields a comprehensive plan for using instructional technology to meet the educational needs of most children participating in large and small-group activities in the early childhood classroom. For typically developing children, the model works well and can support their active engagement and participation. However, in today's early childhood classrooms, both typically developing young children and those who have disabilities are often served together. This means that the same instructional technologies and strategies used in small- and large-group settings may not ensure both the inclusion and participation of all children who have disabilities. Consider the following example.

Aidan is a social, happy kindergartner who likes to play with his friends but has difficulties maintaining his attention on classroom activities. He cannot remember more than two steps in multistep task sequences and therefore cannot complete the SMART Board activities that other students use for learning. The difficulties Aidan experiences during planned small-group activities cause frustration and acting-out behavior, which disrupts others during the planned SMART Board activity.

Cherise is a bright, alert preschooler who exhibits curiosity about many classroom technologies used in her curriculum, but she has movement problems caused by cerebral palsy and difficulty speaking in both large- and small-group activities. Cherise has trouble performing most fine motor tasks that require gripping and coordinated hand movements, which prevents her from using many apps on the iPad and the standard keyboard on her classroom computer. Although she does understand others and can produce sounds, Cherise is unintelligible to most people and cannot answer or ask questions orally during large- and small-group activities.

Cody is an active and sociable kindergartener who enjoys listening to stories, but he has cognitive disabilities that pose challenges during early literacy activities in class. Cody cannot recognize words but can identify about 15–20 pictures of common objects. When his classmates are presented with Starfall.com activities that focus on reading comprehension, Cody is unable to make appropriate selections on the computer screen that reflect understanding of stories that are read to him.

Such characteristics of young children with disabilities are not uncommon in today's early childhood classrooms. Classroom activities using instructional technology must therefore be designed with consideration for the *unique* needs of young children with disabilities.

THE LAW AND YOUNG CHILDREN WITH DISABILITIES

This chapter deals with specialized problem-solving methods designed for children with disabilities. Whenever instruction is provided to children with disabilities, teachers must be familiar with educational law and regulations. This is certainly true when a problem-solving process for these children is used. This chapter provides some introductory information on the law and children with disabilities. However, educational law on children with disabilities involves federal and state law and their respective regulations as well as a substantial body of case law from the courts, which makes its understanding both complex and nuanced. Thus, it is essential that teachers expand their knowledge beyond what is described in this chapter.

Federal law incorporates special protections for children with disabilities because they have not always been able to gain access to education. The Individuals with Disabilities Education Improvement Act (IDEA) of 2004 (PL 108-446) is a federal law designed to ensure that every child with disabilities is provided with a free and appropriate public education in the child's least restrictive environment. *Free* means without cost to the family. *Appropriate* means an education that is matched to the child's and family's needs. From a technology perspective, this means that children need to have access to curriculum, instruction, and technology that is appropriate for a young child. It has also come to mean that schools do not have to spend excessive amounts of money on technology or supports as long as they are providing an appropriate curriculum and support for the child with a disabilities. However, if the child truly needs a specialized technology device to have appropriate access to the curriculum, then schools must provide it.

Least restrictive environment means a continuum of services and support ranging from more intensive (e.g., a special class for children with disabilities only) to least intensive (e.g., full-time placement in a classroom with typically developing peers with collaboration support from a special educator). More practically—and most often what is highly effective—young children should be in their natural environment (i.e., home, school, and community settings). *Inclusion*, a central theme of early childhood education, means that children with and without disabilities learn together in an early childhood classroom or other natural setting (Sadao & Robinson, 2010). In inclusive early childhood classrooms, children are learning and accessing the general core curriculum and having their individual learning needs met simultaneously.

The IDEA of 2004 mandates that young children who are at risk and those who have disabilities be identified at an early age and provided services to meet their individual needs. Services are designed to address delays in five critical developmental domains (essential areas of human development), including the following (Beard, Carpenter, & Johnson, 2011):

- Cognitive

- Physical

- Communication

- Social-emotional

- Adaptive development

A *risk factor* is something that increases one's chances that disease, disability, or learning problems will develop in the future. For example, smoking cigarettes is a risk factor for cancer. Identification of risk factors that predict learning problems in young children is possible. Risk factors may include both physical and medical conditions such as low birth weight, chronic illness, or an identified syndrome and environmental risk (e.g., parental substance abuse, abuse and neglect, extreme poverty, parental cognitive impairments; Beard et al., 2011). Children who are at risk for developing delays in one or more of these domains may also receive early intervention and early childhood services under IDEA of 2004. Young children with disabilities such as cerebral palsy, autism spectrum disorders, reduction or limitations in vision or hearing, brain injury, genetic disorders, or other medical conditions have delays in development in one or more of the five critical developmental domains (i.e., cognitive, physical, communicative, social, and emotional or adaptive development).

Individualized Education Programs and Individual Family Service Plans

When using problem solving for technology integration with young children who have disabilities, there are two important educational documents to consider. When

When given instructions by an adult, Aidan will attend to the teacher for 3 of 4 trials for 1 minute by 12/1/12.

When given a simple direction in the classroom, using oral, written and picture cues, Aidan will respond appropriately in 3 out of 4 opportunities.

Using an augmentative and alternative communication system, Cherise will increase her oral participation in class from a level of no oral interaction to one comment per 2 class discussions by 3/15/12.

Cherise will use an augmentative and alternative communication system to independently ask and/or answer questions during structured activities in 4 out of 5 opportunities.

Cody will identify 5 pictures related to a story read orally by the teacher with 85% accuracy.

When asked a question for preferred/non-preferred items in an activity setting, Cody will respond with yes/no as appropriate in 3 out of 4 opportunities.

Figure 5.1. Sample individualized education program objectives for young children with disabilities. (© 2013 C. Blum & H.P. Parette.)

young children age 0–3 are identified with one or more eligible risk factors or disabilities, a qualified educational team (including family members) prepares an individualized family service plan (IFSP). The IFSP describes what services the young child or the child's family will receive, as well as how often, where, and by whom the services will be provided.

When a child with identified disabilities reaches the age of 3 years and becomes eligible for early childhood education, an individualized education program (IEP) is prepared based upon input and decision-making by the qualified educational team collaborating with the child's family. The IEP, updated annually, provides a summary of the child's abilities and needs and establishes measurable educational goals and objectives within the five critical domains previously noted. Examples of the types of IEP objectives that early childhood education professionals might observe in IEPs are noted in Figure 5.1.

IDEA of 2004 clearly requires that all children with disabilities participate in the general education curriculum to the greatest degree possible while still meeting their unique needs. Early childhood education classrooms have a history of inclusively serving children with disabilities. It is important to note that many, if not most, young children with disabilities can be provided with the instruction and educational services documented in their IEPs within inclusive early childhood education programs and classrooms. Federal and state law and regulations, IEPs, and IFSPs have a tremendous positive influence in ensuring young children with disabilities gain access to education. These laws do not specifically govern curriculum or instructional choices; however, they provide a legal and regulatory foundation promoting access to the curriculum and natural environments. Additionally, the law requires that the necessary supports and services to gain that access to the curriculum be in place. The SOLVE IT process discussed in this chapter is a form of problem solving designed to help ensure the law is not only implemented but also expanded upon.

SOLVE IT: INCLUDING YOUNG CHILDREN WITH DISABILITIES

Curriculum standards and learning objectives identified for typically developing young children during the EXPECT IT phase serve as a basis for the curricular goals and objectives identified in IEPs for children with disabilities. When the EXPECT IT-PLAN IT-TEACH IT technology integration framework is used to plan and deliver activities, it results in a comprehensive program for using instructional technology to meet the educational needs of most children participating in large- and small-group activities. However, a young child with disabilities also has goals and objectives identified in the IEP that are selected to meet his or her unique physical, social-emotional, cognitive, communication, and adaptive needs. This requires the teacher to make a connection between the process of making decisions about curricular standards, technology selection, and classroom activities and the process of meeting the unique needs of children with disabilities with specialized supports. This process is called SOLVE IT.

Essentially, SOLVE IT is a supplemental problem-solving approach to meet the unique needs and challenges of young children with disabilities within the context of day-to-day instructional planning. SOLVE IT results in an individual plan for meeting the needs of a specific child at risk for or with disabilities that supplements and enhances the comprehensive instructional technology integration plan. SOLVE IT uses elements of the PLAN IT and TEACH IT processes to make decisions about individual technology solutions.

Problems and Barriers Experienced by Children with Disabilities

Instructional technologies, particularly those that are readily available (see Chapter 2), may address some learning needs of young children with disabilities without further planning or instruction. However, many children with disabilities may encounter significant barriers or experience substantial problems in participating in planned activities developed using the EXPECT IT-PLAN IT-TEACH IT framework. Physical and sensory impairments may create barriers to the children accessing some of the elements of the planned educational activity.

For example, Noah and his classmates go to the literacy center to select and use word recognition apps that Mr. Bivens has downloaded onto several iPads that he uses in his planned instructional activities. The apps require children to make selections on the iPad screen using their fingers. Due to his limited fine motor skills caused by cerebral palsy, Noah has great difficulty using his index finger to make selections within the app.

Communication or social impairments may create barriers to successful participation in the interactions with other children and adults in planned educational activities. For example, Emily, a student with autism spectrum disorder, watches a YouTube video of *The Very Hungry Caterpillar* with her classmates. The video is projected onto a screen by a digital projector. After viewing the video, her teacher poses comprehension questions to the students using a Clicker 6 activity. Students are expected to raise their hands to answer the questions. Emily does not raise her hand to answer any question; when the teacher does call on her to probe her understanding, she looks away and fails to answer.

Finally, cognitive impairments may create problems with the children effectively learning within the planned educational activity. For example, Darian watches a PowerPoint-animated book—*Green Eggs and Ham*—that his teacher prepared for a large-group literacy activity. After viewing the book on a digital projector, the teacher asks comprehension questions about sequences in the story. Darian is functioning at an early emergent literacy level and does not remember the story sequence, so he cannot answer questions in the same way as his peers.

In each of these examples, a student exhibits problems in participating in a planned activity due to a disability. The presence of such disabilities often results in the child's exclusion from the curriculum, calling attention to the need for different technology-based solutions.

Technology-Based Problem Solving

Young children with disabilities need well-designed and carefully implemented supports to overcome the barriers and problems that can result from their disabilities. In the previous examples, the problems demonstrated by children with more significant physical, sensory, communicative, or cognitive disabilities present challenges to designing planned activities that support active participation and maximize learning. At times, the discrepancy between the learning expectations for typically developing young children and the expectations and abilities of those with more significant disabilities may seem daunting. In such instances, teachers may erroneously assume that more specialized and noninclusive classrooms are the best solution for such young children. However, two better complementary solutions available for consideration in the SOLVE IT process are partial participation and assistive technology (AT).

Partial participation occurs when children participate in part of the activity but not all of it. AT, as discussed in Chapters 1 and 3, is a specialized technology that compensates for what a young child cannot do. Both of these solutions require consultation and collaboration among early childhood education professionals, special educators, related service personnel (e.g., occupational therapist, physical therapist, speech and language pathologist), and the families of young children with disabilities.

Common Misconceptions About SOLVE IT Solutions

Decisions on whether or not to include children with significant disabilities in classrooms with typically developing children have often been made based on certain misconceptions about curriculum and instruction for children with disabilities (Baumgart et al., 1982; Ferguson & Baumgart, 1991), such as the following:

- Curricular content, instructional environments, activities, and materials must be matched to a child's current assessed developmental age.

- Prerequisite skills must be mastered before access to instructional environments and activities is allowed.

- There should be an assurance that a student can acquire all the skills in an activity before participation in it is initiated.

- There should be an expectation that the student will be able to perform each skill targeted in the learning activity at an independent level (without assistance or supervision) before instruction is initiated.

Such flawed assumptions may prevent even the possibility of a typical education for students with more significant disabilities (Ferguson & Baumgart, 1991). Other strategies are needed to ensure that these young children are included in planned activities.

Partial Participation   In contrast to the potential errors of assumption noted above, teachers should consider the principle of partial participation when designing planned classroom activities as part of a SOLVE IT solution. Partial participation of young children with disabilities in planned activities is educationally more advantageous than exclusion from such environments and activities.

For example, Cody is a child with cognitive disabilities who is fully included with his typically developing peers in an early childhood classroom. In a small-group activity, each child is expected to speak using a complete sentence to predict parts of *The Very Hungry Caterpillar* electronic book. Cody's IEP goal is for him to express two-word sentences with a subject and a verb. Cody partially participates in the activity, but the expectation is modified to fit his IEP goal. Cody enjoys the partial participation as well as the benefits of peer modeling and the rich curriculum.

Cody's teacher created an opportunity for him to participate in the curriculum. Even though he was not responding exactly how the other children were, he was working to meet his IEP objective. Through partial participation, Cody not only worked on his IEP goal but also heard how children without disabilities responded to the teacher, providing the considerable benefit of peer modeling. Partial participation has increased Cody's access to the core curriculum, making it a superior SOLVE IT solution.

Baumgart et al. (1982) observed that the kinds and degrees of partial participation in school and nonschool environments and activities should be increased through direct and systematic instruction (described in the ARRANGE IT phase; see Chapter 3), beginning at an early age, to ensure that children are able to participate in activities with typically developing peers and adults as much as possible. During the PLAN IT phase, partial participation in planned activities may be supported using personalized and individual adaptations that 1) enhance young children's existing skills, 2) compensate for missing skills that will not likely be acquired, or 3) allow for the acquisition of alternative skills (Baumgart et al., 1982). Five types of individual strategies can be used to achieve these outcomes:

1. *Use or create materials or devices.* Provide objects, equipment, or materials that permit and enhance participation in the steps of the planned activity. For example, Cherise uses an adapted keyboard to type into the SMART Board, thereby partially participating in an IntelliTools Classroom Suite 4 phonics activity.

2. *Use personal assistance.* Provide verbal, physical, or supervisory assistance to the child during transitions to participation in and transition out of the planned activity. For example, a peer provides a visual and verbal model for the reading comprehension activity to Cody, thus allowing partial participation (while other children are expected to participate fully).

3. *Adapt skill sequences.* Rearrange or change the sequence of skills needed to complete a planned activity (see Chapter 3). For example, children are expected to

say letter names upon recognition. Sarah, who has a visual impairment, cannot see letters. Instead, the skill sequence is adapted so that she can learn basic Braille words. She partially participates by typing on an adapted IntelliKeys® keyboard with Braille words on the overlay. The children learn that *A* is for *apple*. The teacher allows Sarah and all the other children in the class to feel and smell the apple. Sarah finds the apple on the IntelliKeys® overlay, presses it, and a short sentence is read about apples. The sensory experience, technology, and adapted curriculum not only benefit Sarah but enhance learning for all the other children.

4. *Adapt rules.* Modify the prescribed guidelines, procedures, or customs for engaging in a planned activity. For example, children are learning to hop on one foot during a Simon Says activity presented on a video created by their teacher. The video was designed to be used at home and school and was placed on the class web site. Freddy, who uses a wheelchair, cannot hop. Alternatively, the rules are adapted so he can push himself up and down on in his chair instead, permitting partial participation and further developing his arm strength.

5. *Social/attitudinal adaptations.* Change the assumptions, judgments, or beliefs that govern the behavior and responses of those who participate in planned activities. For example, when working on the computer with a peer, it takes Isabella longer to press the touch screen to respond. To encourage Isabella to participate, she is permitted to have a slower response because of her poor motor control. The children, who are excited by the game, are taught about diversity and that it is courteous to wait for people to take their turn even if they are a little slower. The children learn tolerance and a new set of norms regarding people with disabilities, and it permits Isabella to partially participate.

Strategies for adapting planned activities such as those presented above serve as the basis for problem solving to optimally increase participation of young children with more severe disabilities. The first two strategies focus on whether individualized materials or devices or individualized personal supports can be used to increase active, effective participation by young children with disabilities. The next two strategies focus on whether changes are needed to help children perform expected skills, even with use of individualized materials or personal supports. The final strategy addresses issues of acceptance of materials, devices, personal supports, or the skill or rule modifications needed on the part of others (e.g., teachers, peers) who participate in planned activities.

Assistive Technology The IDEA of 2004 requires that educational teams consider the child's need for AT devices and AT services. AT is defined within IDEA of 2004 as "any item, piece of equipment or product system, whether acquired commercially or off the shelf, modified, or customized, that is used to increase, maintain, or improve functional capabilities of individuals with disabilities" [20 U.S.C. § 1401(251)]. AT also includes the services that support the acquisition and implementation of the AT. The IDEA of 2004 defines AT services as "any service that directly assists an individual with a disability in the selection, acquisition, or use of an assistive technology device" [20 U.S.C. 1401 § 602(2)]. Such services could include the following [20 U.S.C. 1401 § 602(2)(A-F)]:

- Evaluation of the child's needs, including a functional evaluation of the child in his or her customary environment

- Purchasing, leasing, or otherwise providing for access to AT devices by the child

- Selecting, designing, fitting, customizing, adapting, applying, maintaining, repairing, or replacing AT devices

- Coordinating and using other therapies, interventions, or services with AT devices, such as those associated with existing education and rehabilitation plans and programs

- Providing training or technical assistance for the child, or, when appropriate, the child's family

As discussed in Chapter 3, the IDEA of 2004 places emphasis on the compensatory nature of AT—that is, it compensates for something a young child cannot do or perform. For teachers, AT is a tool (and strategy for using the tool) that allows a young child to do a task he or she could not do without the tool (or strategy) at the expected performance level (Parette, Peterson-Karlan, Wojcik, & Bardi, 2007). For example, Cherise's use of an adapted keyboard may allow her to access a computer program she would not have access to otherwise. Steven uses a communication device to augment his communication because he is nonverbal. Carlos uses a picture schedule with Boardmaker icons to know what activity comes next. All of these are examples of AT wherein the child cannot perform a specific task because of his or her disabilities. Thus, a device or item is provided and, with specialized instruction, the child is able to use the device or item to compensate for what they cannot do at expected levels. Using the specialized child-focused instructional strategies discussed in Chapter 3 is an essential part of the SOLVE IT solutions involving AT.

Although the types of instructional technology discussed thus far are helpful in planned activities using the EXPECT IT-PLAN IT-TEACH IT framework, they are not individualized for young children with disabilities. AT must be individually matched to and uniquely required for a young child with a disability to participate in the curriculum, access the classroom activities, and make educational progress to the fullest degree possible (Parette & Peterson-Karlan, 2010). Although there are many ways to understand the types of AT available (Family Center on Technology and Disability, 2012; Peterson-Karlan & Parette, 2008; Sadao & Robinson, 2010), one effective way to consider AT options that meet most children's needs is to study how they support movement (e.g., mobility, positioning, transition from positioning to movement), communication, and interaction with materials (e.g., objects, toys, instructional materials, computer devices; Mistrett, Lane, & Ruffino, 2005). More specific information about AT is provided in the remaining chapters of this book.

Individual Problem Solving in the EXPECT IT-PLAN IT-TEACH IT Framework

As noted, children with disabilities may experience barriers and problems, even in light of thoughtfully planned and executed activities using EXPECT IT-PLAN

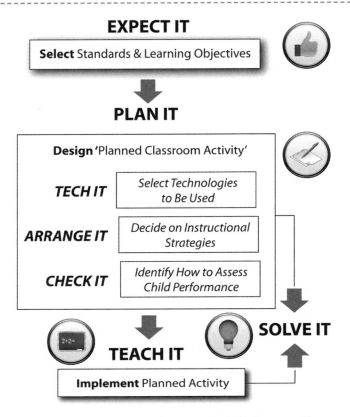

EXPECT IT

Select Standards & Learning Objectives

PLAN IT

Design 'Planned Classroom Activity'

TECH IT — *Select Technologies to Be Used*

ARRANGE IT — *Decide on Instructional Strategies*

CHECK IT — *Identify How to Assess Child Performance*

SOLVE IT

TEACH IT

Implement Planned Activity

Figure 5.2. SOLVE IT in the EXPECT IT-PLAN IT-TEACH IT process. (© 2013 H.P. Parette, C. Blum, & G.R. Peterson-Karlan.)

IT-TEACH IT decision making. These barriers or problems might be anticipated based on the characteristics and severity of a child's disabilities; however, the barriers or problems may not manifest themselves until after the children have begun participating in the planned educational activities. In either case, SOLVE IT (see Figure 5.2) provides a supplemental framework for addressing these anticipated or unanticipated problems. It represents a process for matching the support needs of the young child with disabilities to AT in order to help the child meet the expected performance levels of planned activities.

BREAK IT DOWN: A PRACTICAL APPROACH TO PROBLEM SOLVING

SOLVE IT uses a Break It Down strategy for understanding the problems of the child with disabilities. This approach allows the teacher to select AT solutions that best address the specific barriers or problems that the child with disabilities encounters in the specific planned activity (see Figure 5.3).

When considering the needs of a young child with disabilities, teachers may be tempted to focus on the child and attempt to evaluate the child's abilities in all

---

Name the 'problem' (**NAME IT**)

Break It Down

    Identify the expected performance demands

    Describe the 'gap' between the child's performance and expected performance demands

    Select assistive technology solution/s to 'close the gap' (**ASSISTIVE TECH IT**)

        Consider IFSP/IEP needs

Implement the assistive technology solution in instruction within the planned activity (**ARRANGE IT / CHECK IT**)

Evaluate the effectiveness of the (assistive) technology solution (**TEACH IT-CHECK IT**)

Figure 5.3.   The SOLVE IT-Break It Down problem-solving process. (© 2013 C. Blum, H.P. Parette, & G. Peterson-Karlan.)

relevant areas of functioning, then recommend solutions that might fit all circumstances. When you visit a doctor, you expect him or her to ask questions about specific problems you are having. The doctor may address those concerns personally or refer you to a specialist who can help (e.g., dietician, eye doctor, dermatologist). The specialist and your primary care doctor will only focus on solutions to specific areas of medical need. They do not provide a prescription for your whole life! The SOLVE IT process is a similar approach in that it begins with identifying the problems the child with disabilities experiences in specific areas of activity (e.g., circle time, recess, music, center time) and in the specific planned activity steps in that area (e.g., playing at the water table, shared reading of *Brown Bear, Brown Bear, What Do you See?*, singing songs in a circle).

Before the process of problem solving is initiated, the teacher must name the problem experienced by the child (NAME IT)—that is, the teacher must identify the planned classroom activity and state his or her perception of the child's problem. Some example statements include the following:

- Shawn is having difficulty in making the transition into opening circle.

- Avery is trying but having difficulty answering questions during literacy center.

- Madison has difficulty making on-screen selections during choice time.

The NAME IT step provides a starting place for solving the problems in a specific planned activity. The advantage to this approach is that solutions are tailored to the specific problem. Although they might ultimately prove to be useful across different activity areas and planned activities, the solutions provided by the SOLVE IT process do not initially need to be "super solutions" that attempt to fix everything. The goal of the process is greater inclusion and participation of the child in planned activities.

Once the child's problem has been named, a Break It Down process is used to determine the specific characteristics of the problem in relation to what the planned activity requires the student to DO-SAY-REMEMBER. In Chapter 2, you learned that all planned activities have steps required to complete or participate. DO includes all the physical demands (e.g., standing, moving, walking, making screen selections) and certain perceptual demands (e.g., seeing the computer screen, listening to the voices on a web site activity) that are required to complete a task in a planned activity. SAY includes any oral communication demands that are part of planned activities (e.g., speaking to a peer). REMEMBER includes several key cognitive skills that are required in many steps of planned activities, particularly memory. Memory includes factual demands (e.g., number, word, name, event recognition); remembering sequences of tasks in activities and sequences of daily routines; recalling where things are and spatial relationships; recalling sensory information, such as smells or sounds; and information about social situations (e.g., what greeting to respond with in different situations).

When using the SOLVE IT process, the teacher needs to ask a series of questions and follow a set of corresponding procedures as part of the Break It Down process. These questions and procedures of the Break it Down process are related to what a child has to do, say, or remember and must be completed in sequential order, as presented it Table 5.1.

Table 5.2 provides an example of how the Break It Down format is used in documenting the information generated during the SOLVE IT process for Max, a student having a physical disability. In this example, Max's disability presents barriers to moving around in the classroom, using his hands for fine motor task demands, and communicating with others. Based on what the planned activity steps require typically developing students to DO, SAY, and REMEMBER, and an understanding of Max's abilities and challenges, his teacher identifies the gaps that are present, which helps in identifying AT and partial participation solutions. Max is provided with several AT solutions that give him access to successful completion of or participation in the planned activity tasks.

Two relatively simple AT devices support Max's communication: a Cheap Talk 8 communicator and a simple communication board created with Boardmaker. Both solutions enable Max to meet the SAY demands expected of other students. A simple pointing device with a built-up foam handle is also created by the teacher to enable Max to interact with the SMART Board and tap monkeys on the screen just as other children do. Because he cannot independently push his wheelchair, partial participation is used by having peers position Max in front of the SMART Board so that he can both see the screen presentation and extend his arm using the pointing device to make selections.

Table 5.3 provides an example of how the Break It Down format is used in documenting the information generated during the SOLVE IT process for another child who has attention deficits. In this example, Carrie has trouble attending to the teacher and things that are going on during the planned activity. As a result, she is not learning effectively and disrupts the learning of others when she talks during instruction. Carrie is provided with a Dora the Explorer power card—a

Table 5.1. The Break It Down process with TEACH IT and CHECK IT

Problem question	Break It Down
Identify the expected performance.	
What are the steps of the planned activity?	Write down the steps of the planned activity
What are the DO, SAY, REMEMBER requirements?	For each step, decide what it requires for a typical student to DO-SAY-REMEMBER to complete the planned activity without support
Describe the gap in the child's performance.	
What is the child's performance on each step in the planned activity?	Write down what the child is observed to DO for each step
What is the gap between the child's performance and the expected performance level on the step?	Decide how the problem might relate to the child's ability to DO, SAY, and/or REMEMBER compared to the demands of the planned activity step
Select assistive technology solution(s): ASSISTIVE TECH IT	
If the child had support for DOING in the step, would he or she be better able to perform the step?	Write down the support solution for the step if needed. Consider assistive technology and/or partial participation
If the child had support for SAYING in the step, would he or she be better able to perform the step?	Write down the support solution for the step if needed. Consider assistive technology and/or partial participation
If the student had support for REMEMBERING in the step, would he or she be better able to perform the step?	Write down the support solution for the step if needed. Consider assistive technology and/or partial participation
Implement the assistive technology solution (ARRANGE IT and CHECK IT)	
How will you teach the student to use the assistive technology solution in the step of the planned activity?	Decide how the assistive technology will be used by the child in the planned activity step(s)
	Make a plan for using instructional strategies to teach the student to use the assistive technology to complete the steps of the planned activity (ARRANGE IT)
How will you determine whether the assistive technology solution is working?	Make a plan for how to assess whether the assistive technology is supporting the child in completing the steps of the planned activity (CHECK IT)
Evaluate the effectiveness of the assistive technology solution (TEACH IT-CHECK IT)	
After teaching the child to use the assistive technology solution, what is the child's performance on each step in the planned activity?	Write down what you observe the child actually doing for each step when using the assistive technology solution (TEACH IT-CHECK IT)

(© 2013 by C. Blum, G. Peterson-Karlan, & H.P. Parette.)

small card with pictures of Carrie's preferred hero in a set of instructional steps that she needs to follow directions. Power cards have been used to increase children's compliance or help them follow steps in activities involving social cues. The teacher also uses a feature in Clicker 6 that allows a smiley face to appear when the cursor hovers above a picture that corresponds to a targeted sound. It is accompanied with verbal feedback such as, "Good! The cat makes the /(c)/!" When a student hovers the cursor over a picture that does not correspond to the sound, a straight face appears and no verbal feedback occurs, requiring the student to make another (appropriate) selection. Carrie, like Max, benefits from partial participation as a complement to her AT solution when her teacher has peers give her prompts at transitions.

Table 5.2. Break It Down table for a student with physical disabilities

Define the problem: Max has difficulty participating in a SMART Board literacy activity.

Activity: In this SMART Board small-group activity, the children will watch a YouTube video of *Five Little Monkeys*. Afterward a Smart Board activity will be used in which students will come to the Board and count how many monkeys there are by "tapping" them to disappear. The teacher will ask children to predict what will happen next. After every student takes a turn, the teacher will question the students regarding their discoveries. The instructional strategies for this activity would include modeling, guided discovery, and prompting.

Planned activity steps	Planned activity requirements				Child performance	What's the answer?
	DO	SAY	REMEMBER			
Transition: Students get carpet squares from shelf and seat themselves on squares in front of SMART Board	Listen to teacher's prompt Look at and select carpet square Move to SMART Board and sit	N/A	Recognize SMART Board		Max can hear teacher's prompt He has difficulty gripping a carpet square He cannot move his wheelchair independently Max, sitting in his wheelchair, was pushed by the teacher away from circle and SMART Board	Peer assistance in moving wheelchair and carpet to SMART Board. With assistance Max is close to peers seated on floor*
Watch YouTube video	Look at SMART Board screen during video	N/A	N/A		Max has poor visual acuity and needs to be positioned within 5 feet of objects to see clearly Max sat in wheelchair 7–8 feet from SMART board	Peer positions Max close to the SMART Board.* Max sits next to peers on floor with assistance permitting him to be closer
Count the monkeys on the SMART Board screen	Listen to teacher a she models counting Watch SMART Board screen	Orally count monkeys on screen when called upon	Remember number sequences		Max has a beginning understanding of number concepts. Sometimes at home he attempts to count, but his speech is not intelligible Max sat quietly while the other children counted	Cheap Talk 8 communicator to allow 6 numeral messages (0–5) to be spoken

108

Predict what happens when monkeys are tapped and disappear	Listen to teacher as she gives instructions Watch SMART Board as teacher provides model	Orally predict how many monkeys will be left	Recall steps in instructions provided by teacher	Max can hear and understand simple instructions He has poor visual acuity He cannot use intelligible speech Max sat quietly while other children made predictions	Use Cheap Talk 8 communicator to allow spoken predictions to be made
Tap one monkey away on SMART Board screen	Listen to teacher when called upon Watch SMART Board Come to and stand in front of SMART Board screen Extend hand and tap monkey on screen	N/A	Recall simple rules of subtraction	Max has only been able to count before in one-one situations at home. He has never tried any form of subtraction and just watches other children. Max could not reach the board to tap it Max is able to grasp larger objects Other children showed Max what to touch on SMART Board while he sat in his wheelchair	Boardmaker activity sheet showing combinations of monkeys remaining Provide Max with a simple pointing device made from a classroom pointer with handle wrapped in foam to tap monkey on screen
Transition: Replace carpet squares and go to next activity	Listen to teacher directions Look at carpet square Grasp carpet square and return to shelf Go to next area	N/A	Recall where shelf is located Recall next routine in daily schedule	Max cannot move his wheelchair independently He has poor visual acuity He has difficulty remembering routine sequences during the day Max is moved by the assistant to the next activity before the other children	Max is assisted back in his chair Boardmaker visual schedule of daily routines is available so Max knows what comes next A peer will push Max to his next routine area*

*Partial participation

Table 5.3. Break It Down table for student with attention deficits

Define the problem: Carrie has difficulty making letter-sound matches during large-group story time.

Activity: In this large-group activity, the children will watch an LCD-projected Starfall.com activity—*ABCs. Let's Get Ready to Read.* Students will view animated presentations of four phonemic sounds: /b/, /p/, /k/, and /d/. The teacher will ask children to identify letters and sounds as each is presented and to hold up Boardmaker response cards when she calls out targeted sounds. Students will then participate in a Clicker 5 activity in which sounds are matched with pictures of objects. Students will come to the computer when called and make a selection using the mouse. The instructional strategies for this activity would include direct instruction, modeling, and prompting.

Planned activity steps	Planned activity requirements			Child Performance	What's the Answer?
	DO	SAY	REMEMBER		
Transition: Go to desk	Look at desk in classroom Listen to teacher's prompt	N/A	Recognize desk	Carrie sometimes takes the wrong seat and doesn't seem to hear the teacher's prompt to go to her seat Carrie sat in the free play area and did not go to her desk when prompted; when she saw others moving about she went and sat in another student's desk	Digital photo of Carrie on her desk Peer prompt that it's time to take her seat*
Watch Starfall.com screens for /b/, /p/, /k/, and /d/	Look at screen Listen to audio instructions and teacher questions Hold up response cards	Respond to teacher's questions	Recall letter-sound relationships presented on screen	Carrie often looks around the classroom during instruction and talks with other students Carrie was gazing out the window when instruction began	Power Card having steps for participating Teacher uses prompt, "Look at the screen" before each presentation Peer taps her on shoulder when she is called on*
Watch Clicker 5 screens presenting letter sound matches and make matches	Look at wall screen Listen to teacher instructions Listen to Clicker 5 screens Look at computer screen Click mouse to make selection	Answer teacher questions if asked	Remember directions given by teacher Recall letter-sound relationships presented on screen	Carrie will need to be reminded to watch the screen as others are working She was talking to her friend Katie while the Clicker 5 slides were being presented	Power Card having steps for participating Build in voice prompt in Clicker 5 to get Carrie's attention Build in errorless learning "smiley" feature for mouseover in Clicker 5
Transition: Go to next activity area	Listen to teacher directions Look at next activity area Go to activity area	N/A	Recall routine Remember rules for transitioning Recognize next area to transition to	Carrie sometimes begins talking with others and doesn't follow through with transitions Carrie was talking when the activity ended and students were told to go to literacy center	Power Card having steps for participating Peer prompts her that it's time to transition*

*Partial participation.

FOLLOWING THE STEPS OF THE BREAK IT DOWN PROCESS

Step 1: Identify the Expected Performance

The first step is to identify the expected performance for all young children who participate in the planned activity. Two questions are answered in this step:

1. What are the steps of the planned activity?

2. What are the DO-SAY-REMEMBER requirements of each step?

To answer the first question, the teacher should list the steps of the planned activity (as explained in Chapter 3). As shown in the Planned Activity Steps column of Table 5.2, the teacher writes down what a young child is expected to do to successfully complete a planned activity within an activity area. For example, when considering an opening circle planned activity, the teacher considers step-by-step what the typical young child must do to complete or participate in the opening circle activity. This would include any steps to transition the child into and out of the activity, as well as all parts of the planned activities within opening circle (e.g., calendar, weather, show and tell).

The next question in this step determines the task requirements. Task requirements are what the typical young child needs to DO-SAY-REMEMBER to successfully complete each step of the planned activity. This is written down in the corresponding columns of Table 5.1. In Max's example, to complete the steps of the planned activity, children must DO (e.g., they must use their hands to manipulate objects, make selections on a SMART Board or iPad, or use the computer keyboard; walk to an Activity area or SMART Board; listen to directions or conversations; look at the teacher, technology used, or planned activity area); SAY (e.g., answer questions posed by the teacher; ask questions; socialize/interact with peers); and REMEMBER (e.g., understand task sequences in activities; recognize the sequence of routines during the course of the day). Identification of expected task performance using DO-SAY-REMEMBER for each step permits the teacher to understand all the physical, communication, and cognitive demands that are asked of a child to complete a task. Understanding this will help the teacher to identify challenges and potential solutions.

Step 2: Describe the Gap in the Child's Performance

The next step in problem solving is to describe what the young child with disabilities actually does. As seen in the examples of Max (Table 5.1) and Carrie (Table 5.2), the teacher writes down what is known about the child and his or her observations of the child's actions in the Child Performance column. Therefore, the child must be observed while participating in all steps of the planned activity as they occur in the natural environment, including transitions into and out of the activity. Transitions in and out are key steps in any activity and may present challenges for some children with disabilities. Taking some notes is typically the preferred way most teachers quickly gather these observations. Transferring the notes to the Break It Down table can occur later. However, it is important not to wait too long between when the observation occurred and when the notes are written in the table, or important details may be forgotten!

Once notes have been taken on what the child actually did, it is also necessary to describe any gaps in DO-SAY-REMEMBER—that is, the difference between what was observed and what was expected. The teacher should make decisions about 1) the extent of the gap between the performance of the child with disabilities and the performance that is expected of a typically developing child, and 2) what specific requirements (demands) are not being met by the child across all of the steps of the planned activity. Understanding why a young child was not able to complete a particular step in a planned activity requires some simple investigations on the teacher's part. Because DO-SAY-REMEMBER demands (physical, communication, and cognitive demands) are potentially interrelated in any step of a planned activity (e.g., walking to an area and lining up requires the child to see and remember where to go; speaking to a peer requires that one remember social etiquette rules), the teacher may have to 1) ask the child a question (e.g., to know whether rules or steps are understood or whether directions are heard); 2) observe the response (which provides a clue whether all demands of the planned activity steps are met); and/or 3) consider how the child has responded in previous situations (as prior performance of certain demands might rule out inability to perform the task).

Interpreting DO-SAY-REMEMBER   When examining the demands of planned activity steps, one must first consider what each activity step demanded the child to DO (see the Do column of Tables 5.1 and 5.2). If a child completes an activity step correctly without extra help, there is no need to further evaluate it; in this instance, he or she is completing the activity step correctly. Various forms of scaffolding and prompting discussed in Chapter 3 are available to all children. The gaps or discrepancies that exist for children with disabilities are 1) what they did not do, and 2) what extra help is needed beyond what would be provided for a typical child. What the child with disabilities is able to do, what the child attempts to do unsuccessfully, and maybe what the student does not do is also noted in the Child Performance column.

For example, Max has a lot done for him (see Table 5.2). In inclusive settings where paraprofessionals or other early childhood education professionals are providing considerable assistance, providing physical prompts (e.g., using hand over hand), or just doing things for the child, is an indication that there are physical barriers for the child. Some physical barriers will be obvious. For instance, Max uses a wheelchair and cannot push himself. He also has difficulty reaching and holding things, so he needs a pointer. Other examples include children who might not be able to grip a crayon or use a keyboard.

Other physical barriers, however, may be created by teachers. If the teacher is doing things for Max simply to move the activity along quickly, it may not be seen as a barrier. For example, if Max were able to retrieve his art materials from a bin, but it took considerably longer than other children, the teacher might simply perform this task for him in the interests of time. Similarly, if Max is able to communicate his preferences using a picture communication board, but it requires the teacher to wait longer than for typical students, a decision might simply be made to assume what Max's preference is and not take the time to ask him a question that requires him to use his communication board. In either instance, the goal is to make Max as independent as possible, and doing things for him may be reinforcing his dependence on others.

If a child is not engaging in a step and a physical barrier is suspected, it is important to ensure that it is not related to SAY or REMEMBER demands. For example, Ava may not be participating in the physical activity of Simon Says because she is having difficulty with SAY and is discouraged by the need to verbalize. When multiple demands are placed on the child, it is important to rule out other potential reasons for not completing a step. Ava's teacher rules out the presence of a DO barrier based on her observations of Ava completing other tasks requiring gross motor skills with no associated SAY demand.

Doing also includes perceptual tasks such as seeing and hearing. All young children should have appropriate vision and hearing screenings conducted by qualified professionals. This will identify many perceptual challenges related to seeing and hearing that young children can face. However, other aspects of perception can be difficult to assess. For example, some children with autism spectrum disorders make little or no eye contact with other people. However, this does not mean they are not listening. Young children in particular have the unique ability to acquire language and listen to what is happening around them even though they may actively be doing other things. If a young child appears not to be attending, it is best to confirm first by 1) asking the child to repeat the instruction provided, 2) observing the child while performing a requested task, 3) asking the child a comprehension question, or 4) requesting that the child do something to demonstrate comprehension of what was heard. If the child can repeat what is said or do what is expected, he or she must be listening, even though it appears otherwise. If that is the case, the teacher might consider a behavioral support approach to increase motivation (e.g., positive reinforcement; see Chapter 3) for different attending behaviors.

In addition, if a child is having difficulty remembering a routine, it may not be related to inability to listen. To rule this out, the teacher should consider such things as how many times the task has been repeated and if the child should be able to recall it. For example, after a month, the children in a preschool classroom should know their school routine. If a child continues to have difficulty with the routine, it may simply be that they do not remember the steps of the task yet. This would be more common with a child who has an intellectual disability and difficulty with memory. Other children may have difficulty with responding to natural cues (see Chapter 3), even though they have normal vision and hearing.

Learning how to respond to different kinds of cues is a common learning problem in young children, which can be supported using child-focused instructional strategies (see Chapter 3) combined with AT supports such as picture schedules. The teacher can identify this type of problem if the child does not seem to be responding to natural cues in the same way as typically developing children in the classroom (e.g., wandering around the classroom, staying in one place, not appearing to know what to do). Response to natural cues typically occurs quickly, so if children wait too long, they miss other natural cues that may be important for completing a task.

Like some aspects of perception, observing what the child remembers is somewhat more difficult. It requires that the early childhood educator make inferences from what the child does and what he or she seems to remember and not remember. Identifying memory issues can be difficult through naturalistic observation; if the educator suspects their presence, it may be appropriate for a school psychologist or other medical professional to assess the child. For children in special education, this kind of testing is standard and test results should be in their respective files. However, tests do not always identify everything, and young children develop and change constantly, often revealing educational learning problems that were not previously apparent.

Before the teacher can consider if there is a potential memory problem, he or she must not only know what needs to be remembered but how well other children remember particular tasks. As previously suggested, in early childhood education classrooms, there is substantial scaffolding and prompting that occur to remind young children to do things. This is natural, and young children are not developmentally capable of remembering everything. However, if a child still does not remember things that most of the class has started to remember, it is the first indication that remembering is a potential barrier.

For children with intellectual disabilities, it may be difficult to distinguish between their ability to discriminate a natural cue and remember steps because there may be interrelated learning problems. For this and other reasons already discussed, it is important, when possible, to first rule out DO and SAY demands as primary barriers to completing a task. Clearly, if a child cannot communicate well because of his or her speech or if the child is not attending to directions (listening), it has nothing to do with the child's ability to remember a task. The teacher can rule out these possibilities through observations of the child with disabilities in other classroom activities. For example, suppose that Max's teacher suspects that he has difficulty remembering task sequences (see Table 5.2). The teacher observed that this behavior was consistent in many tasks, especially more complex ones with many steps. His teacher further observed that he could respond to some natural cues. However, as tasks became longer, Max seemed to be more confused about the natural cues. Such a scenario might require support for Max that addresses both natural cues and AT that supports him in learning the steps of an activity.

However, in Carrie's case (see Table 5.3), memory is clearly not an issue. This is because difficulty in attending to a task or listening to instructions both have behavioral components, and it is most likely not a memory problem causing her not to follow directions but a behavioral issue. The teacher observed that Carrie could recall many things when she was attending. This ruled out memory as a probable learning challenge. Although identifying gaps in remembering can be tricky, if the teacher uses simple observations, he or she can rule out different potential explanations of the problem.

When making decisions about the performance of a young child with disabilities, it is helpful to consider whether and how effectively the child can complete a step. For example, Max (see Table 5.2) sits quietly rather than counting the monkeys. For Max, a key learning objective of this planned activity is to practice counting. Sitting passively will diminish his ability to learn how to count. Similarly, skipping steps in daily routines, such as not putting soap on one's hands when washing them, makes the child's attempt to wash hands ineffective. All activities in the early childhood classroom have some kind of effectiveness factor, whether the children are learning something new or practicing routines, such as lining up, washing their hands, or using the bathroom.

In some instances, a young child with a disability may be able to complete all of the steps, although less efficiently than a typically developing child. For example, Andy has underdeveloped fine and gross motor control. By the time Andy picks up one toy and puts it away, all the other children are in a circle awaiting the next activity. Although Andy can perform the steps in the planned activity, it takes him much longer than it does the other children. During this part of the decision-making process, it may be helpful for the teacher to consult with other members of the child's IFSP or IEP team to think about solutions to Andy's problems. They may have insights from their own observations of the young child about the extent of the performance gap or the specific demands not being met.

 ### Step 3: Select AT Solutions (ASSISTIVE TECH IT)

Once it has been decided which steps the child is not completing effectively or efficiently, AT solutions can be selected to help him or her complete the planned activity. Working together with the IFSP or IEP team and the family, AT solutions should be identified for each step with which the young child with disabilities has difficulty (see the What's the Answer? column in Tables 5.2 and 5.3). The team should attempt to list AT solutions based on the questions in Table 5.1 for Step 3. These solutions will support the young child with disabilities to DO the step, SAY what needs to be said, and REMEMBER information or procedures more effectively or efficiently (i.e., using less effort and time and with better quality). The goal here is to list several possible AT tools that will help the child complete the step, and then select the system of tools that will benefit the child the most in the planned activity as a whole. In the process, the teacher should consider issues such as the following: the complexity of the tool, the time needed for the child to learn to use the tool, and the familiarity of educational professionals and family with the technology.

Although the cost of AT may also be a factor, it should never be the first consideration. An inexpensive tool (e.g., a Boardmaker communication board or simple six-message voice output communication device) may be just as effective as a more expensive one (e.g., a voice output communication app for an iPad) if the child needs to express only a limited range of messages in the planned activity. In addition, it may even be a better fit for certain contexts (e.g., using the restroom, expressing a desire to eat lunch).

In some instances, the educational team may conclude that the child may not be able to fully complete all the steps of the planned activity, even with AT. In this case, the educational team may decide to employ other partial participation strategies. For example, a peer pushing Max in his wheelchair (see Table 5.2) is an instance of partial participation. Partial participation strategies should not be used instead of AT but rather as a complement to it; partial participation can even be stopped if AT alone becomes sufficient.

Partial participation may initially be necessary until the young child with disabilities develops more skill or different technology solutions become available that enable the child to fully participate. A young child with cerebral palsy who uses a wheelchair may need a communication device to tell the person who pushes the wheelchair (partial participation strategy) where he or she wants to go. However, later, if a powered wheelchair is provided, the young child with disabilities can independently go from place to place (no partial participation strategy needed). When using partial participation, it is always important to consider how AT could be used to support the performance of the young child with disabilities prior to reducing the amount or type of participation in the planned activity.

Step 4: Implement the AT Solution (TEACH IT-CHECK IT)

The problem-solving process for considering the use of AT with the young child with disabilities does not end when the AT has been selected. Depending on the type of technology selected, members of the child's IFSP or IEP team then may need to acquire the technology, install it (if it is added to a computer system or to a portable device; e.g., an iPad), and learn to use it themselves. For other AT that is created, (e.g., a visual choice board for free play, an audio cueing system for getting ready to go home), a member of the child's educational team, perhaps even the early childhood education professional, will need to prepare the display, making it durable, age-appropriate, and professional.

After acquiring or creating the AT, the teacher should make a plan for instructing the young child with disabilities to use the AT in the context of the planned activity. The teacher should also plan to determine whether the AT is effective in supporting the young child with disabilities in effectively or efficiently completing the planned activity.

TEACH THE CHILD TO USE THE AT SOLUTIONS (ARRANGE IT-CHECK IT)

As with the implementation of instructional technologies for all young children (see Chapter 2), the teacher will need to plan and then teach the young child with disabilities to use the AT solutions within the context of the planned activity.

ARRANGE IT

Planning requires decisions about selecting instructional strategies to be used within instructional arrangements. The members of the child's IFSP or IEP team collaborate in designing this AT instructional plan using their different areas of expertise. Next, a written plan is developed with the instructional objective of having the child gain *functional competence* in the use of the AT within the context of the planned activity. Functional competence refers to the child being able to successfully complete the activity within the time allowed in a step of a planned activity at the desired level of quality. With some AT (e.g., a voice-output communication aid, an iPad-based task prompt system), it may be necessary to create a two-objective plan. One objective produces *operational competence* for the child with disabilities in using the device. Operational competence here refers to the young child's ability to make the device "work" (operate). A second objective of the instructional plan produces functional competence (i.e., the ability to use the AT to get something done). Depending on the complexity of the AT, one integrated instructional plan with both objectives might be developed; alternatively, two distinct plans might be taught sequentially.

CHECK IT

As part of planning for instruction in the use of the AT solutions, the teacher, together with the IFSP or IEP team, will choose assessment strategies that will inform them as to whether the AT is effective in addressing the problems the young child with disabilities demonstrates when attempting to complete a planned activity. The simplest strategy for assessment would be to repeat the original observations of the child attempting to complete each step of the planned activity and to note whether or how the child meets the DO-SAY-REMEMBER requirements for each step. It will also be important to note how the child uses the AT and any problems the child might have in getting access to the AT during the planned activity. Sometimes, the inability of the child to effectively use the AT is not the fault of the child or the instructional plan, but a problem with access to the AT during the planned activity itself. The environment must be arranged such that the AT does not get in the way of the activity, nor should it be out of reach of the child. A simple way to assess the effectiveness of the AT in helping the child is to use an ecological assessment strategy, described in the next section.

Using Activity Probes in the SOLVE IT Process

In Chapter 4, a number of assessment tools and data collection strategies were described. When using the SOLVE IT process to make decisions about AT for young children with disabilities, another kind of approach is helpful to understand whether an AT tool really makes a difference in a planned activity. As previously noted in this chapter, AT is compensatory and thus helps a young child to do something he or she could not do without the AT at some expected level of performance.

Starting with this premise, the teacher can assess the child performing a task in the planned activity both with and without the AT. Changes in child performance can be very subtle and difficult to discern without collecting data. Using probes (i.e., systematic assessments of a skill at selected times with no support provided for that skill) provides an effective and efficient strategy for collecting data to help make problem-solving decisions. It enables the teacher to document a child's performance with and without AT prior to AT selection and implementation (i.e., when several AT alternatives are being considered to determine which AT is most effective). Once a decision is made about AT, the probe approach helps the teacher to determine if the AT is effective in planned activities. Finally, the approach is helpful for progress monitoring over time (i.e., across the school year to determine if the AT continues to be effective in planned activities; Parette, Blum, & Boeckmann, 2009; Parette, Peterson-Karlan, Wojcik, & Bardi, 2007).

Probes should also be used periodically to examine the child's performance without the AT when performing a particular AT-supported task in the child's planned activity. Data on the child's performance is collected before an AT intervention is introduced for a series of days/sessions. The AT intervention for a specific task is then introduced, and data are collected on the child's performance. Probes are made periodically (e.g., weekly) on the same day in which the child also uses the AT for a particular task completion. This is the distinguishing aspect of this particular data collection strategy: Data are collected regularly (e.g., daily) to examine the child's performance on a task using AT, while probes in which the student is asked to perform a task without his or her AT are less frequent (see Figure 5.4).

In Chapter 2, a vignette of Mrs. Hearns was presented in which decisions were made about readily available technologies that supported her curriculum. In her classroom, there is also a young child named Brooke, who has some significant

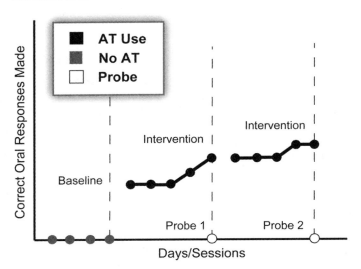

Figure 5.4. Using probes to determine if an assistive technology solution makes a difference. (© 2013 H.P. Parette.)

physical disabilities and uses a wheelchair. Brooke can make sounds and can point to pictures to communicate her intent, and she seems to have good attending skills in group activities. She expresses excitement when Mrs. Hearns asks other students to orally express themselves or use response cards to make choices or respond to questions. Because of Brooke's disability, she cannot participate effectively in any of the small- and large-group settings by orally participating. Consider how Mrs. Hearns approaches problem solving to identify appropriate AT to support Brooke's participation in the curriculum.

During circle time, children are asked to select from among four cards that represent the beginning sounds of pictures and hold an appropriate card up in response to questions. Mrs. Hearns also intermittently asks children to orally sound out their selection. Based on the data that she has collected in four sessions, Brooke can point to sounds represented by pictures placed in front of her but cannot verbalize a choice. This data that was collected is called the *baseline*—that is, the natural occurrence of an academic, social, or life skills task or behavior prior to some new instruction and/or the introduction of AT (Alberto & Troutman, 2012). Mrs. Hearns recognizes that Brooke's physical disability prevents her from verbally selecting a card to demonstrate her understanding and communicate choices about beginning sounds, but pointing to pictures is deemed an appropriate alternative to holding up a card.

The curriculum calls for students to orally demonstrate their understanding of beginning sounds, so it is necessary for Brooke to participate in a manner similar to other students. Although there are a number of communication devices that would allow Mrs. Hearns to orally record the four or more responses required in the curriculum, she remembers that Radio Shack sells programmable picture frames that allow a single message to be recorded. The recorded messages can be heard 5–6 feet away. Mrs. Hearns reasons that if four of these frames were positioned using Velcro adjacent to one another on a board, each with a different picture and recorded response, Brooke could communicate the four responses appropriate for any instructional session using her PowerPoint-based curriculum when she touched a small button on the appropriate picture frame.

Mrs. Hearns soon acquires the picture frames and pastes them to a 3-inch three-ring binder so that an inclined surface would be presented to Brooke, thus making it easier for her to both view choices and to depress the buttons on the frames. Mrs. Hearns records the four sound responses and affixes Boardmaker symbols to the frames (the same symbols used on the other students' response cards).

In delivering her instruction the next day, Mrs. Hearns continues with her scripted lesson, asking, "What sound does *door* begin with? Use your cards!" as a picture appears on her SMART Board. Students select from their picture cards and hold up their respective responses. Brooke is able to point to her cards, so Mrs. Hearns positions herself to observe Brooke's choice as she scans the room and observes other students' responses.

When asking questions, Mrs. Hearns also wants children to verbalize their understanding of beginning sounds, so as a picture appears on the screen, she also asks periodically, "What sound does *door* make? Think about it. Now make the sound." Because Mrs. Hearns moves closer to Brooke when she asks the students to orally respond, she is able to both observe what selection Brooke is making and hear her choice. She then makes a tally mark on her data collection sheet regarding Brooke's response (successful or unsuccessful) on this and other response opportunities during the instructional setting. This cumulative data is then plotted at the end of the day on a graph that enables Mrs. Hearns to see if progress is being made.

For the fifth instructional session (see Figure 5.5), Mrs. Hearns uses a probe to see if Brooke is able to verbalize responses without her AT. She does this simply by beginning the lesson without providing Brooke with her recorded picture frames, then she quickly asks students to pronounce the beginning sound targeted in the beginning of the lesson. While listening to the children's choral responses, she is also listening for Brooke to verbally respond. Mrs. Hearns notices that she makes a sound, but she cannot understand whether it is the targeted beginning sound from the previous lesson. She makes a tally on her data collection sheet that Brooke unsuccessfully pronounced the beginning sound and then immediately provides Brooke with her AT board with the four recorded sound options. She says, "Brooke, what sound did the picture make?" and waits for a response. This time, Brooke correctly identified the sound, and Mrs. Hearns continued the

instructional session allowing Brooke to use her AT. Again, at the end of the day she records her data and notices that there is a distinct difference between Brooke's performance: When she had no access to her AT, she could not perform the targeted skill, whereas Brooke's ability to produce sounds rose markedly when AT was available.

Mrs. Hearns uses this approach for several more weeks, making one probe each week to ensure that the AT used to support Brooke's participation in the instructional session remains effective. As students learn all the beginning sounds, Mrs. Hearns shifts the focus of her instruc-

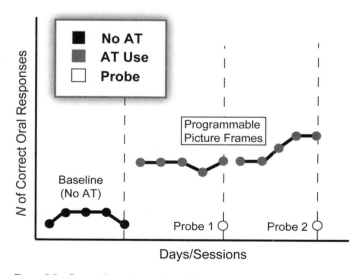

Figure 5.5. Data collected regarding Brooke's performance on oral identification of beginning sounds using the probe approach. (© 2013 H.P. Parette.)

tional activities using the PowerPoint-based curriculum toward word recognition and alliteration. These sessions are designed to present all students with four choices just as with the instructional activities targeting beginning sounds. Brooke uses her AT for all of these instructional sessions because recordings can be changed depending on the focus of instruction. Mrs. Hearns employed the same data collection approach over time, coupled with periodic probes to ensure that Brooke's performance on tasks (i.e., verbally producing responses) was effective.

EVALUATE THE EFFECTIVENESS OF THE ASSISTIVE TECHNOLOGY SOLUTION (TEACH IT-CHECK IT)

The final steps of the SOLVE IT process are to teach the young child with disabilities to use AT to complete the planned activity using the instructional plan and to determine whether the AT is effective in supporting the young child with disabilities. Learning to use AT is just that—a learning process. The child will need time to learn to use the AT (operational competence) and to use it to complete the planned activity (functional competence) more efficiently (with a greater quantity of task steps completed or less time taken to complete task steps) or more effectively (with greater quality responses). Instruction in the use of the AT may be needed over a week or two, with systematic assessments before fully determining if the AT is working.

The IFSP or IEP team should assist the teacher in this decision making. One outcome of the TEACH IT-CHECK IT process is that the AT is effective. It is always hoped that the problem-solving process is quickly successful. However, two other outcomes are also possible. First, the AT may be only partially effective (i.e., the young child with disabilities achieves success in completing some of the steps). Second, for unforeseen reasons, it is possible that the original thinking about the source of the problem was incorrect. Gaining clarity of the problems demonstrated by the child in meeting DO-SAY-REMEMBER requirements might only occur when an attempt is made to instruct the young child in the use of the selected AT. For example, only after addressing the child's ability to do the planned activity with AT to support manipulation will the child's problems in remembering the task steps become apparent. The solution to both outcomes is to rewind the problem-solving process by re-examining the child's performance, generating new AT solutions, and planning and implementing new instruction.

THE DYNAMIC NATURE OF THE BREAK IT DOWN AND SOLVE IT PROCESSES

SOLVE IT is part assessment and part evaluation. Using Break It Down is a naturalistic assessment process to identify the expected steps of a planned activity, the demands of the planned activity steps, and how the child performs each step. The value of authentically and naturally identifying the AT support needed for young children using this assessment process cannot be underestimated. The activity probes and progress monitoring using data collection strategies discussed in Chapter 4 comprise the evaluation. However, SOLVE IT, like all educational problem-solving processes, is dynamic. In dynamic assessment, the assessor intervenes during the course of the assessment with the goal of intentionally inducing changes in the young child's current ability to perform the planned activity. The SOLVE IT process is ongoing and never really stops. As the teacher develops solutions using one Break It Down table, he or she may apply these solutions to many similar activity demand situations. The goal of this is to change the child's level of performance by using AT without going through a full problem-solving process on every occasion. Over time, effective AT solutions identified through the SOLVE IT process are written into a child's IEP. At times, it is overwhelmingly obvious that a child cannot perform a task without AT. For example, Monique has fine motor problems that make it difficult for her to perform many typical classroom tasks that require gripping and/or fine motor coordination, such as pointing with precision or effectively manipulating small objects. Based on her teacher's observation of these demonstrated difficulties, the teacher may reasonably assume that Monique might be anticipated to have problems accurately depressing keyboard keys. It is possible to anticipate that AT support is needed in this instance and therefore sensible to note that Monique cannot complete that step and develop an AT solution (e.g., a keyguard or Big Keys keyboard) in collaboration with a special education teacher or AT specialist.

Finally, children may have AT solutions already identified, such as a communication device, seating and positioning system, or specialized wheelchair. These solutions should not be ignored to complete a Break It Down table with no AT. However, the teacher could complete the Break It Down table with the existing AT to see how effective it is for other planned activity demands. If it is only marginally effective, a new AT solution may need to be developed. Throughout the subsequent chapters, case examples will illustrate AT solutions that have to be developed at almost every step of the process. However, quite frequently, there will be some solutions already in place that can be applied to many demands of planned activities, especially by the time a child is in kindergarten.

SUMMARY

Young children with disabilities present particular challenges to teachers who use instructional technology in planned classroom activities. The nature of their disabilities present barriers to participation, and AT is needed for children to access planned activities. This chapter presents a practical problem solving approach—SOLVE IT—for including young children with disabilities using both partial participation and AT in the context of the EXPECT IT-PLAN IT-TEACH IT framework. A practical CHECK IT data tool—a probe approach—is also described to enable the teacher to make the best decisions about AT to support young children with disabilities. It is important to note that the problem-solving approach requires collaboration between individuals, and it will take some time to implement this process.

ADDITIONAL READINGS

Center for Technology in Education. (2005). *Considering the need for assistive technology within the individualized education program.* Arlington, VA: Technology and Media Division of the Council for Exceptional Children.

Family Center on Technology and Disability. (n.d.). *Assistive technology and the IEP.* Retrieved October 1, 2012, from http://www.fctd.info/uploads//IEP_print.pdf

Gray, T., & Silver-Pacuilla, H. (Eds.). (2011). *Breakthrough teaching and learning: How educational and assistive technologies are driving innovation.* New York, NY: Springer.

Green, J.L. (2011). *The ultimate guide to assistive technology in special education: Resources for education, intervention, and rehabilitation.* Waco, TX: Prufrock Press.

Mistrett, S. (2004). Assistive technology helps young children with disabilities participate in daily activities. *Technology in Action, 1*(4), 1–8.

National Early Childhood Technical Center. (2011). *Assistive technology (AT) for infants, toddlers and young children.* Retrieved October 1, 2012, from http://www.nectac.org/topics/atech/atech.asp

REFERENCES

Alberto, P.A., & Troutman, A.C. (2012). *Applied behavior analysis for teachers* (9th ed.). Upper Saddle River, NJ: Merrill.

Baumgart, D., Brown, L., Pumpian, I., Nisbet, J., Ford, A., Sweet, M., et al. (1982). Principle of partial participation and individualized adaptations in educational programs for severely handicapped students. *TASH Journal, 7,* 17–27.

Beard, L.A., Carpenter, L.B., & Johnston, L.B. (2011). *Assistive technology: Access for all children* (2nd ed.). Boston, MA: Pearson.

Family Center on Technology and Disability. (2012). *Technology solutions.* Retrieved October 1, 2012, from http://www.fctd.info/assets/assets/21/AT_solutions-may2012.pdf ?1338562550

Ferguson, D.L., & Baumgart, D. (1991). Partial participation revisited. *Journal of the Association for Persons with Severe Handicaps, 16,* 218–227.

Individuals with Disabilities Education Act (IDEA) of 2004, PL 108-446, 20 U.S.C. §§ 1400 *et seq.*

Mistrett, S.G., Lane, S.J., & Ruffino, A.G. (2005). Growing and learning through technology. In D. Edyburn, K. Higgins, & R. Boone (Eds.), *Handbook of special education technology research and practice* (pp. 273–307). Whitefish Bay, WI: Knowledge by Design.

Parette, H.P., & Peterson-Karlan, G.R. (2010). Assistive technology and educational practice. In P. Peterson, E. Baker, & B. McGaw (Eds.), *International encyclopedia of education* (3rd ed., Vol. 2, pp. 537–543). Oxford, England: Elsevier.

Peterson-Karlan, G.R., & Parette, H.P. (2008). Integration of technology into the curriculum. In H.P. Parette & G.R. Peterson-Karlan (Eds.), *Research-based practices in developmental disabilities* (2nd ed., pp. 183–214). Austin, TX: PRO-ED.

Parette, H.P., Blum, C., & Boeckmann, N.M. (2009). Evaluating assistive technology in early childhood education: The use of a concurrent time series probe approach. *Early Childhood Education Journal, 37,* 5–12.

Parette, H.P., Peterson-Karlan, G.R., Wojcik, B.W., & Bardi, N. (2007). Monitor that progress! Interpreting data trends for AT decision-making. *Teaching Exceptional Children, 39*(7), 22–29.

Sadao, K.C., & Robinson, N.B. (2010). *Assistive technology for young children: Creating inclusive learning environments.* Baltimore, MD: Paul H. Brookes Publishing Co.

6

Integrating Technology to Support Emergent Reading

Karen H. Douglas, Carrie Anna Courtad, April L. Mustian, and Howard P. Parette, Jr.

After reading this chapter, you should be able to

- Understand the key components of prereading
- Describe how the EXPECT IT-PLAN IT-TEACH IT model is used to integrate readily available technology into literacy activities
- Use the SOLVE IT process and Break It Down framework to solve problems related to prereading skills
- Describe the importance of including families in technology discussions and providing them with resources

LITERACY IN 21ST-CENTURY CLASSROOMS

Literacy skills begin to develop at an early age in children's home settings. Young children become aware of print and its use through experiences with books and other print material, screen presentations on family computers, audio feedback from software and web sites, and other interactions with technology (McGee & Richgels, 2006). These early experiences are gradually shaped and developed into more refined literacy competencies through learning opportunities in preschool and kindergarten, which prepare children for future success in school, community, and work settings. Consider the following examples.

Before dinner, Jenni's parents give her their iPad and she opens an early literacy app, Interactive Touch Books. This app allows Jenni to hear the story read, see the words, and manipulate the objects on the screen (i.e., move items to a different location, touch the animals to hear the sounds they make).

During a playdate, Sean and his friend Kyle want to get on the computer to play a game. Sean navigates to the pbskids.org/lions web site to play a game called Between the Lions. They take turns making selections and help each other with finding the answers. Sean's mom is happy to see the children sharing and collaborating.

While traveling to her grandmother's house, Keisha uses her Leapster Explorer Learning Experience to listen to e-books, play games, watch videos, and use flashcards. She especially likes to test her knowledge with the flashcards. Keisha's parents like the device because they can log in online to see her progress.

These early experiences with technology are integrally connected to language and communication development among today's young children. Language and communication development begins at birth. As children develop and refine these skills over time, literacy skills are developed, refined, and supported by technology (Koppenhaver, Coleman, Kalman, & Yoder, 1991). All early childhood education professionals recognize that children begin communicating their needs at birth by crying or making faces. To understand the communicative intent of infants, adults have to guess at the intention of the cues provided by infants. The early communication methods of infants eventually evolve into gesturing toward desired objects and making word approximations to regulate the behaviors of others, socially interact, or establish joint attention toward an item (i.e., the means to engage another person or respond to another person's initiation of attention in relationship to an object). For example, when a child looks at a sibling and then points at a favorite book (or brings the book to another person) to have it read to him, he has initiated joint attention. If the parent initiated joint attention by pointing at a book and asking the child if he wanted to read it, then the child got the book and handed it to the parent, the child is said to be responding to joint attention. When the child responds by handing the parent the book, he communicates desired intent (i.e., "I want to read the book"). As the previous examples demonstrate, the earliest interactions with books, games, and technologies such as electronic devices and toys promote language and literacy development.

The world of young children is full of symbols communicating varying types of intent. Whether it be television symbols (e.g., icons, print and advertising logos), magazine advertisements, or signage in community settings (e.g., directions, billboards), all are communicating messages to children. As a result, children can identify and discriminate specific environmental cues very early on in life. For example, a young child who watches commercial television (among the earliest technologies with which young children have contact) may call out during a drive in the car, "There is McDonalds!" Or, the child may exclaim, "Every kiss begins with *Kay*," a jingle from a popular jewelry commercial. Such instances call attention to the influence of technology exposure on the language and symbols used by young children. Further, as mobile technologies, such as the iPad, are integrated into the daily lives of families, digital and web-based applications will become as important as television in the development of communication and literacy with the youngest children.

The preferences shown by young children for technology use in their daily lives is also growing and is supported and reinforced by families, developers, marketers, professional organizations, and other constituencies. Messages communicated using web-based and computer application technologies have gained increased prominence in our society. Smartphones, iPads, iPods, personal computers, and web sites associated with children's books, movies, or television characters are now part of many young children's literacy world. As noted in Chapter 1, young children seem to be motivated by the animations, interactivity, and game-like features of current and emerging technologies. Today most children's shows do not present one media platform for a child to watch the show. Now there are web sites that promote literacy and, increasingly, there are applications to download for an iPad, iPhone, or other digital device to help children develop early literacy skills. From the perspective of universal design for learning (UDL), it makes sense to consider multiple means of engagement, action and expression, and representation—features of many instructional technologies with which children are familiar and/or prefer. Thus, the learning environments of young children should include the use of technology in young children's lives when developing classroom literacy experiences.

Emergent Literacy

During early childhood, the social interactions between children and their families and friends are particularly important because they provide the foundation of emergent literacy for young children (Lawhon & Cobb, 2002). Emergent literacy skills are the earliest of the numerous literacy skills acquired by children prior to entering school (Teale & Sulzby, 1986), including phonemic awareness, alphabetic principle, fluency, concepts about print, vocabulary development, and comprehension. Collectively, these skills provide the foundation for the development of reading, which is fundamental for independence in our society (International Reading Association & National Association for the Education of Young Children, 1998). Today's instructional technologies provide teachers with a wide array of supports to teach emergent literacy.

Phonemic awareness refers to the ability to focus on (or discriminate) and manipulate individual sounds in spoken language (McGee & Richgels, 2006), such as being able to isolate, segment, blend, and delete individual sounds of words. For example, after a child hears the word *cat,* he or she should be able to delete the initial sound and say, "at." Among young children, the ability to manipulate words that rhyme is a key emergent literacy skill that can indicate a level of phonemic awareness. For example, Olivia opens a free app, *abc PocketPhonics Lite,* on her iPad. When the app launches, she chooses the word game and hears a voice that pronounces the /a/ sound. She selects the letter *a* from six letters and it appears on a dotted line. A voice asks her to select the /n/ sound. After correctly selecting the letter *n,* the app blends the two letters together and pronounces the word *an.*

Alphabetic principle refers to the relationship between letters and sounds (Hutinger, Bell, Daytner, & Johanson, 2006). Awareness of how letters correspond to sounds is critical for young beginning readers, and developing this emergent skill is an emphasis of many early childhood curricula. For example, Ella and her parents often open Starfall.com on their home computer to play ABCs. This game is also available as an inexpensive app that has been installed on her father's iPad. Ella likes the ABCs game because she can select letters that she is interested in and view multiple screens in which the letters are pronounced and presented with pictures and animation.

Fluency refers to the ability to read text accurately, quickly, and with expression. Development of fluency leads to comprehension (Cooper, Kiger, Robinson, & Slansky, 2011). When reading with family members and in classroom settings, young children begin to recognize words automatically and do not concentrate on decoding words, allowing them to focus on the meaning of text. For example, Alex opens a talking book, *Dog and Cat*, at Starfall.com. She clicks on an icon to open the book presenting text spoken by the dog and cat on each page. Simple sentences are read in a child's voice when an icon is clicked by each character's name. Words are highlighted as each word is read, allowing Alex to hear the text read in a natural way. She then reads the words herself, and can click on any individual word if she needs to hear it pronounced.

Concepts about print refer to the knowledge that print carries meaning (McGee & Richgels, 2006). These concepts include understanding the function of text, how text sources are configured, and how a reader approaches text. This begins with young children understanding how to hold a book upright, differentiating between words and pictures, and turning the pages. For example, Joshua and his mother click on a bookmark on his home computer that leads them to Storybird, a free collaborative storytelling site. His mother reads recently added titles that other young readers have created together and selects one called *A Curious Day at the Zoo*. Joshua clicks on a curled corner of a page and the story book opens. As his mother reads the story to him, Joshua uses a mouse to click on navigation arrows at the bottom to turn pages.

Vocabulary development refers to the ability to understand the meaning of words and to use them effectively in speech (McGee & Richgels, 2006). This emergent literacy skill is particularly important with regard to school achievement and later success in life. For example, Ryan opens a Sesame Street game, Let's Make Words, on his home computer. As one of the show's characters greets him, several screens appear, each of which features parts of an incomplete word that are represented by pictures. When Ryan selects a picture, the first letter of the word that the picture represents appears, and the character pronounces the sound.

Comprehension refers to the understanding of meaning and importance of written and oral text (McGee & Richgels, 2006). In early childhood classrooms, students are typically expected to identify characters in and retell events of stories that are part of the literacy experiences of children. For example, Andy goes with his class on a field trip to the zoo. When they return, his teacher asks him to tell a story about the trip using a free iPad app, Educreations, which allows him to click a recording button and arrange zoo pictures in a sequence as he tells the story. The app captures his voice and the screen movements of photos being placed in sequence as he tells the story. His teacher saves the exercise in a movie format to later share it with others.

Instruction in each of these emergent literacy areas is essential, and teachers are finding that use of instructional technologies

Figure 6.1. A free iPad app, Educreations, allows students to upload pictures, manipulate objects on the screen, draw, record their voices, and replay screen manipulations. (Used by permission of C. Blum and Educreations.)

in their classrooms holds great potential to develop these skills in far more engaging ways than in the past.

What the Research Says

An extensive report called *Developing Early Literacy: Report of the National Early Literacy Panel* (National Institute for Literacy, 2008) identified three major skills with several subskills that predict later reading outcomes: oral language, including listening comprehension and oral language vocabulary; alphabetic code, including alphabet knowledge and phonological/phonemic awareness (i.e., the ability to discriminate sounds in words); and print knowledge/concepts, including environmental print and concepts about print (Strickland & Riley-Ayers, 2006). The panel identified these three areas after synthesizing over 500 research articles that provided correlational data of children's early abilities and skills and their later literacy development. The following vignettes provide snapshots of how technology can be used during early literacy instruction in today's classrooms. Each vignette focuses on a different area of literacy development.

During reading centers, Mr. Bivens creates many individualized opportunities for his students to practice oral language skills. For example, Nicholas and Rihanna are paired together at the listening comprehension station. The two are using the Puppet Pals app on the classroom iPad to work on listening comprehension. Before school started, Mr. Bivens used the Puppet Pals iPad app to create a puppet scene with a prerecorded sentence, "The cowboy found his horse." Mr. Bivens has taught Nicholas and Rihanna how to use Puppet Pals. Once they successfully take turns repeating the sentence Mr. Bivens created, each student gets to create his or her own puppet scene and record a sentence for the other student to practice repeating aloud.

During literacy csenter, Ms. Steele is using her SMART Board to provide phonics instruction to teach alphabetic principle to a small group of students in her kindergarten class. For these skills, she has decided to use the model-lead-test approach, wherein she models a skill to be learned, practices application of the skill together with children, and then has students apply the skill on their own. Using the Construct-A-Word game on the ReadWriteThink web site (www.readwrite think.org; see Figure 6.2), she allows each student to take turns walking up to the SMART Board to construct and say words by combining letters. For example, Ms. Steele begins the activity by choosing the word ending in the letters *-at* and moving it into the second of two connected squares at the bottom of the screen. She then picks the letter *c* and asks the students to state the whole word with her. After modeling this activity, she allows each student to combine a new beginning letter with *-at* to form and say a new word.

During circle time, Mrs. Hearns provides instruction to her preschool students on concepts about print. She projects the Sesame Street e-book, *Big Block Party,* using her digital projector. This

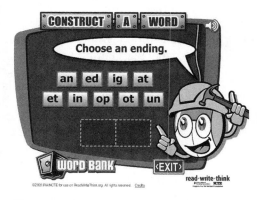

Figure 6.2. Screen view of Construct-A-Word from www.readwritethink.org. (Used by permission of ReadThinkWrite.org.)

e-book is used to model important concepts about books, such as reading left to right, turning pages, and one-to-one correspondence between spoken words and written words. She gives students the opportunity to come up to the laptop to turn the pages of the e-book and trace their fingers along each word that is highlighted as it is read aloud.

TECHNOLOGY'S INFLUENCE ON LITERACY DEVELOPMENT

Opportunities for use of instructional technology to support the development of literacy skills are abundant in classrooms. In using the EXPECT IT-PLAN IT-TEACH IT approach (see Chapter 2), the teacher initially connects literacy standards and learning objectives to the consideration of instructional technology when developing planned activities. During the PLAN IT stage, instructional strategies and groupings (ARRANGE IT) are identified (see Chapter 3). Typical activity areas in both preschool and kindergarten classrooms become the venue for ARRANGE IT prereading activities that are connected to learning objectives (see Table 6.1).

Understanding these activity areas and the kinds of learning tasks that occur in them is a prerequisite to deciding *how* instructional technology can be used (TECH IT). For example, a typical day for many young children might begin when they enter the classroom and find their personal spaces clearly marked with their names. This may be the first introduction to seeing their names and their classmates' names in print. After placing their belongings in their designated spaces, the next stop might be a choice chart with digital pictures representing the type of lunch they want today (hot or cold). Each student will have to make a choice. To do this, the young student will need to locate his or her name on the class list, look at the choices, and circle his or her desired choice. All of these actions are centered on literacy, with the available choices communicated via text along with the children's selections. Therefore, the students are communicating to the teacher that they have read the choices and made a decision.

Teachers usually have some large-group time in which they cover a variety of activities developing literacy. During this large-group circle time, teachers frequently cover calendar information (e.g., date, day, year, weather, number of school days). Often at this point, teachers engage students in a morning message—an interactive literacy activity in which the teacher and class participate in a coconstructed message related to the content information for children while the teacher acts as the facilitator (Mariage, 2001; Wasik & Hindman, 2011). For example, the teacher sequentially presents a series of screens on her SMART Board that allow children to interact with the screen by dragging their names and text for days of the week, and writing numerals on the calendar. Incomplete sentences are present on each screen, allowing both children and the teacher to chorally respond to statements such as, "Today is Monday, March 4, 2013."

After morning message, the teacher may introduce a few new activities (i.e., centers) and then break into small-group centers or choice time. During the small-group activity, teachers are usually working on academic content while other students are working at centers with a literacy focus. For example, a teacher might provide direct instruction on targeted sight words to a small group of students, while other students are at centers either engaged in reading books or drawing pictures about a story they had read. Typically, literacy is interwoven throughout

Table 6.1. Typical preschool and kindergarten prereading activity areas and tasks

Activity area	Typical tasks
Preschool	
Arrival	Identifying where to hang up coats or personal items in cubby or hook by picture or name
	Making snack and/or drink choices using pictures or words
	Coloring at seat (writing)
Circle time/large group	Singing songs (phonemes that rhyme, alphabet awareness)
	Listening to stories
	Participating in calendar tasks (reading words, dates, symbols, pictures)
	Participating in group discussions (interactive discussion about stories)
Choice time/free play	Creating art (writing, name writing)
	Looking at/reading books (left-to-right orientation, awareness of plot, themes)
	Listening to stories
	Engaging in dramatic play (expression of characters and plot elements, language development)
	Constructing projects (e.g., diorama of story)
	Writing
Small group	Listening to stories
	Participating in flannel storyboards
	Engaging in science experiments (following visual steps)
	Cooking (following visual steps)
Departure	Selecting materials for cleanup based on pictures or words
	Gathering home materials (following steps based on pictures)
Kindergarten	
Arrival routine	Identifying where to hang up coats or personal items in cubby or hook by picture or name
	Coloring at seat (writing)
Morning circle/ attendance	Making snack and/or drink choices using pictures or words
	Communicating news to teacher and classmates (use of symbols and communication, words)
	Participating in show-and-tell activity (communication related to self, description of objects)
Reading/literacy	Communicating news to teacher and classmates (use of symbols and words for communication)
	Listening to stories (attending, plot, characters, left-to-right orientation)
	Engaging in dramatic play (expression of characters and plot elements, language development)
	Reading stories and peers' logs
Writing/language arts	Communicating news to teacher and classmates (use of symbols and communication, words)
	Tracing shapes and letters
	Writing name, words, and sentences
	Participating in dramatic play (expression of characters and plot elements, language development)
	Documenting science experiences (writing)
	Journaling

(continued)

Table 6.1 *(continued)*

Activity area	Typical tasks
Math	Counting manipulatives (communication about math concepts)
	Using a cash register and/or calculator (number recognition)
	Engaging in dramatic play (e.g., measuring, communication about relative size of objects)
	Counting the days of attendance (communication about a math concept)
	Using base-10 blocks at calendar time (communication about a math concept)
Art/physical education/ music	Reading labels for art supplies
	Reading task charts for cleaning up areas drawing
	Singing songs about remembering counting and letters
Social studies/science	Writing and communicating observations about the class garden
	Writing (documentation) and communicating height or changes throughout science concepts (e.g., seedling sprouting or chicks hatching)
	Participation in community projects
	Communication and writing about participation in community projects
	Writing to grandparents and parents
	Observing community leaders in their role and writing thank you notes (e.g., firefighter, police officer, principal)
Dismissal routine	Reading and writing lists to collect belongings
	Reading and writing letters, words, symbols for personal organization (e.g., information in correct folder, items to keep at home, items to bring back, put items in pack on back of wheelchair, finding the right bus or car line)

the day into other academic areas. The schedule often includes snack time, lunch, and perhaps even a rest time, which allow the teacher opportunities to show or introduce words, sentences, and concepts, and discuss or reinforce literacy content presented in instructional settings At the end of the day, the students are responsible for packing up their belongings and getting in the correct line to go home (i.e., bus, walking, car, after-school care). In each of these instances, children may be presented with text and opportunities to use language by having to check off their participation in these transitions on a classroom chart or SMART Board screen or read text (sometimes combined with pictures) that provides information about expectations or rules.

LARGE- AND SMALL-GROUP LEARNING ACTIVITIES

The EXPECT IT-PLAN IT-TEACH IT model provides an effective approach for integrating instructional technology into daily literacy instruction for all young children through group activities. The teacher simply initially makes a decision about a particular literacy-related curriculum standard and benchmark that will be addressed (EXPECT IT) and then plans the group activity in the context of a targeted Activity area using the decision-making process related to PLAN IT discussed in Chapter 3. Each of these elements is presented in the following vignettes.

Mrs. Hearns

To ensure a successful planned activity for her preschool children, Mrs. Hearns uses the EXPECT IT-PLAN IT-TEACH IT model to teach emergent literacy skills. This vignette describes how she uses a digital projector in combination with Microsoft Word and a wireless keyboard to support emergent literacy skill development.

 EXPECT IT When examining her school curriculum, Mrs. Hearns recognizes that her students are at a beginning emergent literacy level. She chooses the earliest language arts standard and two related benchmarks that she would like to use for her planned activity: understanding that pictures and symbols have meaning and that print conveys a message.

 PLAN IT A morning schedule serves dual purposes. It is not only a procedure used to discuss upcoming events in the day, but it also reinforces concepts about print. It helps her class understand that letters and words communicate messages about events that happen in the morning. For the planned activity, Mrs. Hearns decides to use a daily whole-group activity called Morning Message (i.e., circle time). This is an interactive reading and writing activity that addresses a variety of early childhood learning goals, including directionality, phonics, letters, words, capitalization, and punctuation. Morning Message also highlights that print communicates a message.

 TECH IT Mrs. Hearns decides that she will use Microsoft Word paired with her digital projection system to complete her Morning Message. In a large font, she will type *Today is* and use her projection system to project the computer display on the screen hanging from a blackboard. She uses a portable wireless keyboard so more than one student can use the keyboard and not worry about cords. To fade out the picture prompts over time, she will progressively fade out the coloring (shading or coloring is a signal prompt; see Chapter 3) so that the picture eventually disappears.

 ARRANGE IT Mrs. Hearns also decides that the whole class will participate in Morning Message together. She decides that she will model and demonstrate the benchmarks she has selected by reading and filling in blanks of a predictable sentence (e.g., "Today is _____"). She will give her students the opportunity to add a sentence about what normally happens on that day of the week or about that day's weather. Each day, students will respond to questions as a whole class, and then one student will type the answer using a wireless keyboard, thus guiding the children using shared writing and providing them with a scaffold. Mrs. Hearns will also call on students who need extra practice on specific skills or to review skills learned the day before.

 CHECK IT Mrs. Hearns will keep a daily checklist of whose turn it is to be the student leader and will record how well students typed the requested information. This checklist will be saved in a PDF file and uploaded to her free iPad app, pdf-notes, which will allow her to make notations directly on her checklist. It will also allow her to collect data on the additional questions she asks particular students to check for progress.

SOLVE IT   While planning her classroom activity, Mrs. Hearns considers her student Josh, who has cerebral palsy and uses a manual wheelchair. The nature of his physical disability prevents him from using it independently to get around in Mrs. Hearns' preschool classroom. Moving from one activity area to another is always difficult. He also has trouble using his hands and fingers for fine motor activities. Josh has average intelligence, but his speech is often unintelligible. Mrs. Hearns uses the SOLVE IT and Break It Down processes to ensure Josh's inclusion and participation in her planned activity (see Table 6.2).

In using the Break It Down process, Mrs. Hearns, the special educator, parents, and the assistive technology (AT) specialist found a variety of solutions to support Josh's participation in her activity. Mrs. Hearns and the team used both partial participation and AT to help Josh perform identified steps in the planned activity. Because he has difficulty moving around independently using his wheelchair, a simple solution to those steps involving movement to and from activity areas was partial participation—simply having another student push his chair for him and provide assistance in positioning. Because Josh's cerebral palsy causes difficulty with performing motor tasks involving his hands, he has trouble using a standard keyboard. The small keys make it hard for him to type and press two keys simultaneously to make a capital letter. She has borrowed a Big Keys keyboard from her state's Department of Education (see Figure 6.3). The Big Keys keyboard has a larger surface area than a typical keyboard and the keys are easier for Josh to use.

Using Sticky Keys, an accessibility feature that is part of the Windows operating system (see http://windows.microsoft.com/en-US/windows-xp/help/using-stickykeys), Mrs. Hearns and the team have provided Josh with AT that allows access to the Big Keys keyboard. Sticky Keys allows Josh to simply depress the large Shift key followed by a letter key to create a capital letter rather than having to use two hands.

Because Josh has trouble speaking, Mrs. Hearns has also borrowed an Attainment Company Go Talk 9+ from her state. The Go Talk 9+ is a lightweight, multilevel communication device that allows up to 45 messages to be easily recorded, allowing for flexibility in customizing language used across planned activities. Using a 12-message overlay template in Boardmaker, Mrs. Hearns has created several overlays containing pictures and words for various settings within the planned activity. Pictures on the overlays have associated voice recordings. As Josh participates in different parts of the planned activity, the overlays can be easily and quickly changed to match the specific planned activity. As these AT solutions are developed, they can be incorporated into similar planned learning activities and become part of the individualized education program.

TEACH IT   After her initial planning in the TECH IT-ARRANGE IT-CHECK IT process and the Break It Down process that took place afterward, the activity planned by Mrs. Hearns took on the following format when implemented again. Before she began, Mrs. Hearns made sure that there was adequate space between chairs, desks, and other classroom materials so that a peer can easily push Josh's wheelchair to the Morning Message area. In delivering her instruction, Mrs. Hearns placed a cursor underneath her Microsoft Word document text projected on her screen and read aloud, "Today is…." Mrs. Hearns used a built-in Windows

Table 6.2. Break It Down table for Josh

Define the Problem: Josh has difficulty moving around the room and using a keyboard to participate in Morning Message.

Activity: During Morning Message, students observe teacher models regarding days of the week and read and fill in blanks of a predictable sentence projected on the screen. Students use the computer keyboard to add sentences about what happens on the target day of the week or type of weather they are having.

Planned activity steps	Planned activity requirements				What's the answer?
	DO	SAY	REMEMBER	Child performance	
To Begin: Go to circle carpet	See circle carpet Move to the rug Sit on carpet Listen to teacher's direction		Remember where to go	Unable to navigate Teacher pushes Josh Late getting to circle because of obstacles through desks to carpet	Peer pushes wheelchair to circle* Rearrange classroom when possible
Identify what is written on the screen	Listen to teacher See screen Look at teacher Sit on carpet	Read sentence Say day of week Say type of weather for that day	Remember day of the week	Cannot speak sentences intelligibly Sits quietly and is not called on	Go Talk 9+ electronic communication device with pre-programmed messages for weather options and days Boardmaker overlay for weather and day messages
Take turn as student leader	See classmates sitting on the carpet See keyboard	Use social etiquette phrases with classmates		Cannot use social phrases due to speech problems Josh runs into peers getting up in front of class; he rolls over peers' fingers trying to get to computer to take his turn	Go Talk 9+ electronic communication device with pre-programmed social etiquette messages Boardmaker overlay for social etiquette messages Path is cleared so Josh can access the front of room

(continued)

Table 6.2 *(continued)*

Planned activity steps	Planned activity requirements			Child performance	What's the answer?
	DO	SAY	REMEMBER		
Write the day of the week and other messages	See the keyboard Use keyboard or pen Transcribe capital letters by using two hands on the computer	Read sentences and say day of the week	Remember the steps to type and make capital letter	Josh is unable to correctly hit one letter of a keyboard at a time He cannot use two hands to depress keys to make a capital letter Josh cannot read Josh does not speak and attempts to write message but does not finish sentences	Big Keys keyboard with larger keys Use the Windows accessibility options and turn on Sticky Keys to allow Josh to push a sequence of keys to get a capital Go Talk 9+ electronic communication device with preprogrammed sentences Boardmaker overlay for sentence responses
To End: Walk to centers upon teacher instruction	See where to go Hear teacher Walk to center upon teacher cue (i.e., a color card matching each center is assigned to a student)	Talk with peers or teacher as needed	Know where to go	Josh runs into keyboard desk when rolling to his next center Teacher pushes Josh	Peer pushes wheelchair to center* Go Talk 9+ electronic communication device with pre-programmed social etiquette messages Boardmaker overlay for social etiquette messages

*Partial participation.

Figure 6.3. The Big Keys keyboard enables access to a computer-based activity and Go Talk 9+ supports communication within a planned activity. (From Attainment Company, Inc.; used by permission.)

accessibility feature to enlarge the cursor arrow, then she had that day's student leader come to the keyboard. She asked the students, "Class, what is today?" They responded with, "Monday, March 4, 2013." Because Josh could not respond with the class, she said, "Josh, can you tell me what day it is?" He responded using his Go Talk 9+ device that had Boardmaker symbols paired with preprogrammed messages to respond.

Mrs. Hearns then turned to Tamika, the class leader for the day, and said, "Great, now let's help Tamika write *Wednesday*. Tamika, do you know what letter Wednesday starts with?" Tamika looked at the keyboard and pushed the *w* key. A lowercase *w* appeared in the Word document on the screen. Then Mrs. Hearns scaffolded the learning activity by explaining that the names of days start with a capital letter. She asked if anyone knew how to create a capital letter, and another student explained how he pushed two keys at once to get a capital letter. Mrs. Hearns then placed a preprinted text model for the complete word by the wireless keyboard so that Tamika could look at the word and find the letters on the keyboard. She then successfully typed the word *Wednesday* to complete the sentence. Mrs. Hearns provided several prompts to assist Tamika by pointing to keys when Tamika exhibited hesitancy.

After the students completed the day and date, Mrs. Hearns reminded them of their Wednesday music class. They used that information to write more sentences. She used the same approach of calling on other students to serve as class leaders. Mrs. Hearns had each student type a word that completed a sentence, thus creating a shared writing activity. The Morning Message sentences that they wrote included, "Today is Monday, March 4, 2013," "Today we will attend music class after snack," "We have been in school 123 days," and "Tomorrow will be Tuesday, March 5, 2013." In each instance, the incomplete messages on the screen served as signals to gain children's attention, and Mrs. Hearns had a typed model ready to help the student leaders type using the wireless keyboard. Mrs. Hearns provided prompts as needed by pointing to the keys to be depressed whenever a student leader seemed unsure.

Josh used his Go Talk 9+ communication device to participate and respond in each component of the Morning Message routine. When he was called upon to come forward as a student leader, a peer was able to easily push him to the computer because an access path had been created for his wheelchair. With his communication device having preprogrammed social etiquette phrases, Josh was able to say, "Excuse me" as he was being pushed to the computer and navigating around others, as well as say "Thank you" to the peer who assisted him with his wheelchair. Mrs. Hearns connected a Big Keys keyboard with large colorful keys to her computer, which allowed Josh to successfully type words in the Morning Message routine. Because Mrs. Hearns had turned on the Sticky Keys Windows accessibility feature, Josh was able to use one finger to make a capital letter when it was his turn to complete a sentence.

Throughout Morning Message, Mrs. Hearns individualized learning experiences for other students based on her understanding of specific problems that they had with emergent literacy skills. For example, Mrs. Hearns realized that Steven was having some problems recognizing the letters in his name, so she asked him if he saw any letters projected on the board that have the same sound and shape as the first letter in his name. She emphasized the /s/ sound. He nodded his head and she asked him to come to the computer and highlight the letter on the screen. He correctly highlighted the s using the text highlighter feature in Microsoft Word (see http://office.microsoft.com/en-us/word-help/apply-or-remove-highlighting -HA102534180.aspx). She asked him, "Why is it capitalized?" He answered that it is a name of a month just like his name is that of a boy. These interactive discussions are just as important as the integration of the technology in making the lesson successful.

When the entire group composition had been completed and conventions such as capitalization, punctuation, and letter sounds were discussed, Mrs. Hearns had the document read back to the class while she pointed along. She uses a text-to-speech feature to narrate the document (see http://office.microsoft.com/en -us/word-help/using-the-speak-text-to-speech-feature-HA102066711.aspx for more about this feature). Mrs. Hearns guided the students by pointing to each word as it was read.

In this teaching scenario, Mrs. Hearns used several readily available technologies that were available on her computer operating system and built into Microsoft Word to deliver her planned activity. She used modeling, scaffolding, and signals in the delivery of the instruction for all her children. Her use of the Break It Down process enabled Josh to effectively participate in the planned activity using several simple solutions. She ensured his access to the activity by arranging the environment such that his wheelchair could be pushed to the computer by a peer. Providing Josh with a means to communicate using preprogrammed messages and an alternative means to type further supported Josh's participation in the shared Morning Message activity.

Mr. Bivens

Mr. Bivens is using the EXPECT IT-PLAN IT-TEACH IT model to enhance the oral language skills of his kindergarten students in a small-group lesson. This vignette describes how he uses a SMART Board and digital photographs to engage his students and provide opportunities for oral language development.

 EXPECT IT A kindergarten standard that Mr. Bivens is working on with his class is to help his students be able to listen and speak effectively in formal and informal situations. More specifically, his students need to focus on several learning objectives: listen with understanding; respond to directions and conversations; and communicate their needs, ideas, and thoughts. This standard and the learning objectives support the development of oral language.

 PLAN IT To enhance his students' oral language, Mr. Bivens wants his students to participate in a digital language experience approach (DLEA; see Entz & Galarza, 2000; Good, 2009 in Additional Resources). DLEA is a multistep process that allows children to talk about a photographic or picture experience (see Figure 6.4). Using the PLAN IT process, Mr. Bivens is able to integrate instructional technology, providing a meaningful language experience for the children in the class based on a recent field trip to a local fire station.

 TECH IT After taking pictures on the field trip with his digital camera, Mr. Bivens uploads his fire station pictures to his computer. Now he has to decide which computer program to use for creating the DLEAs. Possible computer software options include Microsoft PowerPoint, Photo Story, and Clicker 6. A web-based application, VoiceThread (see Chapter 4), is also considered. He wants a program with the capability to insert photos, add text, record sound and video, and play automatically. VoiceThread enables each of these instructional needs to be met, and it allows children to navigate slides and leave comments using voice,

Step	Task	Task Demands
1	Take photographs	Child takes pictures of an experience or someone takes pictures of him/her.
2	Look at photographs	Child looks at a photograph of him/herself or a familiar place or person.
3	Compose a story	Teacher types student dictation or records student recounting the experience for each picture.
4	Interact with story	Child rereads story, prints story to share with others, or listens to the recording of the story.

Figure 6.4. Steps for conducting a digital language experience approach.

text, audio, or video files (see Figure 4.4). VoiceThread is designed for social networking in educational settings by allowing the creation of an interactive thread around the fire station photos (see http://voicethread.com for more information about this tool). Prior to the lesson, Mr. Bivens embeds selected field trip pictures into PowerPoint so that each is presented to the students for them to decide what two pictures they want to use and corresponding comments should be made. He then uploads the student-selected photos to VoiceThread. (He also connects the microphone and his webcam to record the students and gets the wireless keyboard ready to type what they say. He plans to let each student talk about the two pictures that he or she selected.)

On showing the photos in the created VoiceThread, he will prompt each student to comment on it. As each student speaks, his or voice will be recorded. Mr. Bivens will ask the students for sentences that can be said repeatedly stated during the story. Once the group decides on a repeated sentence, it will become a repeated choral response throughout the story as the VoiceThread is developed. This repeated line will allow students to build their choral reading skills. When the story is complete, the students can listen to their recording while looking at the pictures and videos. The students will be asked to say the repeated line before going to the next slide in the VoiceThread. Each group rotates through to share experiences about their field trip. Once completed, Mr. Bivens has a VoiceThread that is developed for the DLEA. Using the SMART Board in small groups of students, everyone can interact with the VoiceThread created for the DLEA. Students may interact with other students' comments even though they are not in the group. Students can rotate through this experience throughout the day or week. They may even come back to at a later point.

 ARRANGE IT   The primary instructional strategy is a DLEA, wherein multiple photographs of the children's field trip serve as signals in the PowerPoint presentation that allow each child to both select and comment on two photographs that become part of a shared reading experience using VoiceThread. The children make comments in response to a teacher prompt: "Emily, tell me about this picture." Each child creates a story by recounting the experience. His or her story is then captured in VoiceThread and can be reread and scaffolded by others, who provide additional comments. A DLEA using VoiceThread can be used to foster the acquisition of language, formation of basic literacy concepts, and development of reading skills for children of varying literacy abilities. The UDL features of an instructional technology like VoiceThread support rich interactive peer-driven discussions that are experiential and connected to the real world.

 CHECK IT   Because Mr. Bivens recorded what each student said using the video feature in VoiceThread, he has a permanent product of the language sample (see Chapter 4). He can transcribe them and will be able to determine the number of words or morphemes spoken and analyze the grammatical errors. In each student's recording, Mr. Bivens can listen for any articulation problems and determine any grammatical errors. He can collect data on these specific language components to see if progress is being made across multiple DLEAs.

 SOLVE IT   Raquel has a cognitive disability that causes her difficulty in remembering routines and task sequences in various classroom activities. Her disability also results in a failure to listen to instructions given by Mr. Bivens and a failure to attend to instructional activities. Although Raquel has speech, she frequently fails to respond to questions and participate in conversations with her classmates. To solve the problems that Raquel will have participating in this planned activity, Mr. Bivens uses the SOLVE IT approach and Break It Down table to identify AT that will ensure her participation (see Table 6.3).

In collaboration with a special educator and other team members (e.g., parents, occupational therapist), Mr. Bivens developed effective solutions for the *What is the answer?* portion of the Break It Down table. Mr. Bivens and the team combine instructional support strategies (e.g., signals, positive reinforcement, physical prompting) with AT solutions to help Raquel participate in the planned activity. He uses his digital camera to create a visual routine schedule to help her with transitioning to the activity and a picture task book using Boardmaker symbols to provide signals and images of what Raquel is expected to do for the activity steps. The schedule presents images of activity areas across the day organized vertically and paired with numbers to help Raquel understand the sequence of routines. The task book shows images that illustrate what to do for each step. Raquel can follow along easily flipping the task book pages with occasional reminders from Mr. Bivens.

Watching peers first will allow Raquel to see other students complete the task and minimize any likelihood that she might have difficulty remembering what to do. Peers play a big role in the solution by making the supports more naturalistic and inclusive. They also limit the choices that Raquel had to make because the number of pictures available to her decrease as each child made their respective two choices. Mr. Bivens will use animation features in PowerPoint to highlight appropriate photos selections when he asks, "Raquel, do you want this picture?" When she makes a choice, he will reinforce her selection. Peers also can help Raquel if she needs a reminder by saying, "Raquel, what do you want to do?" When creating the final product for the planned activity—a printout of the VoiceThread screenshot to take home—Mr. Bivens will laminate the document to minimize possible damage when Raquel takes her schoolwork home to share with family members. Now that Mr. Bivens has implemented these AT solutions for Raquel, they will become part of a set of strategies to enhance her participation in the future.

TEACH IT   Prior to students transitioning to a small-group activity, Mr. Bivens gives a 5-minute warning signal to the children reminding them that a transition to the SMART Board is about to take place. This supports Raquel's ability to make such transitions, given that she often needs reminders to perform tasks in her classroom. Mr. Bivens also provided Raquel with a portable visual schedule that shows digital photos of children performing steps of the activity. Both of these supports enabled Raquel to make a successful transition to the SMART Board. Mr. Bivens opened his PowerPoint presentation and said, "I want each of you to choose two pictures that we will use in a story later." He began showing the slides, each having one picture of one or more students in a scene from the field trip. As the children selected their pictures, Mr. Bivens asked them to say something about the photo. As he progressed through the presentation, he made notations about the slide numbers when a child made a selection, which would allow him to quickly copy and paste them into a new PowerPoint presentation once all choices had been made.

Table 6.3. Break It Down table for Raquel

Define the problem: Raquel has difficulty knowing what to say to comment on her visit to the technology museum and doesn't follow directions.

Activity: A digital language experience approach (DLEA) is used to allow students to comment on their trip to a technology museum. Working with a small group of four students, teacher uses the SMART Board and VoiceThread to show digital pictures taken at the museum and allow students to record comments about their experiences. Each student talks about two pictures for a total of eight pictures.

Planned activity steps	Planned activity requirements			Child performance	What's the answer?
	DO	SAY	REMEMBER		
To begin: Children transition from individual work to small group around the SMART Board	See SMART Board Hear teacher's directions Walk to the SMART Board	N/A	Know where to go for small group Recall rule to walk quietly to SMART Board	She needs to be verbally prompted by the teacher several times Raquel continues to work at desk	Portable visual schedule using images from digital camera Give a 5-minute warning prior to transition*
View PowerPoint field trip pictures on SMART Board	See the teacher Hear the teacher See the pictures Make selection of photos	N/A	Recognize her pictures	Raquel has normal vision and hearing but is often inattentive Raquel looks around the room without *making* a selection	A task book with images of each step from Boardmaker is provided to signal Raquel what to do Use PowerPoint animation feature (entrance and exit) to signal Raquel when a slide having her photo is viewed Use request, "Raquel, do you want this picture?" along with reinforcement for selection*
Describe photos on request	Hear the teacher See the photo Look at photo	Verbally describe the photo when called upon	Recall the field trip experience	Raquel has mild language delays according to speech and language pathologist, and is verbal though she is quiet for the activity. Raquel stares at photo and does not say anything	Use visual signals in task book show Raquel when to respond (i.e., visual of a person talking) paired with a peer model Ask prompting questions to help her think of something to say* with 5-second time delay to encourage a response(see Chapter 3)

Choose two pictures to make comments on, and share ideas about comments	Hear the teacher Raise hand when called on Listen to other student's responses	Share what pictures she selected and idea on what to say	Recall that she needs to select a picture, how to respond when it is her turn, and her idea	Raquel appears to have difficulty remembering when to make a selection Raquel says she does not know what to do and will say "I don't know" or sometimes does not try to participate at all and just sits even after teacher prompts	A task book providing images of each step from Boardmaker is provided to signal Raquel what to do Print photos in handout format in PowerPoint so Raquel can see them all at once and her peers can signal her that that she needs to make a choice Children help simplify the choice-making process for Raquel by narrowing picture options for her to choose from and helping her mark two choices with a highlighter
Upload selected pictures to VoiceThread	Look at screen Sit quietly Make direct selection of photo to be uploaded Tap icon to upload	Ask for help in uploading	N/A	She frequently fails to respond to questions and participate in conversations with her classmates Raquel talks when it's not her turn	A task book with images of each step from Boardmaker is provided to signal Raquel what to do Physical prompt to click on icon*
Children record comments on VoiceThread	Hear the teacher Raise hand to be called on Wait to be called on	Comment into the microphone about the picture	Remember when to respond and what your idea was	Raquel appears to have difficulty remembering what to say and when to say it Raquel sits quietly and watches other children talk into the microphone or makes irrelevant one-word comments about the picture	A task book providing images of each step from Boardmaker is provided to signal Raquel what to do Watches peers complete comment on the VoiceThread first Children can only talk when they are holding the microphone* Peers can provide a reminder prompt if she has difficulty remembering her idea from the previous steps

(continued)

Table 6.3 *(continued)*

	Planned activity requirements				
Planned activity steps	DO	SAY	REMEMBER	Child performance	What's the answer?
To End: Take a printed copy of screenshot of VoiceThread and URL to take home and return to seat	See where to go Walk to desk with screenshot Put screenshot in desk	Children talk to peers on way back to their seat	Know where to go	Rips up screenshot on way back to seat Raquel has tendency to tear up classroom materials	A task book with images of each step from Boardmaker is provided to signal Raquel what to do Have peer buddy talk to Raquel to help her focus on talking with peers vs. ripping up VoiceThread printout Use plastic page cover for screenshot so she cannot rip it up on the way home Provide specialized reinforcement to add extra incentive for Raquel to learn to care for classroom work products (see chapter 3) E-mail the VoiceThread URL to parents

*Instructional strategy.

He waited until the end to say to Raquel, "Now, Raquel, look at your task book. What are you going to do?" He waited for a response as she looked at her task book, and she said, "Choose two pictures." Mr. Bivens responded, "That's right. Let's find two pictures of you to include in our story." He then showed the remaining slides, with two slides having animation features embedded so that an arrow appeared as a signal and pointed to Raquel in the photo, allowing Mr. Bivens to say, "Raquel, do you want this picture?" When she responded "Yes," he provided reinforcement.

Referring to his notes about selected slides, Mr. Bivens then quickly cut and pasted the selected photos into a new PowerPoint presentation. He printed a handout version of the eight-slide presentation with all the slides on a single sheet of paper to later use with Raquel. He opened the presentation and provided a model for the first slide, saying "We went to the fire station and it was fun!" He then moved to the next slide, called on a student, and asked for a comment. When it was Raquel's turn, he asked her to say something about the photo, and she hesitated. Mr. Bivens then continued, "Did you like seeing the fire truck?" He used a time delay of 5 seconds to wait for a response, saw that she smiled, and then provided the model, "Say, 'I liked the fire truck.'" Raquel responded, and Mr. Bivens reinforced her comment. He used the same strategy to support Raquel when she commented about the second photo. These strategies allowed Raquel to successfully choose two photos and comment on them in the same manner as other students.

Mr. Bivens then started the presentation over again, saying, "Now I want each of you to say something about two pictures in our story." He gave Raquel the PowerPoint handout of the eight slides that he printed, thus providing her with a signal for the choices that would be presented. He asked Chad, a peer seated beside her, to narrow her choices by underlining four of the eight photos for her to choose from and marking two that she wanted. As he went through the photos again, he called on children to make comments. When each slide was presented, he would say, "OK, who wants to make a comment?" Students responded with each slide, and when the Raquel's were presented, Chad prompted her to comment. When she did not respond, Mr. Bivens again made a request, "Raquel, what can you say about the picture?" He waited for 5 seconds, and then provided a model, "Say, 'The fire truck was big.'" When she responded to the model, he reinforced her and moved on to the next phase of the activity.

Mr. Bivens had all the photos taken on the field trip saved in a folder on the SMART Board. He opened the folder, in which he quickly moved all the photos that children had not selected for the story into a new folder, with the exception of one that he would use as a model. He opened VoiceThread and said, "Now, we're going to use a program called VoiceThread to allow you to add your pictures. He then said, "Raquel, look at your task book. What are we supposed to do?" He allowed Raquel a moment to look in her task book at snipped images of the three steps for this component of the activity. When she looked back up, he continued by saying, "Each of you will select your two pictures and upload them by tapping on the *Upload* button, selecting your picture, and then tapping the *Open* button." While Mr. Bivens spoke, Raquel looked at the screen as he was modeling for the children the sequence of three keystrokes to upload a picture.

Each student was then allowed to come forward and upload his or her photos by tapping the sequence of icons. When it was Raquel's turn, Mr. Bivens provided a physical prompt by pointing to the icons that she should tap as each photo was selected. Then Mr. Bivens said, "Now we will add our voices to our pictures so you can tell a story. Only one person can talk at a time, so I will give you the microphone when it is your turn, and everyone has to be quiet so we can listen." He then demonstrated on his model slide how to record voice by tapping the Comment, Record, Stop Recording, and Save buttons. Mr. Bivens replayed his comment so that the children understood that they would immediately be able to hear their voices. He then opened the second slide and said, "OK, now who made a comment about this picture earlier?" He waited for a show of hands, called a student forward that had made an earlier comment, and guided him through the four-step sequence of recording a comment. He reinforced the student for his successful comment. Mr. Bivens played back the recording and repeated this sequence with two other students, allowing them to serve as models for Raquel, who was the last to be called.

When Raquel exhibited hesitation about what to say, Mr. Bivens asked her peers to help her by reminding her of what she had said previously. The students orally prompted her, and Raquel was then able to record two responses with physical assistance from Mr. Bivens. When all the comments had been made, Mr. Bivens tapped the icon of the first slide in the VoiceThread and played the comment for the students to hear. He proceeded to tap the arrow key to tab through the remaining slides, listening to the recordings on each slide. When the children had listened to the last slide of the VoiceThread story, Mr. Bivens said, "Let's send our story home to your family so you can watch it. We'll print a screenshot so you can take it with you when class is over." He then captured a screenshot of the page, pasted it into a Word document, and printed copies for the students. He slipped Raquel's paper document into a plastic page cover, as she sometimes tore her classroom materials when transitioning between activities or during her trip home on the bus.

In this scenario, carefully planned instruction using EXPECT IT-PLAN IT-TEACH IT, as well as the Break It Down process in the SOLVE IT phase, resulted in a successful learning activity that included all the students in the small-group activity. Instructional strategies were paired with both instructional technology and AT to support children's participation and learning. Raquel's special needs were addressed using a combination of instructional strategies paired with visual supports (i.e., a task book using digital photos and Boardmaker images) and signaling support using peers and PowerPoint animation features.

FAMILY AND COMMUNITY SUPPORTS

Families and their home environments play a large role in the development of early literacy skills among young children. The use of language through parent-child interactions, storybook readings, singing, experiences with other children, and exposure to print-rich environments helps to develop prereading skills which, in turn, prepares children for a life of learning and reading. In addition, these early literacy experiences help to create positive attitudes among children and contribute to later reading success. Helpful strategies for families to support their children's prereading skill development in home settings are presented in Figure 6.4.

Teachers can also enhance home-school connections by communicating with families about activities occurring in their children's classrooms. Of particular importance is providing suggestions regarding developmental skills that can be supported in home settings. When young children experience similar activities both at school and home, they are more likely to show progress and generalize skills across different environments, materials, and people. Teachers can communicate with families using an array of strategies, including e-mail, VoiceThread, updated classroom web sites, online journaling, and weekly classroom newsletters. iPad apps, such as Doodlecast for Kids, Doodlecast Pro, and Educreations, allow children's recorded work (i.e., drawing and commenting) to be sent to families as e-mail attachments, thus connecting children's classroom work with families. Families can also become connected by volunteering in children's classrooms, checking out books read in class to extend learning at home, and sharing their diverse cultural and linguistic backgrounds with classes.

Additionally, families can be directed to web sites with ready-made activities in engaging, interactive formats that reinforce instruction provided in the classroom as well as guidance for parents. For example, Sesame Street games provide tips for parents on each screen as children are participating in an activity. Starfall.com provides a link for parents from its splash page, providing families with suggestions for how to use the various activities archived on the site. PBSkids.org provides an array of links to content area games and a link to PBS Parents, which has tips and tools for raising children's awareness using their learning activities.

For example, Dan Oliver is a single father with a daughter, Abbey, who is in Mr. Bivens' classroom. He wants to make sure he is supporting Abbey in her literacy development in appropriate and effective ways at home so she will not be behind in learning to read. He tells Mr. Bivens that he reads Abbey a story every night before bed, but he just does not feel that is enough now that Abbey is 5 years old. He wants to make sure she is appropriately supported in her literacy development at home. Mr. Bivens responds by thanking Dan for voicing his concerns. He says he has many resources for literacy activities, books, board and computer games, apps, and web sites that promote reading development and would be glad to share them with Dan and all of the families of his students. He says he will post the list of resources on his classroom's web site and will periodically update the list when he finds new materials. Mr. Bivens will also send an e-mail with weekly class topics so that skills can be reinforced at home. From time to time, Mr. Bivens will also use VoiceThread in the classroom to capture children's artwork and allow them to record their voices to tell a story. The VoiceThread link is also shared with the family using e-mail, allowing Abbey's family members to see and hear her reading-related activities in the classroom.

There are many ways in which teachers can communicate with family members about their children's literacy activities and to help families use their existing technologies to support their children's literacy development. Professionals will be limited in such efforts only by their imaginations in how to use existing technologies to provide needed supports.

SUMMARY

The more children hear words and use them in increasingly complex sentences over time, the greater their literacy proficiency (Bond & Wasik, 2009; Scarborough, 2005). Using the EXPECT IT-PLAN IT-TEACH IT model will help teachers to plan and implement well-designed planned activities that promote literacy development.

Instructional technology integration helps young children develop a greater understanding of the relationship between language, reading, and vocabulary during
active engagements in the learning environment.

When children do not have a strong language-based background, early intervention is instrumental in decreasing the likelihood of later reading problems and
thereby closes the gap between good and poor readers. Thus, it is important for all
teachers to understand the language basis of literacy in order to enhance the reading success of all of their students (Snow, Griffin, & Burns, 2005).

ADDITIONAL RESOURCES

Abbot, M., Walton, C., & Greenwood, C.R. (2002). Phonemic awareness in kindergarten and first grade. *Teaching Exceptional Children, 34*(4), 20–26.

Adams, M. (2001). Alphabetic anxiety and explicit, systematic phonics instruction:
A cognitive science perspective. In S.B. Neuman & D.K. Dickinson (Eds.), *Handbook of early literacy research* (Vol. 1, pp. 66–80). New York, NY: Guilford Press.

Anderson, R.S., Grant, M.M., & Speck, B.W. (2008). *Technology to teach literacy: A
resource for K–8 teachers.* Upper Saddle River, NJ: Pearson Prentice Hall.

Dickinson, D.K., & Neuman, S.B. (Eds.). (2006). *Handbook of early literacy research*
(Vol. 2). New York, NY: Guilford Press.

Entz, S., & Galarza, S.L. (2000). *Digital and instant photography activities for early
childhood learning.* Thousand Oaks, CA: Corwin Press.

Gately, S.E. (2004). Developing concept of word. *Teaching Exceptional Children, 36*(6),
16–22.

Good, L. (2009). *Teaching and learning with digital photography: Tips and tools for early
childhood classrooms.* Thousand Oaks, CA: Corwin Press.

Justice, L.M., & Pullen, P.C. (2003). Promising interventions for promoting emergent literacy skills: Three evidence-based approaches. *Topics in Early Childhood
Special Education, 23,* 99–113.

Pierce, P.L., & McWilliam, P.J. (1993). Emerging literacy and children with severe
speech and physical impairments (SSPI): Issues and possible intervention strategies. *Topics in Language Disorders, 13,* 47–57.

Reutzel, D.R., & Cooter, R.B. (2004). *Teaching children to read: Putting the pieces together* (4th ed.). Upper Saddle River, NJ: Merrill/Prentice Hall.

Stahl, S.A., & Fairbanks, M.M. (1986). The effects of vocabulary instruction: A
model-based meta-analysis. *Review of Educational Research, 56*(1), 72–110.

Strickland, D.S., & Riley-Ayers, S. (2006). *Early literacy: Policy and practice in the
preschool years.* New Brunswick, NJ: National Institute for Early Education
Research.

Strickland, D.S., & Shanahan, T. (2004). Laying the groundwork for literacy. *Educational Leadership, 61,* 74–77.

REFERENCES

Bond, M.A., & Wasik, B.A. (2009). Conversation stations: Promoting language development in young children. *Early Childhood Education Journal, 36,* 467–473.

Cooper, J.D., Kiger, N.D., Robinson, M.D., & Slansky, J.A. (2011). *Literacy: Helping students construct meaning* (8th ed.). Belmont, CA: Wadsworth.

Hutinger, P.L., Bell, C., Daytner, G., & Johanson, J. (2006). Establishing and maintaining an early childhood emergent literacy technology curriculum. *Journal of Special Education Technology, 21*(4), 39–54.

International Reading Association & National Association for the Education of Young Children. (1998). Learning to read and write: Developmentally appropriate practices for young children. A joint position statement of the International Reading Association and the National Association for the Education of Young Children. *Young Children, 53,* 30–46.

Koppenhaver, D.A., Coleman, P.P., Kalman, S.L., & Yoder, D.E. (1991). The implications of emergent literacy research for children with developmental disabilities. *American Journal of Speech and Language Pathology, 1,* 329–335.

Lawhon, T., & Cobb, J.B. (2002). Routines that build emergent literacy skills in infants, toddlers, and preschoolers. *Early Childhood Education Journal, 30,* 113–118.

Mariage, T.V. (2001). Features of an interactive writing discourse; conversational involvement, conventional knowledge, and internalization in 'morning message.' *Journal of Learning Disabilities, 34,* 172–196.

McGee, L.M., & Richgels, D.J. (2006). Can technology support emergent reading and writing? Directions for the future. In M.C. McKenna, L.D. Labbo, R.D. Kieffer, & D. Reinking (Eds.), *International handbook of literacy and technology* (Vol. 2, pp. 369–377). Mahwah, NJ: Erlbaum.

National Institute for Literacy. (2008). *Developing early literacy: Report of the National Early Literacy Panel.* Retrieved October 1, 2012, from http://lincs.ed.gov/publications/pdf/NELPReport09.pdf

Scarborough, H.S. (2005). Developing relationships between language and reading: Reconciling a beautiful hypothesis with some ugly facts. In H.W. Catts & A.G. Kamhi, (Eds.), *The connection between language and reading disabilities* (pp. 3–24). Mahwah, NJ: Erlbaum.

Snow, C.E., Griffin, P., & Burns, M. S. (2005). *Knowledge to support the teaching of reading.* San Francisco, CA: Jossey-Bass.

Teale, W.H., & Sulzby, E. (1986). *Emergent literacy: Writing and reading.* Norwood, NJ: Ablex.

Wasik, B.A., & Hindman, A.H. (2011). Improving vocabulary and pre-literacy skills of at-risk preschoolers through teacher professional development. *Journal of Educational Psychology, 103,* 455–469.

7

Integrating Technology to Support Writing

Emily H. Watts, Yojanna Cuenca-Sanchez, and Howard P. Parette, Jr.

After reading this chapter, you should be able to

- Understand key components of handwriting and written composition
- Integrate readily available technology into writing activities using the EXPECT IT- PLAN IT-TEACH IT model
- Problem solve using the Break It Down framework related to writing skills
- Describe strategies for including families in technology discussions and providing them with resources

---

WRITING IN 21ST-CENTURY CLASSROOMS

Everyone knows that young children express themselves in varying ways as their developmental skills are refined in early childhood. They use their bodies to move in space—often dramatically—in response to sounds, sights, and emotions. They use their voices and their developing language skills to express themselves to others, and they enhance their fine motor skills and understanding of language through practice with drawing and learning to write. These skills are further influenced by interactions between young children and varying technologies that are commonly used today.

For example, Danny sits at his home computer and uses his mouse to draw on a whiteboard, one of numerous choices available to him in Zac Browser (see Figure 7.1), a free Internet browser designed for children with autism. The browser has a colorful, interactive, and engaging interface that reduces the number of controls used to simplify the browsing experience. Danny enjoys writing his name and practicing making words. The browser also provides him with access to an array of literacy choices, including children's television shows, engaging games, music paired with text and animation, and stories.

Figure 7.1. Zac Browser allows young children to draw and write on a whiteboard using a mouse. (Used by permission of People CD, Inc.)

Katie is engrossed with an inexpensive iPad app, LetterWriter, that her mother downloaded for her. In her preschool classroom, students have been practicing writing their letters in the sand table, and use of the app allows her to practice those same letters at home. Sean loves to play with his Draw & Write Touch Board that he received as a gift (see Figure 7.2). He practices drawing and writing his letters, and then starts all over by simply lifting the flap on the drawing surface.

Megan sits at her family computer and types words using a standard QWERTY keyboard. Her teacher has e-mailed her parents the words that she wants Megan to practice transcribing. Megan has selected an 18-point font size that allows her to see the letters on the screen. She finds that using the keyboard to write text is faster than handwriting and easier to read.

In each of the preceding examples, current technologies are used by young children to draw and practice their writing, both prior to or while attending preschool or kindergarten. Although paper and pencils, crayons, and pens were the only tools available to young children in the past, a wide variety of more engaging writing technologies are being used with increasing frequency both by families and teachers. These technologies typically have a number of universal design for learning (UDL) characteristics (see Chapter 1). They often are dynamic, flexible, interactive, and shared, thus making them more engaging to young children and also developmentally appropriate.

The Importance of Writing and a Changing Society

Given the rapid pace of technological advancement, a substantive change is occurring with regard to how individuals read and write. Many technologies are available that allow text to be read for users. These types of technologies are more and more commonly seen for web sites having activities for young children, apps for hand-

Figure 7.2. Lakeshore Learning products, such as the Draw & Write Touch Board, afford young children the opportunity to practice drawing and writing, then refresh their writing surface. (Image courtesy of H.P. Parette.)

held devices, software, and commercially marketed toys and learning materials. Consumers, including young children, have access to "talking books" and digital text that can be read by a variety of handheld devices. The same is true for writing and its importance in our society.

Voice recognition, which allows the human voice to be automatically transcribed into text, is increasingly present in an array of common technologies. Use of keyboards and word processing software is now so common that reliance on traditional handwritten text is less important than in years past. Yet, despite these transformations, great emphasis is still being placed on teaching writing in traditional ways in many of today's education settings. The position taken in this chapter is that—at least for the foreseeable future—teachers will continue the long-held tradition of teaching children to write using traditional approaches. However, use of new and engaging instructional technologies should be considered in supporting the development of writing.

Literacy Means Reading and Writing

The inextricable relationship between the early development of reading and writing skills among young children is well known. Important emergent literacy skills (e.g., phonological awareness, alphabetic knowledge, rapid naming tasks of letters and numbers, writing, and writing one's name) precede and predict fundamental reading and writing skills necessary for later success in schools (National Institute for Literacy, 2008). As young children learn both reading and writing skills, they make connections between the reading of the meaning of the written word, their oral language, and their own attempts at writing. Young children who have difficulty in emergent writing skills frequently have difficulty with reading skills. Thus, teachers must help young children develop emergent writing skills, which then lead to a later understanding that writing has both a purpose and an audience.

Emergent Writing and Technology

Because young children are unaccustomed to writing for a purpose, their writing efforts become a substitute for telling or sharing their experiences (Schickedanz & Casbergue, 2004). The teacher provides a classroom model for writing by using the SMART Board or whiteboard during planned activities, supported by use of visual strategies throughout the day (i.e., print paired with pictures on signs). Providing a model is also accomplished in other authentic ways to show that writing can convey meaning, such as allowing children to make signs and shopping lists, sign their names to art products, or sign up for computer use.

Figure 7.3 shows examples of preschool children's writing samples in such authentic activities, including that of Logan, a 5-year-old at-risk student who was asked to sign his name to an art product; 4-year-old Tucker, who was asked to sign up to use the computer during small-group centers; and Jonathan, a 5-year-old student who was asked to sign his name on the back of a shopping list. In each instance, the writing approximates the real appearance of the text names.

Upon reaching kindergarten, most young children have developed a sense of writing for a purpose and understand the process of writing (Kissel, 2008). Their writing reflects more adult-like structure. For example, in Figure 7.4, writing samples taken during a sign-in activity for Mesha and Holly, both 6 years old, are clearly readable, whereas the writing by younger students (see Figure 7.3) is virtually illegible. By this point in time, the purposes of writing present new challenges for children. Now they are expected to demonstrate such skills as journal writing, story development, and formal letter writing. Additionally, they are expected to use rules and nuances, including punctuation, capitalization, and overall mechanics of writing.

Historically, the writing curriculum for young children typically paired the presentation of letters with pictures. For example, to teach the letter shape *i* required that early childhood education professionals use a picture beginning with

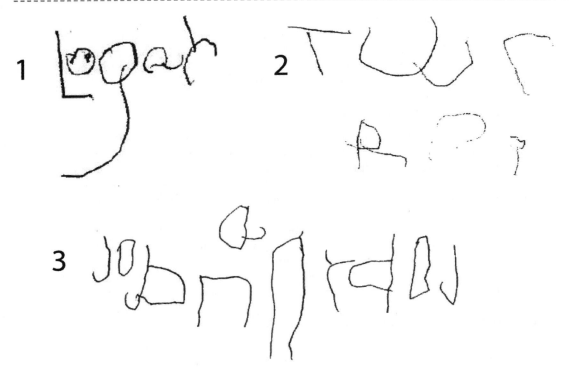

Figure 7.3. Writing samples of preschool children (*1*, Logan; *2*, Tucker; *3*, Jonathan) from authentic classroom activities.

that letter, such as *ice* or *island*. Today, many young children can recognize the letter *i* in print due to the ubiquitous presence of well-known technologies—iPads, iPhones, and iTunes—and their respective advertising in books, magazines, television, and other media. Similarly, the *M* representing the golden arches of McDonalds is well known to young children. The presence of such text when paired with powerful media advertising continues to influence children's understanding of the role of text in our contemporary society.

Early in life children begin to learn about reading and writing by observing and interacting with children and adults across various environments (Strickland & Schickedanz, 2004). These interactions help children understand that writing is a personal method of communication, and they begin to explore and experiment with ways to convey messages through traditional writing methods (e.g., crayons,

Figure 7.4. Authentic sign-in writing samples of kindergarten children (Mesha and Holly).

markers, pencils, varieties of paper). Today such items are still widely used in education settings; however, as previously noted, many current instructional technologies provide engaging supports that enable children to create classroom products, convey meaning, and share what they have written (Parette, Quesenberry, & Blum, 2010; Turja, Endepohls-Ulpe, & Chatoney, 2009).

Progression of Early Writing Skills: What the Research Says

Sulzby, Barnhart, and Hieshima (1989) described writing from the perspective of categories as opposed to a developmental sequence. In examining children's writing behavior, the researchers identified six categories: drawing, scribbling, making letter-like forms, reproducing familiar letter sequences (e.g., one's name), invented spelling, and conventional spelling. These forms may not be linear in progression for a child because both drawing and writing are part of a larger process of organizing the world of materials and strategies (Dyson, 1993).

It is generally recognized that the stages of writing development begin with random marks, scribbles, and drawing pictures (Sulzby, Barnhart, & Hieshima, 1989). As children interact with the environment and have exposure to print, they begin to make a connection that print has form, spaces, and direction. Thus, their writing begins to take shape and look like strings of letter-like forms (Whitehurst & Lonigan, 1998). This evolves through frequent opportunities to practice specific motor movements that ultimately result in greater control and coordination (Bennett-Armistead, Duke, & Moses, 2005).

One of the first letter-like forms that children produce is their name (Bloodgood, 1999). Typically, a child is highly motivated to learn to write the first letter in his or her name. Successful completion of this writing task becomes very personal and bestows a sense of pride or accomplishment in the child (Haney, Bissonnette, & Behnken, 2003).

Today's instructional technologies can support children's progress through the stages of writing. In addition to conventional writing instruments or materials, teachers now have access to many more engaging technologies that involve direct contact with, exploration of, and manipulation of various features. Examples include touchscreens for computer monitors, electronic touch tablets, and an immense array of computer software programs for use with SMART Boards that project on large screens within individual or group activities.

For example, Mrs. Hearns works with her preschool students using her iPads in the writing center to discover letter strokes in their names. Benjamin uses an app for tracing letters. Mrs. Hearns demonstrates tracing of the letter *B* and then asks Benjamin to try tracing the letter. As he traces, sparkling fireflies combine to form the first letter of his name while music plays in the background. Benjamin laughs, and Mrs. Hearns thinks, "How motivating is that!"

In this example, several UDL characteristics are present (see Chapter 2). The app is interactive and things happen as the child's finger moves across the screen. Music plays during these interactions, which serves to engage the child in a different way than if no music were present. The movement of fireflies captures and draws the child's attention to the screen. In addition, the digital nature of the device is part of the child's culture because many people have mobile phones and handheld devices.

Figure 7.5. Readily available web sites, such as Starfall. com, allow early childhood education professionals to use activities targeting use and recognition of letters. (© Starfall Education; used by permission.)

When children begin to recognize letters and identify sounds, typically in the late preschool period, they begin to write letters that have recognizable patterns and a letter name. In this type of writing, known as *invented spelling,* children tend to write words that begin to show emergent phonological awareness and understanding of the alphabetic principle (Bennett-Armistead et al., 2005). This category of writing is often supported by technology-based letter recognition activities. For example, Starfall.com activities present letters in the context of words paired with pictures (see Figure 7.5).

Some research has noted that invented spelling helps children learn how to write as they are making connections between the sound of words and the letters of the alphabet, even though their spelling might not be correct (Whitehurst & Lonigan, 1998). As students develop and become more comfortable with conventional forms of spelling, their writing becomes more structured.

Many schools have basic instructional technologies to support the development of learning in early childhood classrooms. In Chapter 2, key support infrastructure was described, and many classrooms now have some combination of these supports available. This response reflects growing sensitivity to awareness that young children are increasingly exposed to technology in their daily lives (see Chapter 1). For example, with a touchscreen tablet, a child can trace the direction of letters in a word and hear the initial sound and the whole word pronounced. From a UDL perspective, such an experience is both engaging and dynamic because the child receives both visual and auditory feedback even as screens change repeatedly. In addition, children find the interaction with a device to be interesting and motivating. Thus, the activity is developmentally appropriate and should be integrated into existing curricula and instructional practices (Hourcade, Parette, Boeckmann, & Blum, 2010).

Earlier in the day, Mrs. Hearns has discussed and modeled shapes of letters and directions of the strokes. She used individual PowerPoint slides projected on chart paper on the wall during circle time with the large group. Mrs. Hearns encouraged student participation by asking volunteers to come up and help her trace letter-shapes. Later that same morning, Mrs. Hearns planned an activity in which the children were requested to practice three different writing tasks in a small group near the writing center. As students transitioned to the center, they were requested to complete the first task—signing their names in one of the three spaces provided on a notepad labeled *Sign-In Sheet* for the computer use, which had a picture of a computer and spaced lines for the names. Next, students gathered their writing materials: an individual write-on board, a marker, and small eraser. Mrs. Hearns asked one student to launch Starfall.com from the computer desktop using a child-sized mouse. This program has large single images of the letters in the alphabet projected on the monitor accompanied by letter names and letter sounds. The program shows the direction of the strokes and students are prompted by Mrs. Hearns to practice what they have seen on the computer using their boards. This activity lasts until the students are asked to move to the next center choice. Once they are done, students put the materials away and sign out.

Mr. Bivens and his kindergarten class recently took a field trip to the fire station in the neighborhood where they learned fire safety rules, interacted with the firefighters, saw the equipment, and even explored different fire trucks. It was an exciting time for the children, and Mr. Bivens made sure to capture the sequence of activities during the visit with his digital camera. He then prepared a Clicker 6 presentation for the following Friday to be shown on the digital projection unit prior to journal writing time. He also prepared a set of five vocabulary words related to the visit that he modeled in front of the students using the stylus and notepad features of the SMART Board in preparation for their journal writing assignment. He made sure the SMART Board screen had the words visible to all students during their journal writing time. During journal writing time, students were given the directions to write their own entries about the visit and use the words from the SMART Board along with their own drawings.

In each of these instances, instructional technologies have been integrated into classroom instruction to support the writing development of young children. Although the writing tasks vary across the two classrooms, instructional technology is integral to planned activities.

TYPICAL EARLY CHILDHOOD WRITING ACTIVITIES

Writing activities at the preschool and kindergarten levels are as wide-ranging as the diverse purposes for writing that ultimately connect the relationship between print and a meaningful literacy-rich environment. Children write to remember, pretend, label their work, compose a letter or note, make a list, spell, tell a story, contribute and record ideas, enjoy, and share with peers and others. Writing in early childhood is a journey and should not be forced. Children often begin with a great deal of scaffolding and exploration of concepts about print and writing. For example, in many preschool and kindergarten classrooms, children can practice signing in and out of centers, write on an attendance sheet, or identify their work.

When teachers are demonstrating the shapes of the letters of the alphabet, it is not uncommon to introduce the notion that each letter has a name and a sound, thus laying the foundation for basic early literacy skills. Kindergarten students experience more structured and complex writing activities than those experienced in preschool. For example, visual support provided by "word walls" can help kindergarten students write a journal entry about an animal discussed during shared reading. Both preschool and kindergarten students are asked to practice writing throughout the day by completing a variety of writing activities (see Table 7.1).

Large- and Small-Group Learning Activities

Children need repeated opportunities to learn to write. As beginner writers, writing for many purposes is common in daily activities for preschool- and kindergarten-age children. However, writing one's own name may be the most personal and motivating writing task that the preschool child is asked to do. Thus, it becomes a learning benchmark in the curriculum. Teaching students how to make journal entries and write stories are common learning benchmarks at the kindergarten level.

Table 7.1. Preschool and kindergarten activity areas and typical writing tasks

Activity area	Typical writing tasks
Preschool	
Arrival	Sign in on the attendance sheet using a pencil, marker, crayon or name stamp
Large group	Write name (scribble, mock letters, or actual letters in name) on artwork
	Write name (scribble, mock letters, or actual letters in name) on label for locker/cubbie
Choice time/free play	Write a grocery list (scribble, mock letters, or actual letters) on a notepad in the kitchen play area
	Draw with markers and colored pencils in the writing center
	Use stencils for tracing
	In the block area, write an order for construction of a building
Small group	Sign up on sheet for computer use
	Write or draw an individual page for a class book using mock words and sign name
	Trace numbers given a model
	Create a birthday, holiday, or thank-you card for family member or friends
Departure	Write a checkmark to sign out
Kindergarten	
Arrival	Sign in on the attendance sheet using a pencil
Opening/morning meeting	Take turns writing on the daily message board
Reading/literacy	Select a book to "read" then write and draw about it using mock or real words
	Write a mock title and the beginning of a "story" given a stem idea
Writing/language arts	Write entry in daily journal
	Retell orally and write story using mock or real words about a recent field trip
	Participate orally in a shared writing chart with teacher
	Write labels for various centers or bulletin board displays
Math	Use individual write-on board with marker/eraser to write numbers from a model given by teacher
Art/physical education/music	Write labels using words for describing details of artwork
Social studies/science	Draw picture of display objects from nature and label them using directionality and letters
Dismissal routine	Sign out on the attendance sheet using a pencil

To be successful in these activities, children must be provided with ample opportunities to practice writing, thus laying a foundation for the connections among oral language, written language, and reading.

Most preschool education professionals provide supportive environments that lay the foundation for literacy growth (Vukelich & Christie, 2009). Kindergarten professionals scaffold writing skills based upon those preschool experiences (Feldgus & Cardonick, 1999). They strengthen informal, risk-free writing opportunities by providing explicit instruction on more advanced formal types of writing.

Instructional grouping for writing includes a combination of individual, small-group, and large-group activities. The next section includes vignettes to illustrate some activities in which children are expected to develop and understand the purpose of writing. These vignettes will also illustrate how technology can easily be integrated into instruction in writing using the EXPECT IT-PLAN IT-TEACH IT framework.

What the Research Says

Evidence-based teaching strategies of observational learning and incidental learning have been successfully investigated within small-group arrangements of students with learning disabilities, autism spectrum disorders, and intellectual disabilities. Incidental learning has been defined as gaining information or skills that are not directly trained or reinforced (Wolery, Ault, Gast, Doyle, & Mills, 1990). Keel and Gast (1992) taught students target vocabulary words while students learned the observational words of the other students in the group. Campbell and Mechling (2009) investigated the effectiveness of using SMART Board technology to teach letter-sound sets to a small group of kindergarten students with learning disabilities. Observational learning of other group members resulted in the acquisition of nontargeted stimuli (i.e., letter-sound sets), as well as target letter-sound sets.

Mrs. Hearns

Mrs. Hearns is using the EXPECT IT-PLAN IT-TEACH IT technology integration framework to help young children in her preschool classroom explore writing.

EXPECT IT   One of the early childhood standards identified in Mrs. Hearns' curriculum is *writing to communicate for a variety of purposes.* She recognizes that writing letters is important, and so she chooses an associated learning objective in which each child is expected to write most, if not all, of the letters in their first name in recognizable form. Because none of her students can write their first names, she specifically wants to focus on the first letter in their first names.

PLAN IT   To plan an activity for a small group of three students in her writing center, Mrs. Hearns uses a structured approach that considers technologies, instructional strategies, and assessment—three essential planning elements.

TECH IT   Mrs. Hearns knows that her curriculum has a series of recommended letter writing activities that are associated with teaching the learning objectives associated with the writing standard. However, none of the activities incorporate technology, so she decides that she will use her existing classroom instructional technologies that lend themselves to a small group of three students and extend the activities recommended in the curriculum. Because Mrs. Hearns will be working with a small group, she knows that she needs an instructional technology that can be used by all students, and which affords them the opportunity for hands-on experience with the technology.

A digital projector and digital camera will be used to embed photos of children to personalize each of the student's slides, which will connect each child with his or her name (see Figure 7.6). Because Mrs. Hearns has Microsoft Word on her

Figure 7.6. Developmentally appropriate PowerPoint slides are created using children's photos and animation effects to create movement to engage children. (Image courtesy of J. Parette.)

classroom computer, she will create and print three sets of three personalized writing practice sheets containing large-font letters of each of the three students' names (see Figure 7.7). She will also print one set that she will use to model the letter strokes for each student.

Mrs. Hearns creates arrows on her letter figures (see more about inserting shapes at http://office.microsoft.com/en-us/power point-help/add-change-or-delete-shapes -HA010354749.aspx?CTT=1) and she embeds numerals within a text box on each letter to show children the direction of letter strokes to be made in their names. Each personalized three-sheet practice set will be used by the children, who will be given scented markers to trace letters. She also selects a device called MagnaDoodle (see Figure 7.8), which will allow children to write their names after using the writing practice worksheets.

 ARRANGE IT For this planned lesson, Mrs. Hearns will employ a naturalistic approach that allows the children to explore writing their names. Rather than forcing a prerequisite sequence of skills, Mrs. Hearns will allow children attempts at writing their name while using modeling and scaffolding. Young children tend to master what is easiest for them first, and rely on scaffolding for help in completing the more difficult aspects of writing their names. Mrs. Hearns is aware that children in her class are proud to write their names and want to share them with the teacher and classmates. This child centered approach creates an easy-to-hard sequence and permits exploration of the written word without judgment. Mrs. Hearns also models how the scaffold works with the practice sheet (see Figure 7.7) followed by use of the MagnaDoodle to practice writing names.

Although the focus of the lesson is name writing, Mrs. Hearns discusses sounds of letters during the lesson while embedding other important literacy concepts. She shows children how to write and how to hold the writing stylus they are going to use in MagnaDoodle. Consistent with the standard, she asks the students to share their names with her and peers when they have completed their writing. The goal is not perfection, but rather for the children to enjoy and explore letters when writing their names. Young children often create "mock letters"—letters that are similar in shape to the actual letters in their names but are *not* the letters themselves. When children write on the MagnaDoodle, this will be evident. Mrs. Hearns provides encouragement and is not critical of this natural stage of writing development in young children.

 CHECK IT Because Mrs. Hearns uses writing practice sheets for each student, these become permanent products that can be placed in their student files and/or shared with family members. Mrs. Hearns also will use her digital camera to take pictures of each student as he or she completes the MagnaDoodle writing task. These photos can then be filed in her digital student folders for the children and shared with family members.

SOLVE IT Subsequent to the initial planning in TECH IT-ARRANGE IT-CHECK IT steps, the SOLVE IT process occurs to address concerns. Mrs. Hearns recognizes that Davey has a developmental delay that causes him to have a short attention span in planned classroom activities. Based on an authentic assessment that she conducted at the beginning of the year, Mrs. Hearns also knows that Davey lacks awareness of sounds of letters, has limited oral language, and has only scribbled on paper. To ensure that Davey is included in her planned activity, Mrs. Hearns uses the Break It Down approach to make decisions about assistive technology and strategies that might be needed to support his participation (see Table 7.2).

Figure 7.7. Personalized writing practice sheets may be created using Word Art and shapes features in Microsoft Word. (Figure courtesy of H.P. Parette.)

In collaboration with a special education professional, Mrs. Hearns has identified several child-focused instructional strategies designed to enhance Davey's participation. Some solutions are simple, such as ensuring that Davey receives prompting to get to the writing center. It is essential that these prompts are consistently stated to Davey, so Mrs. Hearns writes down what she is comfortable using and attempts to use them regularly. Child-focused instructional strategies for young children with disabilities require that modeling be explicit. During the discussion of writing names, Davey needs explicit modeling to participate in interactive discussions and respond to open-ended questions.

To increase the likelihood that Davey initiates verbally during interaction discussions, Mrs. Hearns decides to give specific feedback and praise for participation, even if it was an approximation (e.g., saying something rather than saying nothing). Using verbal prompts for Davey to say letters in the PowerPoint presentation provides the extra support he needs during that step of the planned activity.

Several signaling strategies are used with Davey to address discrepancies between what he and his peers can do during the writing on the practice sheets. Use of Boardmaker symbols provides a signal for him to watch, listen, and work. Davey will need to be taught what these symbols mean and should be praised for responding.

In this example, the target child is Davey, but all children can be taught to use these symbols if desired. The highlighting is also a signal where children should write. Use of verbal and physical assistance is provided as needed. A prompting scaffold is used by watching when

Figure 7.8. The MagnaDoodle allows young children to stamp, draw, and erase letters of their names. (Image courtesy of H.P. Parette.)

Table 7.2. The Break It Down process for Davey

Define the problem: Davey has a short attention span, doesn't follow instructions, and lacks awareness of alphabetical principle, which causes difficulties during writing center activities.

Activity: Children will be presented with a 4-slide PowerPoint presentation that calls attention to letters in their first names. They will be provided with a model for writing their names on three Microsoft Word writing practice sheets. They will then write their names on a MagnaDoodle.

| Planned activity steps | Planned activity requirements | | | Child performance | What's the answer? |
	DO	SAY	REMEMBER		
To begin: Children transition to writing center	Hear the teacher's instructions Look at the center area Walk to the center Sit in chair	N/A	Recall location of writing center Remember rules for transitioning quietly	Davey sometimes has trouble with transitions between activities Davey stays in his seat when instructed to go to the writing center	Verbal prompt: "Find a friend and go to the writing center"
Participate in discussion about importance of writing names	Listen to teacher See the teacher	Offer ideas regarding importance of names	Recall etiquette rules for participating in group discussion	Davey sometimes doesn't participate in group discussions due to distractibility Davey didn't offer any ideas why names are important	Model ideas suggested by other students and ask Davey to repeat using prompt and reinforcement (praise specific to Davey's participation)
Watch the PowerPoint presentation	Look at the teacher Look at PowerPoint presentation on screen Listen to teacher's model of letters	Say letters in first name	Recognizes picture and own name in print Remembers sequence of letters in first name	Davey says only the first letter in his name Davey says first letter after teacher model is provided, but doesn't pronounce last three letters	Provide verbal model and prompt for each of the last three letters in name

160

Task	Do/See	Say	Remember	Problem	Solution
Write name on Microsoft Word writing practice sheets	Look at the teacher; Hear the teacher's instructions; See the worksheet; See the circle, arrows, and numerals on worksheet; Grip scented marker; Make letter strokes	Say letters as they are written	Remember steps for making strokes	Davey has difficulty making letters and doesn't recognize all the letters in his first name; he also has difficulty following directions. Davey didn't attend to teacher instructions, and made his letter strokes from the wrong direction and appeared confused	Boardmaker rule chart containing three symbols: Watch, Listen, Work. Use highlighter marker to call attention to stroke directions. Model letter names if needed. Verbalize the directionality of the strokes and ask Davey to say the steps out loud. Provide physical assistance
Place practice sheets in writing bins and return markers	Listen to teacher's directions; See writing bin; Place practice sheets in bin; Place markers in can		Know where writing bin is located; Know where marker can is located	Davey sometimes doesn't follow directions. Davey placed practice sheets in bin and returned his marker to the appropriate can	No solution needed
Writes name on MagnaDoodle	See MagnaDoodle; Grip stylus; Write letters	Say letters of name	Remember the letter names; Remember sequence of letters	Davey scribbles palming the pen of the MagnaDoodle. Davey looked at the teacher when prompted to write his name	Use Boardmaker rule chart containing three symbols: Watch, Listen, Work. Verbal prompt. Hand-over-hand assistance. Use verbal praise
To end: Transition to next activity	Listen to teacher's instructions; Look at transition activity area		Remember location of next activity	Davey sometimes has trouble with transitions between activities. Davey stood up from seat and went over to writing materials and began playing with them	Use Boardmaker rule chart containing three symbols: Watch, Listen, Work. Verbal prompt

Davey most needs assistance and only providing support at those moments. This same process is used with the MagnaDoodle. At the end of the activity, use of the Boardmaker symbols will provide a signal, and verbal prompts are an extra reminder that is sometimes needed. All signaling and prompting strategies are considered temporary supports until Davey can become more independent.

Over the year, Mrs. Hearns will make systematic efforts to reduce physical prompting by gradually reducing this support. Additionally, Mrs. Hearns will eventually introduce time delay, in which she waits 5 seconds before giving a verbal prompt, with the ultimate goal of not providing verbal prompts at all. All of these solutions in the Break It Down chart, once confirmed as effective, will be introduced into other activities with similar steps.

TEACH IT   Based on the careful planning Mrs. Hearns did to prepare for her planned lesson, the activity unfolded in a predictable sequence. She opened her four-slide PowerPoint presentation before the children arrived, and the first slide was blinking the word *names*. As the three children transitioned into the writing center, Mrs. Hearns observed that Davey was with a friend (i.e., Alex) as prompted, and he was able to successfully get to the center without distraction.

Mrs. Hearns asked the children to be seated at the writing table and directed their attention toward the screen, on which she provided a preview of the planned activity by stating the children were going to practice writing their names. She said, "Each of us has something that is personal, and that is your own name. You have learned that someone has called your name, so now you need to learn how to write it. Why do think it is important that you know how to write your name?" Mrs. Hearns allowed students to come up with reasons regarding why this is important. She noticed that Davey offered no ideas, so she stated each idea offered by Alex and Chloe, and said, "Davey, writing names helps us to sign in the class in the morning and label our work. So you tell me, why is writing our names important?" She waited for a response, saw hesitation, and then modeled a possible response, "To sign in the class in the morning and label our work." Davey repeated the model provided, and Mrs. Hearns reinforced his response. Then she said, "Today we're going to practice writing our names."

Mrs. Hearns called attention to a Boardmaker chart that she had prepared, containing three picture symbols representing *Watch, Listen,* and *Work*. She pointed to the chart and said, "It's important for all of us to *watch* the teacher, *listen* to what she says, and then to do our *work*." She noticed that Davey was not listening and watching while she made this statement, so she said, "Davey, what are we going to do now?" Mrs. Hearns waited for Davey to respond. When no response was forthcoming, she prompted, "Watch, listen, work," waited for him to respond, and reinforced his response.

Mrs. Hearns continued, "We'll look at each of your names, say the letters, and then we're going to write the letters in your names." She showed the second slide of her presentation in which Alex's picture and name appeared, while saying, "Here is Alex's name" (see Figure 7.6). Mrs. Hearns pronounced each letter from left to right, and then asked Alex to say the letters. Then she opened the third slide presenting Davey's name, and, after modeling the letters, she observed Davey only pronouncing the first letter before he hesitated. She immediately pointed to the second letter *a* and pronounced it, then looked at Davey and awaited a response.

Davey responded to the model, and she then moved to the next two letters, repeating the procedure to get a response from Davey. She opened the fourth slide with Chloe's name, using the same modeling procedure, which Chloe responded to without difficulty.

Mrs. Hearns then distributed the writing practice sheets to each student. She held up her own practice sheet with her own name on it and said, "Now we're going to practice writing our names on some writing practice sheets." She took a scented marker from a bin on the table and said, "I'm going to take my marker and start at the circle. The arrows and numbers [it is easier for children this age to follow the arrows, but this strengthens the concept of number sequence] tell me where to start and which way to go. I start at the *1* and follow the arrow, like this." She demonstrated the strokes, calling attention to the numerals and direction of the lines, and pronounced each letter as it was completed. She observed that Davey was watching the model she provided.

The students selected their own markers and began tracing the letters on their practice sheets. Davey immediately began at the wrong place when he began his tracing, and Mrs. Hearns immediately directed him to look for the number *1* on the practice sheet while highlighting it with a yellow marker. Mrs. Hearns said, "Davey, start with the number *1* and follow the arrows" while modeling with her finger the direction of the strokes. Mrs. Hearns had to provide prompts several times to both Alex and Chloe to help them know where to begin on their writing practice sheets, and she provided positive reinforcement as children completed their work. She asked the children to place their completed writing practice sheets in the writing bin and return the markers to the Writing Shelf, and she was pleased to see that Davey completed this task.

When the students were reseated at the writing table, Mrs. Hearns held up the MagnaDoodle, introduced its use for writing, and showed the students the pen that was attached which they would use to write their names. She modeled writing the name *Mrs. Hearns,* calling out each letter as it was written while observing whether Davey was attending to her model and instructions. She then gave each child the MagnaDoodle, asking him or her to write the letters of their name and say the letters as they were writing. Alex and Chloe wrote their names on the Magna-Doodle; both had some mock lettering and some letters that looked like the letters in their name. Mrs. Hearns captured a digital picture to document their progress. She also made sure that Davey was successful by calling attention to the Boardmaker Watch, Listen, Work chart and went through the steps expected of him: watch Mrs. Hearns as she wrote his name on the MagnaDoodle, listen as she named the letters, and then take his turn by working.

Davey took the writing pen of the MagnaDoodle and scribbled while palming the writing pen. Mrs. Hearns provided a physical prompt by pointing to where he needed to begin his letter, and then provided hand-over-hand assistance (this was considered a temporary support) when she saw that he was going to be unable to complete the task independently. As each letter was created, Mrs. Hearns asked Davey to name it. When Davey did not, she named the letter for him as a prompt and had him repeat it, followed by giving him praise for a correct response. She made several quick notations on the screen to record the type of assistance given to Davey (*P* for prompt, *PG* for physical guidance) and then took a digital photo of his work.

Davey, because of his disability, received a more child-focused, systematic, and directive instructional strategy than Alex and Chloe. All the children showed and shared their name with the group. Mrs. Hearns then said, "All of you did good work today. Now it's time to move to our next center." All three students got up from the writing table, but only Alex and Chloe began moving toward the next center area. Davey instead began playing with some of the markers on the writing shelf. Mrs. Hearns again called attention to the Boardmaker rule chart and said, "Davey, look at the chart. You *watched* me, but now you need to *listen*. It's time to go to the next center." Davey listened, so Mrs. Hearns continued, "Now it's time to work and *go* to the next center." She pointed in the direction of the center and Davey made the transition.

In this teaching scenario, Mrs. Hearns used several instructional technologies that supported her teaching of a targeted learning objective. She also used her readily available software application, Boardmaker, coupled with instructional strategies to ensure that Davey stayed on task and participated in her planned activity.

Mr. Bivens

Mr. Bivens uses the EXPECT IT-PLAN IT-TEACH IT technology integration model to help the children in his kindergarten classroom learn some of the basics of composition.

EXPECT IT   One of the kindergarten standards in Mr. Bivens' curriculum is to *compose well-organized and coherent writing for specific purposes and audiences.* Mr. Bivens has used a variety of planned activities in his class in the past, but he knows that his students need additional work in this area. Mr. Bivens chooses a learning objective identified under this standard: *use a combination of drawing, dictating, and writing to compose informative/explanatory texts to name what they are writing about and supply some information about the topic,* which will become the focus of his planned activity.

PLAN IT   To effectively plan his classroom activity, Mr. Bivens wants to capitalize on a recent class trip to the zoo. He uses the three components of PLAN IT in the context of a large-group format to develop his planned activity, followed by transition into the writing center, where small groups of children can focus on their writing.

TECH IT   Mr. Bivens decides to use his SMART Board to write down student's brainstorming ideas during the large-group brainstorming session at the beginning of his planned activity. He will upload 10 photos of targeted animals from a field trip to the zoo, which he knew students really liked. These same photos will also be used in his Clicker 5 activity. The SMART Board photos will be on a blank Notebook page, allowing him to move them around during the group discussion. He will also use his SMART Board to find and present a zoo activity that can be used with Clicker 5, which is installed on his classroom computer.

Mr. Bivens did a quick search of two sites, the Spectronics Activity Exchange and LearningGridsWorld, to find a zoo activity. He has learned that many readily available activities have been created by teachers and uploaded to these exchanges;

they can be downloaded and quickly modified to meet the needs of instruction in early childhood settings. On searching the Spectronics site, he found and downloaded Zoo Excursion for Clicker 5. This grid download provides a template for children to compose a report about a recent field trip to the zoo. It also provides an opportunity for students to record their own reading of the story. Mr. Bivens had observed which animals children were most interested in at the zoo, so the same photos used in the initial discussion were embedded in the Clicker 5 presentation. Two animals were presented on each page, which would allow children to make a choice. Mr. Bivens also inserted the names of both animals and attributes to include targeted vocabulary that might be possible for each of the pictures (e.g., for the bear and tiger pictures, the words *bear, tiger, big, brown,* and *mean* would be inserted). Mr. Bivens does this to ensure that minimal time will be required to add new words to the pop-up menu during the planned activity while children are brainstorming ideas. He also adds words to the title page's pop-up menu that include *at, the, zoo, we,* and *saw,* which will allow children to select words that would then be typed on the screen.

When children transition into the writing center during the day, Mr. Bivens also wants to use an iPad app, Doodlecast for Kids, that will allow children to write on a blank template, draw an animal, and record their voices while drawing and telling a story about the animals in the zoo experience (see Figure 7.9). Children can control their voice recording in the app by starting and stopping the record button, and all their writing is captured on the screen as soon as a blank template is opened. When the *Done* button is pressed, everything—drawing, writing, and voice recording—is saved as a movie that can be replayed over and over and shared with others. Mr. Bivens will use pictures of the zoo animals taken with his iPad and printed on his classroom printer as a support for the planned writing center activity used with a flannel board. Blank cards and a marker will be used to write words associated with the animals and the class story, which will be placed on the flannel board.

 ARRANGE IT Mr. Bivens decides he wants to use an interactive discussion and writing composition project with his kindergarten class that is based on a zoo field trip. He will use both large- and small-group activities, beginning with large group and following up with work at the writing center. He will discuss with groups animals that children saw at the zoo. He will also model writing names of animals next to pictures on the SMART Board and facilitate an interactive discussion about them. The principle strategy on the SMART board is a shared writing, which is a process in

Figure 7.9. The Doodlecast for Kids app for the iPad allows children to draw, write, and record their voices simultaneously and their writing strokes are saved in a movie format that can be played back immediately. (Used by permission of zinc Roe Design.)

which the teacher and all children are engaged in jointly composing text. It will be quickly paced and error free, taking no more than 10-15 minutes. In shared writing, children think aloud about the writing in the experience. The teacher serves as the scribe in shared writing (in this case, it will be on the SMART Board). The discussion is not solely tied to the zoo experience, but it is connected to multiple narrative texts that help build lexical (vocabulary) networks. This strategy connects writing and reading with technology supporting the instructional strategy. When the children are at the writing center, Mr. Bivens models use of Doodlecast for Kids and scaffolds children's writing.

 CHECK IT   Mr. Bivens decides to use his iPad camera to capture permanent product images of the students who work at the SMART Board during his planned activity. These will be archived on his computer and can then be viewed, printed, and/or shared electronically with families. Given the recording features in Doodlecast for Kids, student drawings and stories will be recorded as movies, allowing yet more permanent products of children's work to be captured, stored, and shared as needed.

 SOLVE IT   Subsequent to the initial planning that occurred in the TECH IT-ARRANGE IT-CHECK IT steps above, Mr. Bivens used the SOLVE IT process to address concerns that were occurring with Anna during writing center (see Table 7.3). Mr. Bivens knows that Anna has a speech and language delay, and that she needs many opportunities to observe others using more complex language structures and practice the use of language in the classroom. He knows that most students in his class are using five- and six-word sentences, although Anna's speech typically reflects use of two- to three-word sentences. (It is a goal to expand Anna's speech to three- to four-word sentences.)

Anna also has some weakness in her hands that make it difficult for her to grip a pencil for writing tasks or use her fingers to draw letters in a small space, such as the iPad screen. However, Mr. Bivens knows that Anna can make crude drawings using her fingers based on her prior work in class in the art center. To support her participation in making a flannel board list of words used in the Clicker 5 story, Mr. Bivens will use a 5-second time delay prompting strategy by specifically asking her, "Anna, what word do you remember?" He will then allow 5 seconds for a response before providing a prompt using one of the words from the story. If Anna fails to respond, a visual Boardmaker symbol will be provided, which allows Anna to use the symbol as a reminder of what to say. Experience working with Anna has demonstrated that she will respond verbally when presented with these symbols. Mr. Bivens will do this for each of the five animals discussed by the students during the writing center.

Anna also has used a computer keyboard in the classroom for text transcription previously, so Mr. Bivens decides that one solution for her participation in the writing center would be to use the Writing Buddy app, which is a talking word processor developed for young children. This app would allow Anna to use an on-screen keyboard to write text on the iPad screen. Further, she could save any writing work and send it to Mr. Bivens' e-mail account, which was set up previously in the app. To further help Anna with her writing—and not expect her to rely on looking at the flannel board words and then back to the keyboard to transcribe

Table 7.3. The Break It Down table for Anna

Define the problem: Anna's speech and language delays have resulted in her using only two- to three-word phrases in her conversational speech and writing during writing center activities. Her fine motor problems make it difficult for her to use a pencil or her fingers for transcription of text.

Activity: After a shared reading activity in which the SMART Board and Clicker 5 are used with the class to write a story about a zoo field trip, a writing center activity based on the shared reading will be presented to a small group of three students. The children will be given iPads and shown how to use Doodlecast to draw the five animals identified by the class for the shared story. They will then be shown how to write and record stories about each of the five animals using the app.

Planned activity steps	Planned activity requirements			Child performance	What's the answer?
	DO	SAY	REMEMBER		
To begin: Transition to writing center	Look at the writing center area Go to writing center Listen to teacher provide directions	N/A	Recall location of writing center Remember rules for quiet transitions	Anna generally makes transitions between activities without difficulty Anna transitioned from large-group activity with SMART Board to the writing center with her two peers	N/A
Draw picture of zoo animals	See the teacher Listen to the teacher See flannel board See and hold the iPad See the Doodlecast and blank template icons See and tap icons and buttons on screen Draw animals using fingers	Ask questions if help is needed	Remember trip to the zoo and the animals they saw Recall sequence of steps to using drawing features in Doodlecast	Anna draws crude pictures using her fingers Anna was a little confused in finding the Doodlecast icon but had no difficulty using her index finger to draw animals that were identified in the story; she had problems finding and tapping the picture icon at the bottom of the Photo tray	Prompt using pointing if needed to help Anna find icon Provide hand-over-hand assistance for tapping small icons

(continued)

Table 7.3 (continued)

Planned activity steps	Planned activity requirements				Child performance	What's the answer?
	DO	SAY	REMEMBER			
Suggest words for Mr. Bivens to place on flannel board	See the teacher Listen to the teacher See the flannel board and words	Say words to be placed on flannel board	Remember words from Clicker 5 large-group activity and zoo animals		Anna sits quietly Anna often had difficulty with remembering new words and saying things because of limited vocabulary	Use of 5-second time delay to encourage independence Boardmaker visual prompt to encourage use of vocabulary tied to lesson
Write animal story using Doodlecast app	See the teacher Listen to the teacher See the flannel board and words See and hold the iPad See the Doodlecast and blank template icons See and tap Record, Done, and Play buttons on screen Write sentence using finger	Say words used in shared story Comment on individual story as it is played	Remember trip to the zoo and the animals they saw Recall sequence of steps to write and save stories in Doodlecast		Anna has difficulty writing using her finger and only uses 2-word sentences when writing Anna didn't offer story words to be used; could not use the iPad screen for writing sentences with her fingers due to her fine motor limitations	Use Writing Buddy app, a talking word processor, to write story Use word "stem sheet" to provide sentence templates during writing on each animal story page Prompting with 5-second time delay as needed
Share animal story with peers	See the teacher Listen to the teacher See and hold the iPad See saved story in iPad Photo tray See and tap Play button on screen Listen to stories played by other students	Make comments about story Ask questions about stories	Remember sequence of finding story in Photo tray and playing story for others		Anna has used a keyboard previously; she has difficulty using her fingers for some fine motor tasks Anna could not use Doodlecast to create a story and thus could not tell a story using its features	Use Writing Buddy app and click "Play" to tell story
To end: Transition to next activity center	See the teacher Listen to the teacher's directions Replace iPad on writing center shelf See the next activity center		Remember location of activity centers Remember rules for quiet transitions			N/A

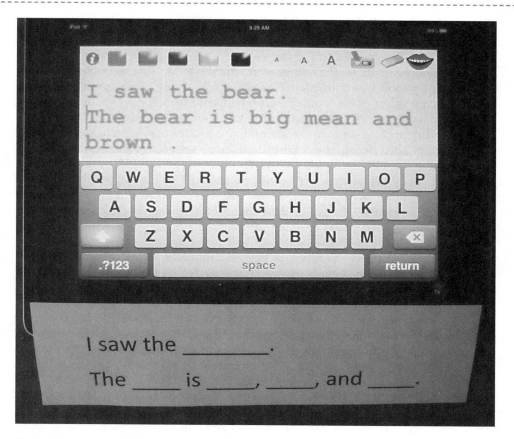

Figure 7.10. Using the WritingBuddy app combined with stem sheets, young children can write sentences about their classroom experiences. (Image courtesy of H.P. Parette.)

them—Mr. Bivens will create and print a stem sheet using Microsoft Word, and which has two sentence starters: *I saw the [animal name]* and *The [animal name] is ____, ____, and ____ [attributes from story]*. The stem sheet will serve as a model that can be placed next to the keyboard for Anna to refer to while writing (see Figure 7.10).

Each of these solutions identified through problem solving were included in the Break It Down chart. Each assistive technology solution addresses direct discrepancies created by the planned activity demands and Anna's ability to meet those demands because of her disability. Providing these compensatory tools will drastically improve Anna's participation level and may eventually improve her performance level. As these solutions are developed, they may become permanent parts of her individualized education program and can be used in other similar situations, hence limiting the need for future problem solving using the Break It Down chart.

 TEACH IT Based on Mr. Bivens' attention to PLAN IT, his subsequent planned activity unfolded with great success. He showed the entire class the SMART Board page having 10 photos of zoo animals they had seen, and he said "Let's talk about our trip to the zoo." He called attention to each of the 10 animals, shown in pairs just as they were presented in the subsequent Clicker 5 activity slides, and asked children to name them. As the names were called out, Mr. Bivens wrote the names next to their pictures on the SMART Board, while saying, "We saw a bear and a lion." He then grouped each photo in the pair with its respective word name, allowing a pair of two pictures and words to be moved as a unit on the SMART Board. He did this four more times, creating five groups of two pictures and words in each group. Then he told the children that they were going to write a story about five of these animals. He showed the students the first animal pair of two pictures/words and said, "Which one shall we write about? The lion or bear? Raise your hands if you want to write about the lion. OK, and if you want to write about the bear, raise your hands." He tallied the count each time and wrote the number beside the pair, and then called attention to the animal in the pair that received the most votes (the bear).

Rather than circling the name as he had originally planned, Mr. Bivens ungrouped the two-picture/word pair so that only the picture of the bear and the word *bear* could be moved. He quickly drew a crude book on the screen and dragged the bear picture/word over to a drawn page on the book. He went through this process for the remaining four two-animal photo/word pairs, resulting in five animals and their word names being on the drawing of a book page. Mr. Bivens then asked the class to say the words as he pointed to each. Then he opened the Zoo Excursion Clicker 5 activity to the first slide presenting two animals from among the 10 originally presented in the group discussion.

Mr. Bivens said, "OK, now let's choose some words to describe the bear." Anna appeared confused, so Mr. Bivens asked her, "Which of the two animals did we select to write about?" Anna simply chose an animal with which she was familiar, but which was not of the two targeted animals. In response, Mr. Bivens clicked on the notebook page that they had used in the initial discussion and voting, called attention to the five names on the drawn book page, and asked the students to say the names again. The repetition seemed to help Anna and she now appeared more engaged in the lesson. He proceeded by clicking on the *Words* button and his previously created pop-up word bank appeared with preselected words (*bear, lion, mean, brown, big*). He said, "Some words that we might use for our story of the bear are big, mean, and brown." He then asked the class, "What are some other words that we might use?" Students answered with several words, including *scary* and *ugly,* which Mr. Bivens typed into the cells of the pop-up screen.

Mr. Bivens went through each of the next four pages, with students selecting one animal from the pair presented and identifying several additional words to add to those Mr. Bivens had previously embedded in the pop-up screen. The animals selected for these pages were *tiger, hippo, wolf,* and *parrot.* When all five pages were completed, he went to the title page of the Clicker 5 activity and asked students to name the story. He listened to several suggestions from the class and wrote the titles on the SMART Board screen. He said each title and asked the class to vote on the title they liked best; they selected *Mr. Bivens's Class Goes to the Zoo,* which he quickly typed into the Clicker 5 tile cell. He then modeled to the class how to tap the *Words* icon, whereon students saw a pop-up window with the words *at, the, zoo, we,* and *saw.* Mr. Bivens modeled tapping the words in sequence so that children saw the words transcribed on the screen and spoken as he made selections. He then called on Marcus to come to the SMART Board and to type the words in the story. Marcus came forward and tapped the sequence of words, whereon they appeared on the screen and were spoken.

Mr. Bivens used the same procedure for the next five slides in which *bear, tiger, hippo, wolf,* and *parrot* were presented and students were called to the SMART Board to write. Several times, Mr. Bivens had to provide prompts for the sequence of words and remind students to tap the period symbol when they were finished so that the sentence could be spoken. When students put words in the wrong sequence, he cleared the cell selection where the text appears and modeled the appropriate sequence of words, followed by clearing it again and asking the student to make the correct word sequence. When they were through, Mr. Bivens praised the class for writing *Mr. Bivens's Class Goes to the Zoo.*

Mr. Bivens then said, "OK, let's go to our centers." When Mr. Bivens went to the writing center, Anna, Georgie, and Sarah were seated at the writing table. He went to the writing shelf and retrieved four iPads, which he handed to each student while saying, "Now that our class wrote a story about our trip to the zoo together, we'll use our iPads for each of you to write your own story." Mr. Bivens used his flannel board to point to pictures of each of the animals selected in the story. He demonstrated where to find the Doodlecast for Kids icon, and he modeled tapping the icon and selecting a blank template for the students to work. He noticed that Anna seemed confused in trying to find the icon, so he used a gesture (pointing) prompt to help her find the icon. He then modeled tapping the icon to launch Doodlecast for Kids and observed whether they selected the blank template. Each student was successful.

Mr. Bivens said, "Now let's draw a picture of the five zoo animals that we wrote about earlier. I'm going to draw a bear." He showed them how to draw a bear on the screen using the nine colors available to them and how to erase their text using a left arrow icon. He also modeled how to click the *Done* button when their drawing is completed, allowing the work to immediately be replayed. Mr. Bivens then showed them how to find it again by looking in the photo tray at the bottom of the screen. The children immediately became engaged in using their drawing tools and creating animal drawings. Mr. Bivens closely observed Anna, who he knew had fine motor difficulties due to poor strength in her hands, but she was enthusiastic about drawing on the iPad screen and playing her pictures. However, finding her work in the photo tray was problematic for Anna because the photo icons were so small, so Mr. Bivens had to provide physical hand-over-hand assistance to help her find her pictures and tap them to make them appear. He provided encouragement to each of the children as they created their drawings, commenting on them and asking them to show the others.

After all the drawings were created, Mr. Bivens told them that they were going to write a story about each animal. He said, "We're going to use some of the words that all of you suggested earlier." Pointing to the flannel board, Mr. Bivens asked students what words they remembered from the Clicker 5 story that were used to describe each animal. As the students offered words, he wrote them down on paper cards, said the word, asked students to echo the word, and placed them below the picture of each animal on the flannel board. Because Anna had a language delay and was only using two- and three-word sentences, Mr. Bivens made sure that she offered a word for each animal by saying, "Anna, what word do you remember?" He would wait for a response, and after a 5-second delay, provided a visual prompt of a picture of a word that might be suggested so that she contributed to creating the words to be used for the subsequent writing activity. (In collaboration with a special education teacher, Mr. Bivens would be provided with visual cards made from Boardmaker symbols to support Anna's language, which would facilitate various lessons and center activities, such as this one.)

Mr. Bivens said, "Now, let's select another blank template and write about your animals using some of the words we've identified. You can talk as you are writing." He modeled the process for children using his iPad by writing a sentence about the first animal (bear) and used three of the words from the flannel board: "The bear is big, mean, and brown." He showed the children how to tap *Done* when they were through, how it was automatically replayed, and how to tap the *Save* button so that it could be viewed later. Mr. Bivens showed Anna the Writing-Buddy app and said, "Anna, we're going to use WritingBuddy to help you write your sentences." He opened the app and demonstrated the basic features of selecting a font color from the four options available, erasing mistakes, tapping the *mouth* icon to have all text spoken, and using the space bar to create text on a new line.

Mr. Bivens then showed Anna the writing stem sheet having the sentences that she would type for each of the five animals in her story. He said, "Anna, these are the sentences that we are going to type for your story. What is the first animal in our story?" He pointed to the flannel board and waited for Anna to respond, "Bear" which she did without need of a prompt. He then said, "OK, so now we need to write your sentences about each animal and fill in the words that we have on our flannel board. Watch me." Mr. Bivens then modeled the typing of the two stem sentences for *bear*, followed by saying, "Now it's your turn." He monitored the progress of other students and provided prompts as needed if they had questions. He noticed that Anna was successful with the typing, although she needed several prompts for two animals that she was writing about.

When Anna finished each of her stories, Mr. Bivens showed her how to send the writing document to him as an e-mail attachment using the classroom e-mail account. Georgie was the first child to finish a story, so Mr. Bivens signaled him to turn up the volume on his iPad so others could hear his story. He helped Georgie find the recorded story in the photos tray at the bottom of the iPad screen, and then asked him to share the story by tapping the *Play* button. Each child was allowed to share their respective stories with others, and the children were delighted each time to see the work of others. On completing their writing work and sharing it with one another, Mr. Bivens signaled them that it was time to transition to their next center.

In this instance, Mr. Bivens used several instructional technologies for a large-group shared writing activity, and he used scaffolding to build on the writing experience in a small-group writing center activity. The instructional experiences connected children across the two activities, while affording the opportunity for individual students to practice their writing in the writing center using an innovative iPad app. Anna's difficulties were addressed by allowing her to use the same app as others for drawing animals, but then WritingBuddy was used to allow her to successfully write using a talking word processor and to share her writing with others. Anna was supported by a stem sheet that provided a model for her writing work. Additionally, Mr. Bivens provided models regarding how to use various features of the app, as well as prompts throughout the writing process to support Anna's successful completion of the writing task.

FAMILY AND COMMUNITY SUPPORTS

Learning that writing can convey meaning and that individuals write for different purposes are critical foundational literacy skills. In the early childhood classroom, many opportunities exist to open children's eyes and ears to stories in books. Through planned writing activities, teachers create "alphabetic doors" to help children understand that circles, marks, and various line shapes are connected to discoveries that their names and other labels in print represent objects in their everyday experiences.

During reading moments in which text is present to both the child and caring adults, older siblings, or friends, emergent writing skill development can be supported by emphasizing that words have letters while pointing to and naming letters aloud with the child (International Reading Association, 1998). Name writing is a highly motivating, personal task. Learning how to do this should be a priority with respect to the first letter in any preschool child's name. Sharing a sing-along of the alphabet song with a young child has been a traditional literacy mainstay that lends itself to a variety of settings whether it is done in the home, child care, preschool, playground, travel times, or bath routines. Calling attention to uppercase letters in alphabet books or in everyday print materials, such as magazines or advertisements, is a quick and easy activity that requires no planning. It is developmentally appropriate to accept strings of "mock letters" as actual letters in the young child's experimental writing. Family members and caregivers can encourage children's learning about concepts of print, such as directionality with regard to where to begin reading or writing. They can demonstrate that current and emerging technologies allow one to write a phone number in a contact list, make a grocery list on scrap paper, or write a message on a card to a friend.

With more advanced writing tasks, kindergarten students are expected to recall and write about their experiences; write stories to accompany pictures they draw that can be made into a book; make journal entries; and begin to understand writing conventions such as sentence structure, basic punctuation marks, and spacing between words. Often, families can support children by showing them that writing is an important way of communicating with others. A family member can leave a note to the child about what after-school activities are acceptable for the child to do that day, and the child can circle or check the activities they did in a note to the parent. If parents write a note to the teacher, encourage the child to write their own note to the teacher with their signature. Families can foster children's experimentation with writing by accepting invented spelling and understanding that a child's spelling skills will develop over time.

When teachers send signed drawings or samples of written products home, the family can see the ways that the child experiments with writing and can gain a sense of the literacy activities occurring at school. Home–school collaboration on curriculum activities can foster the child's literacy development of writing skills across environments. In turn, teachers can encourage families to practice writing at home and send to school any of their child's writing samples along with a note sharing the story behind a particular sample (e.g., under what circumstances did the child produce the writing). Regardless of whether samples are from home or school, teachers should display children's written work in the classroom. In addition, teachers should keep dated samples and descriptive notes for portfolio review that can show the progression of a child's writing development over time.

Community literacy supports are abundant in the signage on buildings and along the roadways. Some libraries offer events focusing on developmentally appropriate art activities in which name writing is required to identify each child's product. Schools will display children's writing samples at family events or during visits by community leaders. On the walls of local businesses, proprietors may display drawings with thank-you notes from appreciative school children. Furthermore, public libraries offer low-cost or no-cost venues for accessing a variety of books in print or on computer stations.

This vignette describes a family's worry that their 4-year-old child, Zachary, is going to have learning problems when he enters kindergarten. In a conference with Mrs. Hearns, Zachary's parents discussed concerns that when he writes his name, it always results in multiple errors, such as backward letters and malformed letters. Zachary's older cousin was diagnosed with a learning disability when he was in third grade, and the parents see Zachary's faulty writing as a foreboding expectation of future difficulties in school. As a kindergarten teacher, Mrs. Hearns values parent–school involvement and asks for a convenient time to hear their concerns. She thanks them for bringing their concerns to her. During the conference, Mrs. Hearns displays a web site that shows the stages of writing development. She asks the parents to watch for and point out examples from the web site that are errors just like the ones that Zachary makes (e.g., reversals and inconsistencies). As they make several comparisons, she underscores the point that his errors are typical for children's writing samples at the kindergarten level. In addition, Mrs. Hearns shows samples of children's writing taken from resources ranging from preschool to second grade; all levels have the same kind of errors that Zachary makes. She asks what the family thinks about what they have seen on stages of writing development as it relates to their son. Mrs. Hearns reassures the family that Zachary's writing is developing normally with his peers. She says that she will continue to expose Zachary to a variety of print experiences and asked them to continue to involve him in fun, unstructured activities at home that support his experimentation with writing.

SUMMARY

Teachers who use instructional technology, particularly those having numerous UDL features, know that dynamic, engaging, interactive, and shared writing experiences can be supported in todays' classrooms. The EXPECT IT-PLAN IT-TEACH IT technology integration framework provides guidance for successfully integrating these technologies into meaningful writing experiences for young learners. When teaching early writing skills, instructional technology can support practice in fine motor movements required for transcription of text. Later, to support conventional writing skills in which children write for different purposes and audiences, technology can be incorporated to help lay a foundation for connecting oral language, written language, and reading skills together.

What is particularly challenging in the field of early childhood education is the question of the importance of writing in the future. As new technologies are developed, voice recognition has emerged as a powerful tool that allows everyone to simply speak and have text transcribed. On the other hand, the connection between writing and other aspects of literacy is undisputable. Awareness of print will continue to be critical for young children, as will the use of modern tools for writing (e.g., iPad, tablet computers, laptops). Audio recording features (e.g., in smartphones, digital cameras, PowerPoint, apps, VoiceThread) enable children to record and hear their language use. Keyboards (available with both computers and handheld devices) are a preferred means of transcription in our society beyond the public school experience. Such changes in the importance of handwriting compared with text transcription using today's technologies pose questions regarding the nature of the early childhood writing curriculum. However, the question should guide decisions that the teacher makes with regard to how instructional technologies should be integrated to help children develop basic writing skills, while also supporting new digital writing skills important for participation in a 21st-century world.

ADDITIONAL RESOURCES

Merchant, G. (2007). Writing the future in the digital age. *Literacy, 41,* 118–128.

Copple, C., Neuman, S., & Bredekamp, S. (2000). *Learning to read and write.* Washington, DC: National Association for the Education of Young Children.

Roskos, K.A., Tabors, P.O., & Lenhart, L.A. (2005). *Oral language and early literacy in preschool: Talking, reading, and writing.* Newark, DE: International Reading Association.

Schickedanz, J. (1999). *Much more than the ABCs: The early stages of reading and writing.* Washington, DC: National Association for the Education of Young Children.

REFERENCES

Bennett-Armistead, V.S., Duke, N.K., & Moses, A.M. (2005). The writing center. In V.S. Bennett-Armistead, N.K. Due, & C.E. Snow (Eds.), *Literacy and the youngest learner: Best practices for educators of children from birth to 5* (pp. 141–159). New York, NY: Scholastic

Bloodgood, J.W. (1999). What's in a name? Children's name writing and literacy acquisition. *Reading Research Quarterly, 34,* 342–367.

Campbell, M.L., & Mechling, L.C. (2009). Small group computer-assisted instruction with SMART Board technology: An investigation of observational and incidental learning of nontarget information. *Remedial and Special Education, 30,* 47–57.

Dyson, A.H. (1993). From prop to mediator: The changing role of written language in children's symbolic repertoire. In B. Spodek & O.N. Saracho (Eds.), *Language and literacy in early childhood education* (pp. 21–41). New York, NY: Teacher's College Press.

Feldgus, E.G., & Cardonick, I. (1999). *Kid writing: A systematic approach to phonics, journals, and writing workshop.* Chicago, IL: Wright Group/McGraw-Hill.

Haney, M.R., Bissonnette, V., & Behnken, K.L. (2003). The relationship among name writing and early literacy skills in kindergarten children. *Child Study Journal, 33,* 99–115.

Hourcade, J.J., Parette, Jr., H.P., Boeckmann, N.M., & Blum, C. (2010). Handy Manny and the emergent literacy technology toolkit. *Early Childhood Education Journal, 37,* 483–491.

International Reading Association. (1998). Learning to read and write: Developmentally appropriate practices for young children. *The Reading Teacher, 52,* 193–216.

Keel, M.C., & Gast, D.L. (1992). Small-group instruction for students with learning disabilities: Observational and incidental learning. *Exceptional Children, 58,* 357–368.

Kissel, B. (2008). Promoting writing and preventing writing failure in young children. *Preventing School Failure, 52*(4), 53–56.

National Institute for Literacy. (2008). *Developing early literacy: Report of the National Early Literacy Panel.* Retrieved from October 8, 2012, from http://lincs.ed.gov/publications/pdf/NELPReport09.pdf

Parette, H.P., Quesenberry, A.C., & Blum, C. (2010). Missing the boat with technology usage in early childhood settings: A 21st century view of developmentally appropriate practice. *Early Childhood Education Journal, 37,* 335–343.

Schickedanz, J.A., & Casbergue, R.M. (2004). *Writing in preschool: Learning to orchestrate meaning and marks.* Newark, DE: International Reading Association.

Strickland, D.S., & Schickedanz, J.A. (2004). *Learning about print in preschool: Working with letters, words, and beginning links with phonemic awareness.* Newark, DE: International Reading Association.

Sulzby, E., Barnhart, J., & Hieshima, J. (1989). Forms of writing and rereading from writing: A preliminary report. In J. Mason (Ed.), *Reading and writing connections* (pp. 63–79). Boston, MA: Allyn and Bacon.

Turja, L., Endepohls-Ulpe, M., & Chatoney, M. (2009). A conceptual framework for developing the curriculum and delivery of technology education in early childhood. *International Journal of Technology and Design Education, 19,* 353–365.

Vukelich, C., & Christie, J. (2009). *Building a foundation for preschool literacy: Effective instruction for children's reading and writing development* (2nd ed.). Newark, DE: International Reading Association

Wang, F., Kinzie, M.B., McGuire, P., & Pan, E. (2010). Applying technology to inquiry-based learning in early childhood education. *Early Childhood Education Journal, 37,* 381–389.

Whitehurst, G.J., & Lonigan, C.J. (1998). Child development and emergent literacy. *Child Development, 69,* 848–872.

Wolery, M., Ault, M.L., Gast, D.L., Doyle, P.M., & Mills, B.M. (1990). Use of choral and individual attentional responses with constant time delay when teaching sight word reading. *Remedial and Special Education, 11,* 47–58.

8

Integrating Technology to Support Social Behavior and Social Communication

Amanda C. Quesenberry, April L. Mustian, Christine Clark-Bischke, and Craig Blum

---

After reading this chapter, you should be able to

- Describe and define typical social skill and communication development in young children
- Define social competence in young children
- Explain how social and communication skills are embedded in various early childhood classroom activities by describing what children are expected to DO, SAY, and REMEMBER
- Identify how to use the EXPECT IT-PLAN IT-TEACH IT framework to embed technology into social and communication skill instruction
- Use the SOLVE IT process when teaching children who may be struggling to develop social and/or communication skills
- Identify various uses of readily available technologies in early childhood classrooms to support the development of social and communication skills

---

SOCIAL BEHAVIOR AND SOCIAL-COMMUNICATION IN 21ST-CENTURY CLASSROOMS

Developing social and communication skills is an important facet of the overall development of young children. Thus, a key role for early childhood education professionals is to help young children develop these skills. Generally, social skills may be viewed as specific behaviors or strategies children use to successfully carry out specific social tasks (Gresham, Sugai, & Horner, 2001). Important social skills that young children must develop typically include the following:

- Emotional self-regulation (e.g., seeking the teacher's assistance when stressed or hungry) and self-awareness (e.g., awareness of one's preferences or strengths)

- Social knowledge and understanding (e.g., a student takes a cup from a peer because he does not know how to ask for a cup)

- Social skills (e.g., learning how to take turns or problem solving an issue with a peer)

- Social disposition (e.g., helping a child increase patience while waiting for her turn with a book; Epstein, 2007)

Social tasks that are important for successful participation in today's classroom settings include the following:

- Responding to and initiating interactions between caregivers, siblings, other adults, and peers

- Participating in play activities

- Managing behavior and resolving conflicts

- Understanding oneself and others

- Showing empathy

- Developing self-image

Social behavior and communication skills are embedded in all facets of early childhood classroom routines. For example, every morning when children arrive at school, they greet each other and the teacher as they enter the room. After they get out their folders and put away their backpacks, they take turns using the bathroom and talk with one another as they wash their hands and prepare for breakfast. Before the other children arrive at the tables for breakfast, the table helpers pass out plates, napkins, silverware, and cups. At breakfast, the children pass the food to each other as they share in family-style dining. As they eat their food, an adult facilitates conversation among the children about the food and what the children will do in school today.

What the Research Says

Some researchers (Clements & Sarama, 2003) have suggested that integrating technology in the classroom may support social skill development, although others remain skeptical (Cordes & Miller, 2000). Heft and Swaminathan (2002) found that when developmentally appropriate software was used, children engage in a variety of peer interactions while using the computer. In a randomized controlled experiment, researchers at the University of Alabama found that children with autism benefitted from the use of avatars (computer images that represent a person) comprised of animated photos of real people (Hopkins et al., 2011). The social skills software program FaceSay (see http://www.facesay.com) has three different games that help children identify emotions in people's faces. The interactive format, the repetition the program provides, and the realism of these faces appears to help children who have difficulty learning this type of skill. What is encouraging about this research is that the children were able to take what they learned from the computer program and apply it in natural social situations.

Research also demonstrated how young children benefit from video self-modeling, wherein children watch themselves performing desired social skills. A meta-analysis (i.e., an analysis of many studies on a particular topic and the strength of the effect) on video modeling and self-video modeling found that these two strategies can be considered evidence-based practice for children with autism (Bellini & Akullian, 2007). These two techniques can be used to teach social-communication, functional skills (life skills), and behavioral skills.

Communication

When a young child is successful with communication, he or she sends a message to a peer, teacher, family member, or other persons and the message is both received and understood. Without this full communication loop, young children will fail to communicate any number of messages. The ability to use oral language is an extremely important facet of communication for most young children. Oral language is typically divided into two components: receptive and expressive vocabulary. Receptive vocabulary is connected with a young child's understanding of oral language. Expressive vocabulary refers to the words that the child can express. Although the terms expressive and receptive vocabulary refer to the language a young child has acquired, teachers are more often concerned with expressive and receptive communication skills in classroom settings (Downing, 2005). Indicators of receptive communication can include such behaviors as gestures, facial expressions, or even the giggle of a young child. Expressive communication is any behavior wherein a young child communicates thought. In young children, expressive communication is closely linked to receptive communication. The young child who expresses a giggle in response to a funny animation feature on PowerPoint slide is expressing that he or she finds the slide humorous. Teachers work hard to expand young children's ability to use expressive and receptive communication skills because communication is so essential to a young child's development. Technology can play an extensive role in this because children can communicate both about and with technology.

Communication Form, Function, and Content Teachers can use basic principles of communication among human beings to learn how to better integrate technology into their classrooms. Young children express themselves using a variety of communication forms (e.g., gestures, facial expressions, verbalizations, showing an object or symbol). Frequently these different forms of communication are used in combination with each other. For example, children may point to a web site and comment on it, or they may tell a story while drawing using an iPad app.

Regardless of its form, all communication has a purpose or function (Browder, Spooner, & Mims, 2011). When a young child is communicating with a person in his or her environment, each attempt at communication serves some purpose for the child to express himself or herself and to the person receiving the communication. There are many purposes for communication ranging from requesting/ rejecting (e.g., objects, food, actions); social functions (e.g., greeting, initiate conversations, obtain/direct attention, turn taking); and comments, labeling, or asking questions. Content is simply what young children have to say. Early childhood classrooms generate themes used in the curriculum, shared readings, interactive discussions, and a variety of planned activities that provide opportunities for all children to participate by communicating.

Communication and Technology When integrating instructional technology into the early childhood classroom, teachers must consider the form, function, and content of communication related to technology. Young children may already have some vocabulary about technology, and they quickly acquire it as they hear it used in the classroom. Thus, it is desirable to continue to expand on that vocabulary during classroom instruction. Because the presence of instructional technology related to computers, wireless Internet access, printers, monitors, tablets, and telephones is now so universal young children need language to comment on, talk about, label, and use these technologies in their home environments and daily lives. For young children, it is just as important that they can talk about computers and their application in daily life as they can about kitchen appliances and their toys. Communication and oral language skills are strongly related to the development of literacy skills (Downing, 2005; Pence & Justice, 2008). Further, children must be able to communicate to engage in play that involves interactions with others. These topics are explored more directly in Chapters 6 and 9, although technology is part of learning in each of those areas. Some children with disabilities may require special problem solving related to communication so that they can better participate in a planned activity.

This chapter focuses on social-communication skills. Communication is inherently tied to social competence of young children (Brown, Odom, & McConnell, 2008). To become socially competent, young children must have the communication skills necessary to interact with peers, communicate with adults and peers, and express their wants or needs. Throughout the chapter, an emphasis is placed on the role of instructional technology and its use by teachers to provide better instruction that supports young children's communication and social skills development, thus helping them become confident and socially competent individuals.

DEVELOPMENT OF SOCIAL SKILLS

Erickson (1993) identified three stages of development necessary for growth in social skill development. Through these stages, children can gain a sense of trust (birth to 12 months of age) in those within their lives, a sense of autonomy (1–3 years of age) or ability to do things on their own, and a sense of initiative (4–5 years of age) in seeking out opportunities to learn. As children move through these stages, their social and communication skill development can be encouraged and supported through appropriate ARRANGE IT strategies (see Chapter 3 for a discussion of these strategies). These strategies may include the use of small groups (e.g., two to three students) to encourage participation in planned activities. Use of developmentally appropriate materials and instructional technologies having universal design for learning (UDL) features during instructional activities (see Chapter 1 for a discussion of UDL) would reduce children's frustration and support optimal learning by providing multiple means of engagement, representation, and expression in planned activities. Using such materials and instructional technologies in activities that require cooperation among children would also support social and communication development.

Young children must select social behaviors that are appropriate for the environment (i.e., school, home, community) and must meet their own social goals to demonstrate social competence with the peers and adults with which they interact (Brown et al., 2008). Social competency has been defined as

> the ability to understand, manage, and express the social and emotional aspects of one's life in ways that enable the successful management of life's tasks such as learning, forming relationships, solving everyday problems, and adapting to the complex demands of growth and development. (Elias et al., 1997, p. 2)

For example, at the end of circle time, Mrs. Smith asked each child what they would like to do during center time. Ally, Simone, and Raj asked to play on the three computers in the classroom. When Jordan heard that the computers were no longer available, he complained out loud, "But I haven't had a turn at the computers forever!" Recognizing his frustration, Mrs. Smith said, "Jordan, maybe you can have a turn at the computers after Ally, Simone, or Raj are done." Jordan put his head down and stomped off to the science center. After about 2 minutes, Jordan went to the computer center and announced that it was now his turn. Ally and Simone replied, "But we just got here!" Raj said, "Jordan, if you want to, you can play with me." In response, Jordan pulled up a chair and the two children played the game together.

In this example, Ally, Simone, and Jordan understood the concept of sharing and taking turns, but Raj demonstrated social competence by both sharing his time on the computer and independently using problem-solving skills. Raj is demonstrating socially appropriate expectations for their classroom, and he is recognizing how he can have fun with Jordan and meet his own social goal of having someone with whom to play. When young children develop strong social competency early, it helps them function successfully in many environments throughout their lives. Hence, in early childhood settings, children are taught social skills needed to be successful in school and in life.

This chapter focuses on how to easily integrate instructional technologies into the classroom schedule to support the social and communication development of young children. To accomplish this, an array of tools is available for consideration when implementing the EXPECT IT-PLAN IT-TEACH IT technology integration model.

What the Research Says

It is possible to evaluate social competence by others' judgment of a young child's social functioning. When individuals implement specific social behaviors competently while performing social tasks, social skills are the outcome. Social competence then is demonstrated as the ability to evaluate important outcomes that indicate a person's ability to effectively and efficiently perform specific social behaviors or skills within or across situations over time (Gresham, Sugai, & Horner, 2001). The specific tasks that may be presented as social skills include initiating peer relations by entering an ongoing playgroup or smiling socially and making eye contact, compliance skills when transitioning to new activities at identified times, or self-management skills through sharing toys or taking turns with peers.

Gresham et al. (2001) noted that as educators develop classroom activities to support social skill development, it is important to identify specific deficit areas (e.g., acquisition, performance, fluency). Children who have difficulty performing a skill or understanding the appropriate behavior required during a given activity may have acquisition deficits, whereas performance deficits occur when a student is unable to perform a specific skill consistently. Fluency deficits may occur when a child has limited exposure to appropriate modeling of the desired skill or behavior. As each specific deficit is identified, appropriate activities may be created that will address the students' specific needs (Baker, Parks-Savage, & Rehfus, 2009; Cumming, 2010; Ogilvie, 2011).

TYPICAL EARLY CHILDHOOD ACTIVITIES

To help young children develop social and related communication skills, teachers must help children develop awareness of social expectations, cues (i.e., natural signals that tell children how and when a particular social response is needed), and appropriate responses in social situations that meet social goals. From the time a child first enters a classroom in the morning, there are expectations to interact with peers and respond to the teacher's request for information. For example, during the first week of school, Mrs. Steele greeted Jamal as he entered the room, then asked him to hang up his coat, find a buddy, and share a book. Possibly because Jamal was not aware of or did not understand these expectations, he did not respond appropriately; hence, he could be considered as lacking in social competence. It is also possible that Jamal lacked the social and/or communication skills needed to seek out and read with a friend. In turn, Mrs. Steele felt that Jamal was not following directions and missed an opportunity to relate socially with a peer.

Although children may not enter school with a strong understanding of the social demands of the environment or with stellar social and/or communication skills, most children develop these skills very quickly and easily with proper teaching and guidance. Right away, Mrs. Steele recognized that Jamal needed additional supports to be successful in completing the demands of the morning routines. Therefore, she developed a visual schedule to teach Jamal and his classmates the morning routine. In addition, Mrs. Steele worked individually with Jamal to help him develop basic social and communication skills, such as saying, "Do you want to play?" or tapping peers on the shoulder when he wants their attention. As a result, all children in the classroom better understood the demands that they were to remember during the morning routine.

From arrival to snack time to departure, young children encounter numerous situations throughout a typical day that require the use of a variety of social and communication skills. In all early childhood settings, social demands and related communication skills are connected to the daily activities. Social expectations (rules), social courtesy, and norms within these activities help children gain access to rich learning experiences. Social-communication helps young children navigate the social environment so they can achieve their social goals. Table 8.1 presents typical social behavior and communication tasks that are embedded in classroom activities in preschool and kindergarten settings.

LARGE-GROUP AND SMALL-GROUP LEARNING ACTIVITIES

All activities during the school day require social and communication skills. Although standards vary across states and programs, there are common social and

Table 8.1. Preschool and kindergarten activity areas and typical planned social behavior and communication activity tasks

Activity area	Typical social behavior and related communication tasks
Preschool	
Arrival	Greeting teachers and/or peers by name as they enter the classroom
Circle time/large group	Selecting who they sit by to encourage peer interactions
	Playing games and singing songs that encourage peer interactions
	Selecting a friend to play with during choice time
	Deciding (with a friend) where to play first
	Following directions given by the teacher
	Actively participating in cooperative activities
Choice time/free play	Sharing materials and toys
	Taking turns on computer and when playing games
	Problem solving
	Resolving conflicts
	Complimenting
	Being helpful
Mealtime	Working with others to pass out napkins and snack/mealtime materials to others
	Passing food and drinks to one another
	Using social etiquette (e.g., saying "please" and "thank you")
	Participating in teacher-initiated discussions
Outdoor play	Taking turns using play equipment
	Using equipment cooperatively
Small group	Participating in cooperative projects having shared materials
	Using board games that require sharing and taking turns
Departure	Saying nice things about peers (e.g., using a compliment-stuffed animal that is passed around at closing circle)
	Saying "goodbye" to peers
Kindergarten	
Arrival routine	Interacting with "bus buddies" while walking together to and from bus pick-up/drop-off
	Helping peers hang up coats, bags, etc.
Morning circle/attendance	Passing out materials needed for an activity
	Sharing information about themselves (show and tell) and calling on friends who have questions about what they brought
Reading/literacy	Discussing stories about friendships
Writing/language arts	Writing and illustrating a story on a topic that two children agree on (encourages peer interaction, problem solving)
Math	Teachers purposely provide too few manipulatives for a small group of children so they have to share to solve math problems
Lunch	Using social etiquette (e.g., saying "please" and "thank you")
	Participating in teacher-initiated discussions about the food they are eating
Recess/break	Teacher encouraging peer interaction and problem solving through games and activities

(continued)

Table 8.1 *(continued)*

Activity area	Typical social behavior and related communication tasks
Art/physical education/music	Sharing art materials Helping one another (e.g., help their friend put on art smock) Playing cooperative games that promote turn-taking Singing songs about friendship, singing songs with movements that encourage peer interaction, musical chairs
Social studies/science	Discussing and voting on classroom rules Complimenting one another when they see a peer following the rules Working in small groups and using problem-solving skills to complete a science experiment
Dismissal routine	Helping pass out backpacks to peers Saying "goodbye" to peers

emotional expectations for young children in all classroom settings, such as demonstrating responsibility for self and others, engaging in cooperative group play, and beginning to share materials and taking turns. For instance, sharing toys, playing games, and taking turns are an integral part of small-group and circle time activities in preschool and kindergarten classrooms. To be successful with such tasks, children must be provided with the opportunities to learn and practice these skills in planned activities. Because social behavior and related communication skills are used throughout the day, instruction in these skills is often provided in conjunction with other skill areas, such as preliteracy (see Table 8.1).

Ideally, teachers should schedule designated times during each school day to provide explicit instruction in social behavior. For instance, Mr. Bivens sets aside 5–10 minutes each day to provide direct social skill instruction to his students using projected video modeling during circle time at the start of the day, showing modeling of peers in different settings (e.g., playground, centers) following expectations (Parette, Quesenberry, & Blum, 2010). Mr. Bivens uses embedded learning opportunities to make sure social-communication is modeled during activities and reinforces children for success.

The following vignettes illustrate how instructional technology can easily be integrated into planned activities designed to target social behavior and related communication skills using the EXPECT IT-PLAN IT-TEACH IT technology integration model.

Mrs. Hearns

Mrs. Hearns embeds teaching social skills into a natural literacy activity. This vignette illustrates how she plans for technology integration to accomplish this task.

 EXPECT IT A common early childhood standard for language arts is for preschool children to develop word analysis and vocabulary skills. An important benchmark or learning objective associated with this standard is for children to be able to make letter-sound matches. Mrs. Hearns would like to conduct a group activity during circle time that will meet this learning objective.

PLAN IT This literacy activity will also provide Mrs. Hearns with the opportunity to address an important social-emotional standard: *perform effectively as a member of a group.* Thus, she also selects a learning objective that targets appropriate turn taking and following directions. These two learning objectives align with the social and emotional learning standards for her students.

TECH IT Mrs. Hearns would like to use an online alphabet activity that can be found on Starfall's web site (http://www.starfall.com/n/level-k/index/load .htm?f). Additionally, she would like to use Boardmaker to create response cards for the entire class, each containing one of four sounds (/f/, /s/, /b/, /u/) that the children will be working on during this activity. Mrs. Hearns will embed images of screenshots from the Starfall activity into a PowerPoint instructional sequence presentation to model turn taking and children's use of response cards. The PowerPoint slides will present steps in the activity, including a turn-taking expectation. A laser pointer for signaling and prompting children to the presentation on the classroom screen will be used.

ARRANGE IT Mrs. Hearns will be using a Model-Lead-Test approach in this activity (i.e., "My turn," "Our turn," "Your turn"). This is a direct instruction technique that provides scaffolding as students work toward independence of a task by showing them what to do, allowing them to practice, and then evaluating their demonstrated social and related communication skills. Here the PowerPoint visuals provide a model for what they are expected to do during the Starfall activity (i.e., select one of the four sounds on their response cards, click the sound, repeat the sound, show their card that makes the sound, chorally respond with the class in response to the teacher's signal, and then call on another student to take a turn). Mrs. Hearns will have the students practice turn taking and then try it independently to see what they learned. Also, if children participate out of turn, Mrs. Hearns can quickly toggle to her PowerPoint presentation, show the slides that present the sequence of the activity, and focus their attention to the screen with the laser pointer. Children in Mrs. Hearn's class are accustomed to this cue; as soon as they see her use it, they correct their error.

CHECK IT By using response cards and choral responding, Mrs. Hearns decides that she can formatively assess student learning during this activity. She will be able to clearly see and hear responses among children in the group. To ensure students meet the social-emotional standards of taking turns and following directions, Mrs. Hearns will use a free iPad app, pdf-notes, to upload a checklist that she has created to allow her to assess each student's ability to walk up to the computer and make a selection when called on, raise the response card when provided the signal, and chorally respond when requested.

SOLVE IT In planning her classroom activity, Mrs. Hearns considers Samantha, a child who has been diagnosed with attention-deficit/hyperactivity disorder by her physician. After all children were seated for her initial planned activity, Mrs. Hearns reviewed with the children the classroom expectations for behavior during circle time. She reminded students to use listening ears, keep their hands and feet to themselves, and help others when needed. Next, she led the students through the online Starfall.com alphabet activity as she had planned it. Before she could get through the overview of the activity, Samantha began talking with the children beside her. Mrs. Hearns reminded Samantha that she should "turn her voice off while the teacher is talking." A few minutes later, Samantha got up to go use the computer when it was not her turn. Mrs. Hearns worked through these problems using the Break It Down table for SOLVE IT (see Table 8.2).

 TEACH IT   Based on the planning that occurred in the TECH IT-ARRANGE IT-CHECK IT steps above, the activity crafted by Mrs. Hearns took on the following format when implemented. Prior to the planned activity, she created a short video modeling movie that presented three key components of the social behaviors expected of the children: use listening ears, keep their hands and feet to themselves, and help others when needed. She had made a set of three cards using Boardmaker, which presented pictures representing each of the social expectations. These cards were given to Samantha, who was also positioned close to Mrs. Hearns. The video modeling movie was created using a digital camera, wherein Mrs. Hearns captured three short clips of Samantha and one other student demonstrating the expected behavior while she provided short audio statements with each video clip as it was being recorded. Samantha was the "star" in two of the three video clips. These clips were then placed into Windows Movie Maker, which is provided as standard software on most PCs.

When the children transitioned into the circle time space, Mrs. Hearns noted that Samantha assumed her position in the circle with no problems. Mrs. Hearns opened the activity by showing the movie, calling attention to each of the three social expectations. It appeared that Samantha attended to this movie and did not demonstrate off-task behavior as the lesson continued. Mrs. Hearns then orally stated and used her PowerPoint presentation to visually show the steps to complete the Starfall activity, using her laser pointer to draw the children's attention to each slide (see Figure 8.1). Mrs. Hearns intentionally asked one of the students who typically demonstrated appropriate classroom behavior to sit beside Samantha as a classroom buddy and thus model good behavior for Samantha.

As Mrs. Hearns began her model (using the Model-Lead-Test approach) of the activity, she noticed that Samantha was starting to whisper to a peer. Mrs. Hearns said, "Samantha, think about our movie. Show me what we are expected to do." She waited momentarily, and then prompted Samantha by pointing to the appropriate card and asking her to repeat the behavior represented—use listening ears—and calling attention to the peer buddy seated beside Samantha who was exhibiting good listening behavior. Once Mrs. Hearns had Samantha's attention again, she had all the children practice use of the response card and turn taking, guiding the children through their use.

Mrs. Hearns then said, "Now we're going to look at the Starfall activity and practice finding some sounds." She opened the web site for the alphabet activity and said, "First, I am going to walk quietly to the computer, hold the mouse, and make a selection of one of the four sounds on our cards (/f/, /s/, /b/, /u/)." She modeled each step again as the students followed along. After selecting and listening to a sound, Mrs. Hearns asked students to hold up their cards showing the sound they heard. She then called on a student to come to the computer and select a letter, click on the letter to make a sound, hold up his or her card representing the sound, and then called on another student to come forward for a turn.

Table 8.2. Break It Down table for Samantha

Define the Problem: Samantha gets up to go to the computer when it is not her turn, frequently disrupting the flow of the lesson; she also talks to peers sitting beside her when Mrs. Hearns is talking during the literacy activity for circle time.

Activity: Circle time alphabet activity where students take turns and use response cards using the Starfall.com web site coupled with the LCD projection system. Children are reminded of expectations using PowerPoint at the start of the lesson.

Planned activity steps	Planned activity requirements				Child performance	What's the answer?
	DO	SAY	REMEMBER			
To begin: Children transition from free time to circle time	See the circle area Listen/Hear other children speaking Go to circle	Address other children if needed when walking to circle	Know where to go for circle		Samantha is familiar with the classroom arrangement Samantha goes to her assigned spot with no problems	Continue current transition routine
Observe PowerPoint presentation of teacher models of response card usage	Hear the teacher See the screen Look at teacher while staying seated quietly	Verbally respond to any questions	Recall taught response card procedures if called upon		Samantha is often distractible during instructional sessions Samantha talks to the peer or runs up to the computer screen	Some video self-modeling with Samantha as the "star" (only 1 minute) to model expectations during circle (Note: Other children can participate, but it is important to include Samantha for the strategy to work) Boardmaker cards presenting three key social expectations for circle time
Teacher models correct use of the "Alphabet" activity	Hear the teacher See the screen Look at teacher while staying seated quietly/ orally use speech to provide correct response when teacher asks question regarding procedure	Say a response individually or in unison with class when teacher provides signal	Recall correct directions for completing activity		Samantha likes to talk to others during classroom activities While the teacher is modeling appropriate procedures for the activity, Samantha begins whispering to a peer sitting beside her	Mrs. Hearns places Samantha close to her at the front of the room at the start of the activity Assigns her a peer buddy that also models good behavior Boardmaker cards presenting three key social expectations for circle time Positively reinforces Samantha's "sitting quietly" behavior

(continued)

187

Table 8.2 (continued)

Planned activity steps	Planned activity requirements			Child performance	What's the answer?
	DO	SAY	REMEMBER		
Come up to the computer to take turns playing "Alphabet" when called upon	Hear the teacher See the response cards See the computer and screen Look at teacher while staying seated Select correct required response card Walk to the computer to make choice (for one designated student at a time)	Call on another student Say a response in unison with class when teacher provides signal Orally respond to teacher prompt	Remember sequence for the activity steps Recall correct letter sound	Samantha acts out of turn in class activities After teacher calls the name of another student to come up to the computer, Samantha gets up to attempt a turn out of order	In anticipation of this happening (just before this step occurs) Mrs. Hearns reminds the class of expectations and quickly brings up the slides in the PowerPoint to act as signal and scaffold. She points with her laser pointer to the PowerPoint to emphasize turn-taking procedures. Mrs. Hearns asks a child what behavior is expected that they saw in the self-modeling video from Sam. This provides an extra signal about what is expected for this step. Keeping the pace of the lesson she brings the Starfall web site back up.
To End: Students walk to centers upon teacher instruction	See where to go Walk to center upon teacher cue	Talk with peers or teacher as needed	Know where to go	Samantha has no problems moving around the classroom Walks to correct center	Continue current transition routine

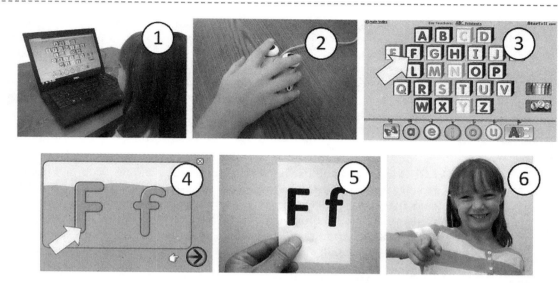

Figure 8.1. Sample PowerPoint instructional sequence used to model steps of a planned literacy activity with embedded turn-taking skills. (Images from B. Wojcik; ABC activity images © Starfall Education. Used by permission.)

Whenever she saw any student not attending to the activity, Mrs. Hearns called attention to the self-modeling video that the class had seen, then asked a student what rule was expected in this step of the planned activity to provide an extra signal about what was expected. On several occasions, Mrs. Hearns noticed that Samantha would begin talking to others as another student was coming forward to the computer, so she would quickly pull up the PowerPoint presentation and tab through several of the slides that presented the model for the steps in the activity. As each student called on another, Mrs. Hearns praised the students for turn taking.

Mrs. Hearns used formative assessment by observing the children's responses with the cards and their choral responses to check for correct answers for the literacy activity. Use of the app, pdf-notes, enabled Mrs. Hearns to use a checklist regarding children's performance on both letter-sound matches and turn-taking skills. If all responses were correct, Mrs. Hearns provided a praise statement such as "Good job, you answered that correctly!" However, Mrs. Hearns did more than provide corrective feedback for literacy responses, as seen in other chapters. Because the embedded social skill of turn taking was just as essential for lesson success and the development of the children in her class, Mrs. Hearns made sure to evaluate the children's performance and give feedback as the lesson proceeded. Mrs. Hearns never stopped the pace for long periods, but rather used prompts (i.e., PowerPoint slides and video modeling) and signals (i.e., asking students what behavior was expected during the activity) to ensure children's participation and success in the activity.

Mr. Bivens

Mr. Bivens uses instructional technology for a direct instruction lesson in social skills. Direct instruction and child-focused instructional strategies help young children know exactly what is expected.

EXPECT IT Mr. Bivens would like to target the kindergarten social-emotional learning standard of using appropriate communication skills to express needs, wants, and feelings with others. He wants to address this standard with a small group of students during center time. Mr. Bivens specifically chooses a learning objective that addresses expression of feelings based on behavior he has observed in his classroom.

 PLAN IT Mr. Bivens will be using *The Incredible Years: Dina Dinosaur Classroom Curriculum* (Webster-Stratton, 1990).

 TECH IT Mr. Bivens will use his iPad and the free iPad application, Puppet Pals HD, which affords children the opportunity to select background templates and characters that appear on the screen. The characters can be moved by children using their fingers and voice comments may be recorded (see Figure 8.2). This app will allow the small group to create their own role play scenario on expressing feelings during the social skill activity.

 ARRANGE IT Mr. Bivens decides that he will use 20-minute small-group skill practice with three or four students, real-life scenarios, and both puppet and virtual role playing. In addition to the modeling and role playing, Mr. Bivens is also incorporating direct instruction and problem solving. The explicit and direct instruction allows Mr. Bivens to provide immediate performance feedback and reinforcement for appropriate behaviors. Additionally, role playing with peers using the iPad application allows students to use problem-solving skills as they work together through the real-life scenarios. Other students in the class will be working in small-group centers during this time.

Because Rashod, Cierra, and Calvin have exhibited skill deficits related to appropriately communicating wants, needs, and feelings during class time, Mr. Bivens has chosen to work with them specifically to provide this direct social skills instruction. Because Mr. Bivens will be working directly with these three students during this activity, he can provide immediate feedback and reinforcement to students.

 CHECK IT Using Doodlecast Pro, an inexpensive app available for the iPad, Mr. Bivens will document children's behavior using anecdotal notes and brief recordings of children's responses to document their expressions. Notes about teacher encouragements and prompting can be included using the app, which is particularly useful because it permits the teacher to collect recorded observations and store them on the iPad.

 SOLVE IT In planning his classroom activity, Mr. Bivens considers Cierra, a child with an intellectual disability who has language delays. Mr. Bivens chooses to develop a lesson using the Feeling Wheel found on the Center on the Social Emotional Foundation for Early Learning's web site (http://csefel.vanderbilt.edu/modules/2006/feelingchart.pdf; see Figure 8.3). This wheel could be printed and then mounted on a board with a dowel stick in the center such that it could be spun. In previous lessons, the students learned one to two feelings at a time. It is now time to review eight of the feelings they have learned (i.e., happy, scared, sad, mad, nervous, embarrassed, frustrated, and lonely). Mr. Bivens first spins the Feeling Wheel and asks children to demonstrate how each feeling looks on their faces.

Mr. Bivens then has each student name the word for the feeling. Mr. Bivens role plays several situations by using two of the puppets, Wally and Molly, that are available with the *Dina Dinosaur Classroom Curriculum* (Webster-Stratton, 1990) and asks children to act out and point to the Feeling Wheel picture of how they would feel in that circumstance. Mr. Bivens also has each student point to a feeling on the wheel and share a story about a time when he or she felt the way the feeling face on their chosen card looks.

Figure 8.2. iPad apps, such as Puppet Pals, can be used for role playing to allow children to express and act out their feelings by moving figures on the screen and recording dialogue. (Used by permission of Polished Play LLC.)

Finally, Mr. Bivens allows all three students to work together to create a role-play story using the Puppet Pals HD application on the classroom iPad. Mr. Bivens will promote several important social skills concepts by praising children who are following directions, praising children's descriptions of their feeling states, and praising children using their words to express themselves. While the students were working together, Cierra became frustrated. Table 8.3 indicates why she was frustrated and what Mr. Bivens did to solve the problem using the Break It Down process.

Although there were many steps of the planned activity that Cierra could participate in, she had difficulty with remembering what words to use in Step 3 (REMEMBER) and expressing herself in Step 4 (SAY). Mr. Bivens inferred that Cierra may be having trouble with remembering because she did not know what words to recall even after they have reviewed them many times. He checked with a school psychologist, who confirmed that previous testing suggested that Cierra has some difficulty remembering words.

Social-communication problems such as these are common with young children with intellectual disabilities. Using Boardmaker is one method of providing compensatory support (i.e., support that compensates for the inability of a child to accomplish a given task related to his or her disability) for these communication needs. In Step 3, the visual cues provided using Boardmaker symbols support Cierra in remembering what to say. Because the symbols can be paired with words, they also promote her emergent literacy skill development. Although Cierra has some verbal skills, there are occasions when she needs support. In Step 5, the Boardmaker symbol cards not only serve as signals for what to say, but, if she chooses, Cierra may use the card instead of the word to respond in the activity. Research suggests that using augmented speech (e.g., Boardmaker symbols) as a compensatory support will not limit Cierra's ability to speak; rather, it will support and help develop her ability (Downing, 2005).

Feeling Wheel

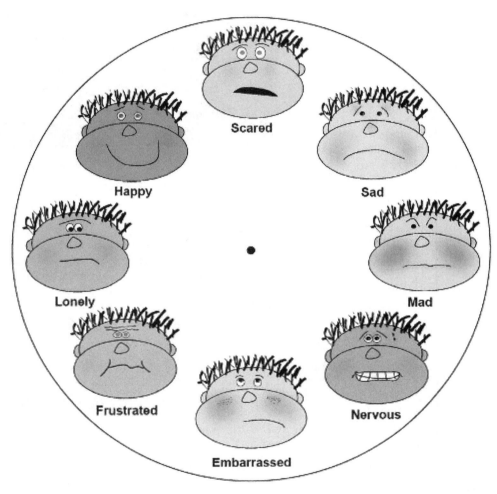

Figure 8.3. The Feeling Wheel is an example of a web-accessible resource that can be used to help children identify their feelings. (© Center on the Social and Emotional Foundations for Early Learning; used by permission.)

TEACH IT Subsequent to the initial planning that occurred in TECH IT-ARRANGE IT-CHECK IT steps and the SOLVE IT process that took place afterward, the activity planned by Mr. Bivens took on the following format when implemented again. Mr. Bivens chose to incorporate a lesson using a Feeling Wheel that was a readily available web-based resource. He first spun the Feeling Wheel (i.e., happy, scared, sad, mad, nervous, embarrassed, frustrated, and lonely) and asked children to demonstrate how each feeling looked on their faces. He visually

Table 8.3. The Break It Down table for Cierra

Define the problem: Despite being able to verbally state the seven feeling words, Cierra has difficulty providing the oral responses on cue when Mr. Bivens uses choral responding.

Activity: Using Feeling Wheel with role play to identify and express feelings using iPad

Planned activity steps	Planned activity requirements			Child performance	What's the answer?
	DO	SAY	REMEMBER		
To begin: Transition from free time to center time	See the circle area Hear other children speaking Go to circle	Address other children if needed when walking to circle	Know where to go for circle Remember to walk quietly to correct center	Cierra typically makes transitions appropriately Cierra goes to her assigned area with Rashod and Calvin with no problems	Continue current transition routine
Demonstrate how each feeling looks on one's respective face	See the spinner Hear the teacher Look at teacher while staying seated quietly/ provide correct facial gesture for feeling when Mr. Bivens provides prompt	(Cierra should say nothing) Show facial gesture	Understand how the facial gesture for each feeling physically feels	Cierra uses expressions in her daily activities Cierra correctly provides facial gesture for each feeling	Continue this step of the activity as planned
Watch role-play "feelings" scenarios with Wally and Molly puppets	See the puppets Hear the teacher Look at teacher while staying seated quietly/ orally use speech to provide correct response if Mr. Bivens asks questions	Say a response in unison with other students when teacher provides signal	Recall correct feeling words	Cierra sometimes used the wrong feeling word to describe what is occurring in the scenario Cierra's limited vocabulary causes problems in communicating in class	Use Boardmaker to provide Cierra with Feeling Faces cue cards; she can show the cue card that corresponds with the right feeling

(continued)

Table 8.3 (continued)

Planned activity steps	Planned activity requirements				Child performance	What's the answer?
	DO	SAY	REMEMBER			
Point to a feeling and share a feeling experience	See the spinner Hear the teacher Point to a feeling and share a story related to that feeling	Individually say the name of a feeling	Remember which feeling word matches real experience		Cierra has limited verbal skills Cierra doesn't form complete sentences but response is still deemed appropriate	Continue this step of activity
Use iPad and Puppet Pals HD app to create feelings and role-play scenario using appropriate feeling words	Hear other students See the iPad screen Tap the iPad screen Work in group to build role-play puppet scenario with feeling word	Talk to each other to share, take turns, and build role play	Remember important rules when working with others, remember feeling words		Cierra enjoys being around other students Cierra works cooperatively with the other two students but cannot provide feeling word orally	Use Boardmaker feeling faces cue cards so that Cierra can use the cards to use in place of words or as reminders of what to say. Other children are taught that they should respond to Cierra's cards like speech when she uses them
To end: Walk to next center upon teacher instruction	Hear other students and teacher See the students Students walk to next center upon teacher cue	Talk with peers or teacher as needed	Know where to go and how to walk quietly		Cierra is able to walk in the classroom Cierra walks to correct center	Continue current transition routine

194

surveyed the class as the children responded with facial gestures, making notations on his iPad checklist that had been created in Doodlecast Pro. He observed that all the students could show the facial gestures that were associated with feelings on the wheel. He then had each student name the word for the feeling while using his iPad to capture pictures of each student. Mr. Bivens then role played several situations using two of the puppets, Wally and Molly, that were available with the *Dina Dinosaur Classroom Curriculum* (Webster-Stratton, 1990) and asked children to act out and point to the picture on the Feeling Wheel of how they would feel in that circumstance.

Cierra had been provided with Boardmaker faces cue cards to help express the appropriate feeling, and she successfully used the cards to identify feelings when called upon. Mr. Bivens then asked each student to point to a feeling on the wheel and share a story about a time when they felt the way the feeling face on their chosen card looked. When it was Cierra's turn, she did not use complete sentences while providing her description, but her responses were appropriate. Finally, Mr. Bivens allowed all three students to work together to create a role-play story using the Puppet Pals HD application on the classroom iPad.

After role playing with the Wally and Molly puppets for the scenario of "Wally being sad that he didn't hit the baseball," Mr. Bivens provided Rashod with a scenario that required his response: "Your mommy really liked a picture you drew for her, so she put it up on the refrigerator. How would you feel?" Rashod responded, "I would look at it." Mr. Bivens immediately stated, "Is that a feeling? How did Wally feel when he couldn't hit the baseball?" Rashod said, "He was sad." Mr. Bivens said, "So, use one of your feeling words to tell me how you might feel if your mommy puts your drawing on the refrigerator?" Rashod then provided Mr. Bivens with the appropriate response, saying "Happy." Mr. Bivens provided immediate verbal encouragement, "Great! I'm sure you would be excited if your mommy put your picture on the refrigerator!"

Mr. Bivens used the same strategy with both Calvin and Cierra. Calvin successfully responded to the instructional strategies. When it was Cierra's turn, she was encouraged to use her Boardmaker cue cards to both remind her of feelings and to support communication of a feeling when responding to Mr. Bivens. The planned activity supported several important social skills concepts by praising children who followed directions, praising children's descriptions of their feeling states, and praising children who use their words to express themselves.

FAMILY SUPPORTS

In this chapter, the EXPECT IT-PLAN IT-TEACH IT-SOLVE IT process is examined for Mrs. Hearns and Mr. Bivens, providing suggestions on ways that instructional technology tools and strategies can be used in the classroom setting. However, the use of these technologies to support development should not be limited to the classroom. In addition to classroom integration, technology should also be used in the home setting to support the development of social behavior and communication skills in young children. Whenever possible, teachers should work with families to extend classroom learning to learning at home. The following vignettes illustrate ways that technology use can be carried over to the home to support children's ongoing social behavior and communication development.

Since the beginning of the school year, Mrs. Hearns has been using PowerPoint to teach mini-lessons on social skill development during circle time. The students respond well to the use of this instructional technology tool. During parent-teacher conferences in October, Mr. and Mrs. Santos share with Mrs. Hearns that their daughter, Sophia, has told them all about learning to make friends from the "big screen." Sensing that they were interested in learning more, Mrs. Hearns offered to e-mail Sophia's parents some PowerPoint presentations with voiceovers (using VoiceThread) for them to use to extend Sophia's learning at home.

For several years, Mr. Bivens has had a SMART Board in his classroom. He uses it on a daily basis to implement lessons he develops himself or downloads from the SMART Activity Exchange. Last year during an open house, he provided a demonstration for parents on how SMART Boards are used in classrooms. He highlighted the many ways that SMART Boards can support children's academic and social development. This year, the principal at his school asked Mr. Bivens to create a wiki (i.e., a publicly available web site where content can be uploaded, edited, and shared with others) for the school to be unveiled at this year's open house.

As Mr. Bivens explored the many uses of wikis (see wikispaces.com), he decided to create one for his classroom as well. On his classroom wiki, he shares general information about his class schedule, class routines, and student products. In addition, he has created a password-protected electronic portfolio for each child, highlighting their growth and progress throughout the year. Each electronic portfolio has samples of children's work as well as digital photos and videos of children developing social and communication skills. These portfolios can only be accessed by Mr. Bivens and each child's parent.

SUMMARY

This chapter provides an overview of the typical social and communication skills that young learners develop in the early childhood years. Within preschool and kindergarten settings, planned classroom activities allow children the opportunity to DO, SAY, and REMEMBER important social and communication skills, such as problem solving, turn taking, following directions, initiating and responding to peers, and making choices. Further, today's classrooms provide educators with a plethora of readily available technologies to support social and emotional growth and overall social competence in children. There is substantial research to support the inclusion of such technology into social and communication skill instruction.

The vignettes featuring Mrs. Hearns and Mr. Bivens illustrate how instructional technologies, ranging from a single computer to classroom iPads, can easily be integrated into both explicit and embedded instruction on social behavior and communication skills using the EXPECT IT-PLAN IT-TEACH IT framework. Additionally, these vignettes examine the versatility of the framework across early childhood classrooms with diverse learning needs.

The EXPECT IT-PLAN IT-TEACH IT framework is an approach for purposefully linking technology to social behavior and social-communication instruction rather than viewing technology integration as an afterthought. Integrating technology into the classroom provides a 21st-century approach to providing high-quality instruction in social behavior and social-communication skills of young children.

ADDITIONAL READINGS

Buggy, T., & Hoomes, G. (2011). Using video self-modeling with preschoolers with autism spectrum disorder: Seeing can be believing. *Young Exceptional Children, 4*(2), 2–12.

Good, L. (2009). *Teaching and learning with digital photography: Tips and tools for early childhood classrooms.* Thousand Oaks, CA: Corwin Press.

Janney, R., & Snell, M.E. (2008). *Behavior support* (2nd ed.). Baltimore, MD: Paul H. Brookes Publishing Co.

Snell, M.E., & Janney, R. (2006). *Social relationships and peer supports* (2nd ed.). Baltimore, MD: Paul H. Brookes Publishing Co.

USEFUL WEB SITES

Technology and Young Children Interest Forum (http://www.techandyoung children.org/research.html)

Developmentally Appropriate Practice in Early Childhood Programs Serving Children from Birth Through Age 8 (http://www.naeyc.org/files/naeyc/file/positions/position%20statement%20Web.pdf)

Center on the Social and Emotional Foundations for Early Learning (http://csefel.vanderbilt.edu)

Research Synthesis on Screening and Assessing Social-Emotional Competence (http://csefel.vanderbilt.edu/documents/rs_screening_assessment.pdf)

REFERENCES

Baker, J., Parks-Savage, A., & Rehfuss, M. (2009). Teaching social skills in a virtual environment: An exploratory study. *Journal for Specialists in Group Work, 34*, 209–226.

Bellini, S., & Akullian, J. (2007). A meta-analysis of video modeling and video self-modeling interventions for children and adolescents with autism spectrum disorders. *Exceptional Children, 73*, 261–284.

Browder, D.M., Spooner, F., & Mims, P. (2011). Communication skills. In D.M Browder & F. Spooner (Eds.), *Teaching students with moderate and severe disabilities* (pp. 262–282). New York, NY: Guilford Press.

Brown, W.H., Odom, S.L., & McConnell, S.R. (2008). *Social competence of young children: Risk, disability, and intervention.* Baltimore, MD: Paul H. Brookes Publishing Co.

Clements, D., & Sarama, J. (2003). Strip mining for gold: Research and policy in educational technology: A response to "Fool's Gold." *AACE Journal, 11*(1), 7–69.

Cordes, C., & Miller, E. (2000). *Fool's gold: A critical look at computers in childhood.* College Park, MD: Alliance for Childhood.

Cumming, T.M. (2010). Using technology to create motivating social skills lessons. *Intervention in School and Clinic, 45*, 242–250.

Downing, J.E. (2005). *Teaching communication skills to students with severe disabilities.* Baltimore, MD: Paul H. Brookes Publishing Co.

Elias, M.J., Zins, J.E., Weissberg, K.S., Frey, M.T., Greenberg, N.M., Kessler, R., et al. (1997). *Promoting social and emotional learning. Guidelines for educators.* Alexandria, VA: Association for Supervision and Curriculum Development.

Epstein, A.S. (2007). *The intentional teacher.* Washington, DC: National Association for the Education of Young Children.

Erickson, E.H. (1993). *Childhood and society.* New York, NY: Norton.

Gresham, F.M., Sugai, G., & Horner, R.H. (2001). Interpreting outcomes of social skills training for students with high-incidence disabilities. *Exceptional Children, 67,* 331–344.

Heft, T., & Swaminathan, S. (2002). The effects of computers on the social behavior of preschoolers. *Journal of Research in Childhood Education, 16,* 162–174.

Hopkins, I.M., Gower, M.G., Perez, T.A., Smith, D.S., Amthor, F.R., Wimsatt, F.C., et al. (2011). Avatar assistant: Improving social skills in students with an ASD through a computer-based intervention. *Journal of Autism and Developmental Disorders, 41,* 1543–1555.

Ogilvie, C.R. (2011). Step by step: Social skills instruction for students with autism spectrum disorder using video models and peer mentors. *Teaching Exceptional Children, 43*(6), 20–26.

Parette, H.P., Quesenberry, A.C., & Blum, C. (2010). Missing the boat with technology usage in early childhood setting: A 21st century view of developmentally appropriate practice. *Early Childhood Educational Journal, 37,* 335–343.

Pence, K.L., & Justice, L.M. (2008). *Language and development from theory to practice.* Upper Saddle River, NJ: Pearson Education.

Webster-Stratton, C. (1990). *Dina dinosaur's social skills and problem-solving curriculum.* Seattle, WA: 1990.

9

Integrating Technology to Support Play

Christine Clark-Bischke, Emily H. Watts, and Howard P. Parette, Jr.

After reading this chapter, you should be able to

- Describe and define typical play skill development in young children
- Describe how play skills and activities are embedded in various early childhood classroom activities using instructional technology
- Describe potential long-term impacts when young children do not develop play skills
- Identify uses of instructional technologies in early childhood classrooms to support the development of play skills

---

INTRODUCTION

Children's development involves a diverse array of learning experiences, yet it is the area of play that captures the imagination of families and teachers alike. In today's early childhood classrooms, play is an important component of any curriculum for young children (Isenberg & Quisenberry, 2002). Play has been called the "work of children" because it consists of a cadre of meaningful work activities that help a child to relate to his or her surroundings in a serious way (Rieber, Smith, & Noah, 1998). From a developmental perspective, this work is reflected in the role of play in helping young children develop the following:

- Self-regulation (e.g., following rules or taking turns)
- Language skills (e.g., communicating verbally, signing, or using pictures of the words that are necessary to interact with a peer)
- Cognition (e.g., developing problem-solving skills and understanding of the importance of symbols)

- Social competence (e.g., interacting appropriately with peers and stimulating development of the imagination)

Often, play activities that help children develop these work skills are simple, non rule-based, enjoyable games created by young children who observe their daily lives and creatively act out their observations (Piaget, 1962). As children grow older, their cognitive, social, and language work skills increase. Their corresponding play behaviors are often characterized by rule-driven and more complex language-based and problem-solving activities involving one or more individuals. In many play activities—both in home and school environments—all children have increasing access to and preference for technologies, and the form of play behavior using technology undergoes change over time (Downey, Hayes, & O'Neill, 2007).

For example, Lucinda sits in front of the television with her family after dinner and is engaged with her father's iPad. She loves playing with several of the free iTunes apps that he has downloaded. Her father brought home a new Play-Doh package and told Lucinda about a new app that had ideas for things that can be made with the package. She opens the app and selects Fresh Ideas for Characters, which then leads her to make a choice about six different characters that could be made with her Play-Doh. She selects Mr. Potato Head, which is followed by a series of pictures showing various stages of making Mr. Potato Head using her available Play-Doh.

Seth logs on to his family computer and clicks on the icon for Zac Browser. From the brilliant seascape desktop, he clicks on an icon of a soccer ball, which leads him to an array of choices for games located on the Internet. He selects whiz kidgames.com and is taken to a screen in which he types his name on an onscreen keyboard. He clicks on Robbie the Robot, and a robot with a smiling human head greets him and presents a series of games related to emotions.

After school, Bonnie sits at her mother's computer and selects Tux Paint from the program menu. Her class went on a field trip to the local fire station earlier that day, and Bonnie wants to create a drawing to share with her class the next day during a show-and-tell activity. Using various shapes, tools, and color choices presented to her on the drawing palette, Bonnie completes a colorful drawing of a fire truck carrying her classmates through town. She prints a copy on the family printer.

Chloe and Mia are paired together in dramatic play in their kindergarten classroom. Their teacher had just shown the class a video about going to the doctor. In the play area, Chloe and Mia constructed a doctor's office from materials that the teacher had, and they role played patient and doctor. Dr. Mia used a free iPad app, EyeChart, to give Chloe an examination.

Given the presence of technology in the lives of young children, varying types of play often involve technologies in the early years (Blake, Winsor, & Allen, 2011). For example, infants and toddlers are drawn to and typically want to interact with cell phones, iPods, iPads, and computer screens because these technologies are used by family members. Children watch television with their families and see technology being used by others on popular shows and movies. Many young children now have technology-based toys and learning games, such as LeapFrog products, and they use these technologies in play activities to develop emergent literacy skills.

As children grow older, more and more models are present in which they become aware that more than one individual can use these technologies. Also, children are introduced to interactive games and activities on web sites and handheld devices that allow sharing and turn taking in supportive classroom environments.

In each of the preceding examples, technology use is a part of young children's lives, although the way in which it used in play activities undergoes change from more solitary, individual interactions with technology to using technology to play with others. Thus, there is a continuum of technologies that may be present through the preschool and kindergarten years that reflect differing levels of developmental appropriateness based on children's experiences and understanding of the world, language development, and cognitive skills.

Recognition of this changing nature of play and its relationship to technology is reflected in the National Association for the Education of Young Children (NAEYC, 2012, p. 7) revised position statement:

> Play is central to children's development and learning. Children's interactions with technology and media mirror their interactions with other play materials and include sensorimotor or practice play, make-believe play, and games with rules. Therefore, children need opportunities to explore technology and interactive media in playful and creative ways. Appropriate experiences with technology and media allow children to control the medium and outcome of the experience, to explore the functionality of these tools, and to pretend how they might be used in real life.

What the Research Says

Parten (1933) provided the most comprehensive description and classification of the various types of play. She observed children between the ages of 2 and 5 years during prearranged 1-minute periods that were systematically varied. During these observations, she collected data on children's play behavior and categorized their play into six types. Each of these types has implications for technology interactions that might be present (Casey, Reeves, & Conner, 2012; see Figure 9.1):

1. *Unoccupied play* is demonstrated when a child does not play with anyone or anything, but merely sits or stands without doing anything observable. For example, Lily moves about her family living room as the television set plays a popular television show. On hearing a catchy song being played on the television, she smiles and begins to sway and move her arms to the music. In this instance, Lily is not engaged in purposeful play, but she responds to a technology that her sensory system recognizes and she responds with movement.

2. *Solitary play* occurs when the child plays alone and appears to be unaware of other children. For example, Mason sits in a pediatrician's waiting room with his mother. Other children are present with their parents and are looking at books and getting in and out of their seats. Mason's eyes are fixed on a Leapster2 touchscreen while he plays a game with a favorite character. Even though other children are talking and looking at books, Mason does not seem to notice. Mason interacts with an engaging technology to the exclusion of everything else going on around him. Other children, although present and involved in activities, do not capture his attention.

3. *Onlooker play* occurs when a child observes the play of other children, and their play is the focus of the child's attention. For example, Grace sits in the free

play area with blocks lying in front of her. She watches two peers who are playing a *Clifford, the Big Red Dog* activity on the classroom computer. Grace's attention is not on her own play activity. Although blocks are in front of her, she regards the technology activity of her peers with focused interest.

4. *Parallel play* occurs when the child is in proximity to one or more other children and the play (i.e., form, toys, and materials) resembles that of others. For example, Michael and two of his peers go to the Literacy Center where they have a choice of big books or iPad books to read. All three boys select iPads and each opens a different story and proceeds to read their respective book. None of the boys shows interest in the stories being read by others, but all three are using the same technology to accomplish the classroom task presented to them.

5. *Associative play* is demonstrated when children interact with one another during play, yet do not play together, although the technology adds to the activity. For example, Avery and her peers sit in a small-group setting and use their iPads and an app, Drawing Pad, to create pictures representing a recent field trip to a local fire station. The app allows each student to use an array of tools to make their drawing and to print or e-mail the drawing to their home. Avery looks at another student's work from time to time and comments about how "cool" his own drawing is. Avery sits in close proximity to others who are using their iPad apps to draw pictures. Avery has some proficiency in using the various drawing tools in the app and notices his peers and the tools they use. He makes statements about other possibilities in how the features might be used, but returns to his own work after comments are made.

6. *Cooperative play* is present when children actively play together. For example, Logan and his classmate, Christopher, go to the dramatic play center and assume roles associated with a bakery. Logan is the customer, and Christopher is the bakery worker. Christopher takes Logan's order and together they use an iPad app, Cookie Doodle, to create and roll the dough, cut cookies with a cutter, and choose from an array of frostings, sprinkles, and candies. Cooperation with a play peer is demonstrated by Logan and Christopher, who share a common goal of acting out a real-world scenario involving a bakery. Each student assumes a role and technology is used to help the students represent real-world actions that might occur in the bakery.

Figure 9.1 shows the various stages of play and their relationship to the form of technology use. Although some teachers may still tend to question the role of technology in today's classroom settings, its use in play activities of young children has increased in their home settings in recent years, and thus its integration into planned play activities is developmentally appropriate (NAEYC and Fred Rogers Center, 2012; Sandall, Hemmeter, Smith, & McLean, 2005).

LOOKING DEEPER INTO THE ROLE OF PLAY

As young children play, particularly using technologies available to them, there is flexibility in their purpose and in how any particular play activity unfolds. Although very young children would typically be involved in solitary and onlooker

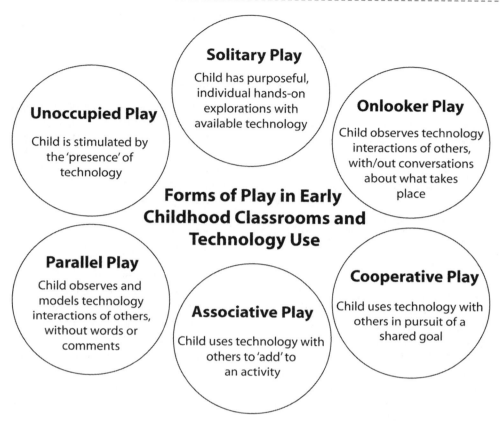

Figure 9.1. The forms of play observed in early childhood classrooms are associated with different ways of using technology. (© 2013 H.P. Parette.)

play, 3- to 5-year-old children move into the arena of true social play in which technologies become the means through which representation of the world is presented. This occurs both in physical or constructive play activities (e.g., using apps or computer software to build, play with wheeled vehicles, create structures using building materials) and dramatic play (e.g., controlling the actions of animated characters on web sites that present options for social roles of families, merchants, and community helpers or the behavior of heroes and heroines).

In the process of play, young children determine what happens in their activities. For example, objects become something else and represent both imagined and real-life things. A box becomes a spaceship and a dowel stick becomes a magic wand. Similarly, an app allows options about certain roles that are assumed by multiple players in cooperative activities. Additionally, there is a nonliteral, nonrealistic aspect to play because it is created from the imagination of children. For example, children may not follow the specific guidelines of a game or career choice by assuming the role of a troll or monster with which they are familiar in an electronic game. A girl may pretend to be the father instead of the mother when playing with another child. A rock or other inanimate object can become alive and take on human traits. Software programs, a SMART activity, or web sites may allow

Figure 9.2. Shidonni.com allows multiple children to draw their own creatures, which become animated and appear in various games and activities. (Used by permission of Shidonni.)

children to draw their own characters and create the worlds in which they live (see Figure 9.2).

Learning from Others

Every child learns something different when engaged in a play activity with others. As children play in the classroom environment, they learn about themselves and their worlds and gain insights regarding possible futures. For example, when dressing up with clothing, young children can practice rules for dressing for the weather, experience a variety of careers in which they have interest, and explore related social and communication skills as they interact with peers. They can also dress avatars or cartoon characters on web sites or when using software programs, which accomplish the same purpose. They can build unique structures with real blocks, thus stimulating their creativity. Similarly, using e-manipulatives, children can create similar structures or manipulate images of common objects, which also challenge their creativity and thinking skills. Physical play (e.g., running, swinging, climbing, stacking blocks, pushing cars, tossing a ball) can also be paired with technologies that allow such actions to be captured, viewed, and commented on (e.g., video recordings, digital pictures, apps). During imaginative play activities (e.g., dressing up, observing a peer playing, imitating play activities, modeling Play-Doh, playing in the sand, playing an iPad app or web-based game), young children increase their cognitive skills and abilities to process information.

Through such play activities—both traditional and technology-supported—children develop skills in ways not possible through typical classroom tasks, such as completion of worksheets, writing, drawing, coloring, or other routine demands placed on them in classroom activities. Play becomes a mechanism through which the teacher can plan classroom activities that are connected to the EXPECT IT-PLAN IT-TEACH IT process.

What the Research Says

Jean Piaget (1952, 1962), a prominent developmental psychologist, found that at approximately 2 years of age young children begin to represent and reconstruct their experiences and knowledge. This process of learning to represent and reconstruct experiences is evident in three types of play, which have been described as exploratory (e.g., inventing new ways to achieve goals or play with objects), functional (e.g., appropriate use of objects), and symbolic (e.g., pretend play).

Exploratory Play and Technology Children may begin exploring objects or exploratory play as early as 9–10 months of age. Through exploratory play, children gain experiences with possible uses of items. For example, a child may find a container or drawer and begin exploring the texture, taste, and sound of items found in the drawer. In family settings, it is not uncommon for families to present various technologies, (e.g., mobile phone, iPod and iPad apps, remote control for the family television) to their children and allow them to play with them, thus piquing their curiosities when things happen (i.e., cause and effect) during these exploratory interactions.

Functional Play and Technology During the first 2 years of life, play assumes a functional role wherein children repeat experiences that include movements in their environments, manipulations of objects, and self-imitations (i.e., reproductions of their own actions). This play allows children to practice and learn about their physical abilities when interacting with their environments and achieve mastery over those movements.

Functional play characterizes infants and toddlers. At age 3, it constitutes 50% of a child's play (Klugman & Fasoli, 1995). In preschool and kindergarten, these play experiences are reflected in such activities as sorting, dumping, filling, categorizing, stacking, and repeating pegboard patterns. A child may push the buttons on a phone or a computer keyboard. They may swipe at an iPad screen to make something happen based on their prior observations and cause-effect experiences with varying apps. Although functional play decreases as a child grows older, it remains important in classroom activities and can be either solitary or parallel.

Symbolic Play and Technology As the cognitive development of young children advances, they develop the ability to remember and thus try out actions that are observed in the world around them. Children also develop the ability to think using symbols—both memories and mental images. This accounts for children's ability to engage in pretend or symbolic play using tools. Through their imagination and creativity, children come to understand that one item can represent another (e.g., a picture of a cat can represent a real cat; through imagination, pencils can represent chopsticks).

In early childhood classrooms, symbolic play allows children to pretend to eat imaginary foods. Children may use a block as a phone, a remote control, a radio, or other technology with which they have had prior experiences. Pretend play, reaching its highest level in preschool and kindergarten, can be both a solitary and a group activity in the classroom (Klugman & Fasoli, 1995). Pretend play helps children process emotions and events in their lives. It also helps them practice social skills, learn values, develop language skills, and create a rich imagination.

Another form of symbolic play is constructive play, wherein a child creates or makes something and solves problems. Traditional classroom examples of such play include building with blocks; playing with arts, crafts, and puppets; and doing puzzles. Increasingly, software, apps, and web site activities provide such technology-based opportunities to engage in this type of play. Approximately 50% of all activity for preschool and kindergarten children is constructive play (Klugman & Fasoli, 1995). Children can play constructively alone as well as with others. This type of play develops thinking and reasoning skills, problem solving, and creativity.

Most children in preschool and kindergarten settings will have symbolic play capabilities. However, some children with disabilities may have only exploratory or functional play skills present.

PLAY IN TODAY'S CLASSROOMS

Many adults may believe that play opportunities only occur indoors with toys or outdoors as children run and interact with their peers or objects. The reality is that exploratory, functional, and symbolic play opportunities can occur in any setting (e.g., classroom or home) and any activity (e.g., preparing for dinner, math center, library time). Even in preschool and kindergarten, exploratory and functional play opportunities exist. Many of these play experiences for preschool and kindergarten children are symbolic in nature. By this point, children have cognitive and language skills that enable them to represent the world around them and to use language during the play. While a mother or father is preparing dinner, a child can prepare a mock meal using cooking utensils. During math center, children can play as they build towers while counting manipulatives or act out story problems. Children can play during library time as they explore real objects related to a story, read the story using different voices, or act out parts of the story.

In early childhood education settings, a range of instructional technology applications having universal design for learning (UDL) characteristics are available to encourage and support children's symbolic play. As discussed in previous chapters, these technologies are engaging, interactive, dynamic, shared, and flexible. Children can now draw on interactive whiteboards rather than on paper, allowing them an opportunity to create while developing fine motor skills. A wide array of iPad apps can be used to allow children to explore content, practice skills that are targeted in the curriculum, or simply provide entertainment. Children can point to or select a digital picture or software-generated icon when they want to request participation in an activity, allowing them an opportunity for independent expression for a preferred activity. They can take turns with various software, apps, and web site activities designed for two or more players.

As some teachers strive to make connections between new instructional technologies and classroom activities, symbolic play may pose some concern. There has been a tendency in recent years for play to be deemphasized as greater emphasis is placed on academics. This may be in large part due to a lack of understanding by early childhood professionals regarding how play can be used to support the curriculum.

Some teachers may have the misperception that most technologies only support a single child's play at any given moment, and thus they have limited utility in the curriculum. Admittedly, children may have home access to technologies that support engagement of one child (or player) at a time. This is anticipated given the way in which play and the availability of technologies in children's lives unfolds (e.g., an iPad app at home is presented to a young child who engages in the interactive elements by himself or herself). Also, many software programs or computerized games, such as the Nintendo Wii, may be used by a single player. However, although the earliest experiences with technology may indeed be at home, most children will have some degree of family involvement/engagement with the child during these early experiences. For example, a father may show his child a smartphone or iPad app and provide assistance in helping the child learn to use some of the features. A mother may read an electronic book as the child clicks a button (or swipes a finger) to turn a page.

In preschool and kindergarten settings, children will naturally understand that some technologies are used by several children at the same time for some expressed educational purpose. Asking children to share technologies encourages social participation and provides an opportunity to take turns responding to questions, playing a game on a particular device (e.g., an iPad app), or using the features within a technology (e.g.., a small group observes a SMART Board literacy activity using Clicker 6 and takes turns making button selections in the activity). As teachers prepare to effectively integrate instructional technology into planned activities in their classrooms, it is encouraging that today's instructional technologies provide an array of opportunities that support the play needs of young children.

For example, for several weeks, Mrs. Hearns has spent time during choice time/free play and other play activity times observing her children as they played independently and with peers. During her observations, Mrs. Hearns also made sure to talk with each child regarding his or her play activity and ask for information about the game, creation, or activity in which children were engaged. As the children excitedly shared information about their play activities with Mrs. Hearns, she used her digital camera over a 2-week period to take pictures of the children and their structures made from blocks and Play-Doh creations, as well as the children when they dressed up and played games. After collecting pictures of all of the children, Mrs. Hearns and her students organized the pictures into groups and the children assisted in identifying the order of the groups by activities in which they had been engaged. The students participated with her in creating a PowerPoint presentation, which Mrs. Hearns then projected onto her screen using her digital projector. The children love to watch the presentation and excitedly point to the pictures of them while they play within the classroom.

Mr. Bivens has created a SMART Board activity that allows his students to interact with the screen during a small-group time in a career/dress-up center. The students select a picture of an individual in uniform/professional dress; additional pictures related to the individual's occupation appear on the screen as children make selections in the SMART Board activity. Mr. Bivens assists the students as they talk about the different pictures and possible responsibilities related to the occupation. During whole-group time, Mr. Bivens revisits the career center by asking individual students to stand and verbally identify their favorite career while acting out what an individual in that field would do as an activity during the day.

As illustrated in preceding vignettes, students were provided opportunities within their daily activities to develop academic skills *and* play skills. Mrs. Hearns and Mr. Bivens created simple activities to assist their students in increasing important play skills through photos and encouraged discussion with peers, turn taking with technology, and opportunities to play as they learn. Basic technology has been easily incorporated into each of the learning settings, creating powerful opportunities for learning.

TYPICAL EARLY CHILDHOOD ACTIVITIES

Within activities that occur in the classroom, there are a variety of DO-SAY-REMEMBER demands presented to young children as they interact with their peers. With guidance from teachers, children can effectively and efficiently respond to specific play demands and learn through these experiences. Play opportunities exist in all activity areas in today's classroom settings. As young children enter their classroom each morning, they should be encouraged to play with objects, available technologies, and their peers. Daily play activities for children in preschool settings vary widely because of the diverse ability levels that are typically present. For example, in many preschool classrooms children can observe a peer dressing up as a mail carrier and then follow through by pretending to mail a letter. When teachers see a child sitting alone during play activities, suggestions can be made regarding possible play activities that present an array of DO-SAY-REMEMBER demands for participating in the activity.

Early play activities for kindergarten students often include similar experiences as those enjoyed by preschool students, especially at the very beginning of the kindergarten year. However, the play tasks of these older children evolve as they grow and learn from new opportunities, challenges, and successes. As the school year progresses, the cognitive, communication, academic, and social skills needed in most kindergarten settings represent greater encouragement for the kindergarten student to take that first step into the world of formal schooling and a second step into becoming more independent. This is not an all-or-nothing path because the kindergarten child is still part of the everyday world of play-supported activities that can lead to experimenting with reading, writing, math, working both alone or in groups, getting along with others, and problem solving. Table 9.1 presents typical play tasks that potentially become steps in planned activities when using the EXPECT IT-PLAN IT-TEACH IT approach.

LARGE-GROUP AND SMALL-GROUP LEARNING ACTIVITIES

On examining the array of typical play tasks in Table 9.1, it is apparent that many play activities can occur in small- and large-group contexts. In using the EXPECT IT-PLAN IT-TEACH IT approach, it is important that any play activity be carefully planned. At this juncture, a distinction should be made between child-directed play and teacher-directed play. Child-directed play typically involves one-to-one interaction between an adult and child in which the child is helped to direct or lead the play activity in any way he or she chooses. Its focus is on supporting the young child's development of self-confidence and self-direction. It is not, however, connected to a specific learning standard in the curriculum. EXPECT IT-PLAN IT-TEACH IT assumes careful planning that is connected to a targeted learning standard and benchmarks. Thus, teacher-directed play (which is planned) becomes a mechanism or strategy (ARRANGE IT) that can be complemented using instructional technology to teach specific skills in the curriculum.

In the following examples, specific strategies for incorporating play into daily activities are presented using the EXPECT IT-PLAN IT-TEACH IT process. Admittedly, there are countless variations of strategies that teachers can use to incorporate play throughout the day in today's classrooms. A number of instructional strategies that can be used in planned activities were described in Chapter 3. These strategies, identified in the PLAN IT phase and used during the TEACH IT phase, have utility in many planned play activities in preschool and kindergarten settings. As noted by Bowman, Donovan, and Burns (2000), good teachers use many

Table 9.1.   Preschool and kindergarten activity areas and typical play tasks

Activity area	Typical tasks
Preschool	
Arrival	Identifying and interacting with toys, activities, or classroom centers as other children arrive
Choice time/free play	Making choices about play items
	Observing play of others
	Initiating activities with peers
	Dressing up
	Stacking blocks
	Playing at water table
	Manipulating cars/trucks
	Putting together puzzles
	Molding Play-Doh
	Using art materials to create products (e.g., drawing, painting)
	Writing with pencil and crayons
Small group	Matching and instructional games
	Art activities
	Singing songs that include actions
Outdoor play	Making choices about play items
	Observing play of others
	Initiating activities with peers
	Swinging on the swing set
	Climbing the monkey bars
	Sliding down the slide
	Creating and playing games with peers
	Kicking/tossing a ball
	Playing in the sand
	Riding a tricycle
	Riding in a wagon
	Playing with a parachute
	Jumping on a trampoline
Departure	Singing songs that include actions
	Participating in free play activities while waiting for parents/ transportation
Kindergarten	
Morning circle/attendance	Participating in calendar activities, including "Days of the Week" song
	Chanting ABCs and familiar poems and songs with rhythmic patterns and expressive movement
Reading/literacy	Choosing books from bookcase during free choice
	Clicking on computer menu of free online read-aloud books and listening using a headset
	Watching puppet play based on book of the week

(continued)

Table 9.1 *(continued)*

Activity area	Typical tasks
Art/physical education/ movement/music	Using different art materials (e.g., sponges, glue sticks, paint brushes) at easels or with work trays and sharing with peers
	Modeling clay figures
	Rolling and bouncing squishy balls
	Navigating scooter boards in relays
	Playing with a hula-hoop to music
	Tossing and catching scarves
	Participating in unison to repeat rhythmic patterns or games of claps and snaps
	Using rhythm instruments (e.g., bells, shakers, wood blocks with sticks)
	Singing songs
	Participating in fingerplays
Recess	Making choices about play activities
	Observing play of others
	Initiating activities with peers
	Swinging on the swing set
	Climbing ladders and monkey bars
	Sliding down the slide
	Creating and playing games with peers
	Kicking/tossing a ball
	Playing on a teeter-totter
	Engaging in pretend play when in a playhouse
Social studies/science	Using math manipulatives and puzzles
	Sorting and counting small objects
	Exploring patterns and shapes
Dismissal routine	Singing songs that include actions
	Participating in free play activities while waiting for parents/ transportation

of these instructional strategies to acknowledge and encourage the classroom efforts of children, model and demonstrate instructional tasks, create challenges in planned activities to help children extend their capabilities, and provide specific directions or instruction. Thus, children benefit when teachers understand varying instructional strategies and select the best strategy to use in a planned activity, depending on the standard, learning objectives, and needs of individual children at that moment. The strategy should include children who may need much more support than others, even in exploration and play (Sandall et al., 2005).

In any early childhood curriculum, the challenge is to provide opportunity for play—exploratory, functional, and symbolic—while embedding instructional experiences for students each day, thus allowing and encouraging important skill development. Figure 9.3 presents the connection between play and PLAN IT-TEACH IT. The following examples demonstrate how several teachers have used the EXPECT IT-PLAN IT-TEACH IT process with regard to play for their students.

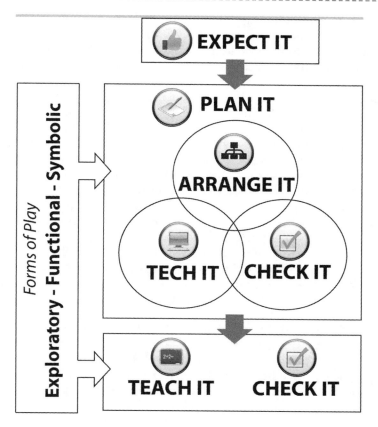

Figure 9.3. Exploratory, functional, and symbolic play are considered both in the PLAN IT and TEACH IT phases of technology integration. (© 2013 H.P. Parette.)

Mrs. Hearns

Mrs. Hearns is hoping to integrate technology and play for learning using the EXPECT IT-PLAN-IT-TEACH IT technology integration model in her preschool class.

 EXPECT IT A standard in Mrs. Hearns's curriculum is development of skills related to classifying and sorting objects by size, color, and shape through play. Mrs. Hearns identifies this standard and targets the learning objective of sorting objects by size and color.

 PLAN IT To effectively plan her classroom activity, Mrs. Hearns wants to plan a functional play activity. She considers in her planning how technology can help the children of her classroom perform an activity.

 TECH IT Mrs. Hearns has prepared a 10-slide PowerPoint presentation in which each page shows attribute blocks that can be stacked on top of each other or arranged in different formations. The first sequence of slides show two items that match in size (or color), whereas the third does not. The pages increase in difficulty with the addition of more items per slide. As Mrs. Hearns presents each page, she will ask the students to find the items that are the same color or size or the item that does not match the other items.

 ARRANGE IT   Mrs. Hearns will model the sorting expectation using the first page of the presentation. As she models, she will locate the items from her set of attribute blocks and place them in the same pattern as those in the page where she sorted the blocks. Mrs. Hearns will then ask the students, as a group, to shout out the items that match or the item that does not match. After modeling the activity, Mrs. Hearns will then assist the students in breaking up into groups of two (or three, as necessary). As a group they will walk through one page together. As each PowerPoint slide is presented, one member of each team will look through his or her items to find the same items and place them in the same pattern as those on the slide, thus providing an opportunity for the students to play while learning. The other student will identify the items that match or the item that does not match. Mrs. Hearns will call students to the screen to point to the objects that should be sorted together. The students will have several opportunities to take turns, identify objects, and verbally identify items that are the same size or color.

 CHECK IT   Through anecdotal notes, Mrs. Hearns can formatively assess student learning during this activity. She will be able to visually monitor each group to identify whether the students have identified the items that match those in the PowerPoint slides, placed them in the correct position, and identified the items that match or the item that does not match. Using an iPad that she just acquired, Mrs. Hearns will take pictures of team work as students complete sorts. These pictures can then be printed and placed in student folders or sent home to family members via e-mail.

 SOLVE IT   As Mrs. Hearns plans her small-group activity that focuses on classifying by size and color, she considers the needs of the individual students who may have difficulty. She is concerned about Madelyne, a student with low vision who will have difficulty seeing both the attribute blocks and any small images in the PowerPoint presentation. Mrs. Hearns works through these problems using the SOLVE IT Break It Down process to help Madelyne independently participate in the small-group activity (see Table 9.2).

Peer participation is an essential part of the SOLVE IT solution that Mrs. Hearns developed. This is important because it helps Madelyne feel that she is a part of the classroom and play activity. Positioning is another important strategy with students who have vision impairments. It is essential for children with vision difficulties to remain engaged in classroom learning activities. A Wiki Stix is a pipe cleaner-type stick that can be used to raise the blocks on the printout of the PowerPoint presentation. Mrs. Hearns collaborates with the low vision specialist to develop these solutions and is provided assistance in preparing materials for activities. Teaching self-advocacy skills to young children with disabilities is also best practice. Many young children, like Madelyne, become frustrated when their needs are not met and simply disengage from classroom activities. Mrs. Hearns provides reinforcement and encouragement to get Madelyne to express her needs. As with all assistive

Table 9.2. The Break It Down process for Madelyne

Define the problem: Madelyne has difficulty seeing print/pictures.

Activity: Students will participate in a PowerPoint activity focusing on classification by size and color. Students will be grouped in pairs for functional play activity and observe teacher modeling selection of attribute blocks on slides. Student pairs assume differing roles of creating the pattern of blocks presented in the PowerPoint presentation and classifying by size or color. As students see each page of the activity, they create a sort. Students are called to the screen so they can show the sort while the class is asked to identify whether it was made by size or color.

Planned activity steps	Planned activity requirements			Child performance	What's the answer?
	DO	SAY	REMEMBER		
To begin: Children transition from whole group to small groups	See where to go Listen to teacher's instructions for transition Move to appropriate small-group area	N/A	Remember where to go for small group activity Remember rule of staying quietly seated	Madelyne often needs help moving around the classroom Madelyne asks for assistance in getting to small group	Peer provides physical assistance in transitioning to small group setting
Observe teacher model of first slide	Look at teacher while staying seated quietly Listen to teacher See the PowerPoint presentation	Say a response individually or in unison with class when teacher provides signal	Recall correct directions for completing activity Remember rule of staying quietly seated	Madelyne's visual impairment affects her ability to see in the classroom Madelyne cannot see the PowerPoint during the presentation	Position Madelyne and her partner close to the screen Make all block images large on PowerPoint slides Use color printer and WikkiStix to create raised tactile sheets of each PowerPoint slide pattern Remind Madelyne to raise her hand to request teacher assistance

(continued)

Table 9.2 *(continued)*

Planned activity steps	Planned activity requirements			Child performance	What's the answer?
	DO	SAY	REMEMBER		
Arrange and categorize attribute blocks	See slides See attribute shapes and colors Hear teacher Arrange blocks in pattern as presented on slides	Say which object is different or which objects are the same when requested to by the teacher	Remember rules for collaboration Recall objects that are the same/different Remember role assigned in partner pair	After the teacher presents the second slide, Madelyne gets frustrated because she cannot see the slide Madelyne's visual impairment affects her ability to see in the classroom	Use color printer and WikkiStix to create raised tactile sheets of each PowerPoint slide pattern Give Madelyne a handheld magnifying glass to use when sorting Remind Madelyne to raise her hand to request Mrs. Hearns attention when she needs assistance
Point to attribute blocks on PowerPoint slide	Hear teacher directions Come to screen See the screen	State classification made in partner pair	Recall sort made in partner pair	Madelyne can see when she is placed close to instructional materials Madelyne was able to come to screen and point to shapes on screen	N/A
To end: Return attribute blocks to storage bin	See the blocks See the storage bin Hear the teacher Pick up blocks and place in can	N/A	Know where blocks are stored	Madelyne cooperates with peers, but has difficulty seeing things at a distance Madelyne works with her partner to put blocks away but cannot see storage area	Peer assistance is provided to return the blocks to the storage area

214

technology solutions, such strategies become part of what Mrs. Hearns routinely uses with Madelyne, reducing the need for future Break It Down tables.

TEACH IT   The activity planned by Mrs. Hearns progresses in a predictable sequence. Mrs. Hearns models the activity using the first PowerPoint slide that she had prepared. She says, "I'm going to use my attribute blocks and make the same arrangement as you see on the screen." She then models selecting the appropriate blocks and places them in front of her. Then Mrs. Hearns says, "Now, I'm going to choose two blocks that are the same size or the same color." She then points to the two blue circles while saying, "These two have the same color."

Mrs. Hearns breaks the children into groups of two and provides each group with a number of varying shapes, colors, and sizes of attribute blocks. She then asks students to look at the screen while the second PowerPoint slide is shown. She asks, "Which two go together? Do we sort by size or color?" Students call out responses, and together the class makes a decision about the sort required. Mrs. Hearns then states why the two blocks go together.

Mrs. Hearns proceeds to the third slide of the PowerPoint presentation and asks each group to number off 1 and 2. She then asks all the students who were assigned 1 to raise their hands. She says, "Good" and provides corrective feedback when needed to several groups. Mrs. Hearns then says, "All the 2s raise your hands" and provides feedback. Mrs. Hearns tells the students, "All the 1s find the blocks and make the pattern that you see. And 2s, you watch." She waits and observes as the children in each group create an arrangement to match the model on the screen, and then she says, "All the 2s find the two that we need to sort by size or shape." Mrs. Hearns then calls Angela, a 2 in one group, to the screen and asks her to show the class the items that were sorted together. Angela points to the shapes on the board and is reinforced by Mrs. Hearns, who comments on the sort, saying, "Class, did Angela sort by size or shape?" Mrs. Hearns listens to their responses and provides feedback. She proceeds through each slide in the same manner, providing opportunities for students to use functional play as a context for the embedded instruction focusing on the targeted learning objective—sorting by size and color.

In this example, Mrs. Hearns's PLAN IT approach resulted in a successful TEACH IT activity for all students, including Madelyne, who was provided with two simple assistive technologies—a handheld magnifying glass and color printed sheets presenting each of the 10 slides used and having raised outlines of the attribute blocks.This helped Madelyne to be included in the planned functional play activity and supported her successful participation as a class member.

Mr. Bivens

Mr. Bivens wants to use the EXPECT IT-PLAN IT-TEACH IT technology integration model to use technology during play to support social skills instruction.

EXPECT IT   On examining his curriculum goals, Mr. Bivens recognizes that his children need to achieve the standard of being able to perform effectively as a member of a group. Because many of his classroom activities involve group participation and working with others, Mr. Bivens decides that he will focus on the learning objective of *sharing materials and experiences and taking turns.*

PLAN IT Integrating technology is an important aspect of Mr. Bivens' instructional planning. Here, Mr. Bivens considers how he is going to meet learning objectives and identify instructional technology that would be useful during cooperative play in the dramatic play center.

TECH IT Mr. Bivens looks through the iTunes store for free and inexpensive apps that support the targeted learning objective. He also wants to connect the apps with a planned cooperative dramatic play activity on "The Bakery." His class had recently gone on a field trip to a local bakery, during which time he took photos of children with his iPad that he e-mailed to himself. He decides to use these photos in a SMART Board activity. He also found an inexpensive app, CookieDoodle, which would allow children to roll out cookies, use a cookie cutter, select frosting colors, affix icing pipings, and add sprinkles and candies. Each child will have access to one iPad having the app.

ARRANGE IT Mr. Bivens decides that, to integrate his TECH IT choices into instruction, the dramatic play center with a small group of six students will be the setting for his planned cooperative play activity. The specific instructional objective lends itself to a logical grouping strategy because students will be cooperating to make, bake, and decorate cookies that might be used at a school party for all the families. Here, Mr. Bivens is not approaching the skills within this activity from an easy-to-hard sequence or from a prerequisites skills sequence, but rather as set of skills connected to the activity of making cookies.

To introduce the lesson, Mr. Bivens will embed eight iPad photos of the bakery field trip into a SMART notebook activity. The pages will represent various phases of the baking process that the students observed on their field trip. He will also select images that align with the process of baking presented in the app the children will be using. He then will provide instructions regarding which app to look for on the iPad, modeling each step of a logical sequence of steps using the app features. Mr. Bivens will model how to take a picture of their work done by showing children how to press the *Home* button and *Power* button on the iPad.

CHECK IT Mr. Bivens has several options for assessment, and he decides that permanent products are appropriate for his planned activity. He knows that his iPad has video recording and screen capture capability. He will use the recording feature in his iPad camera to record footage of children using their iPads to bake cookies at varying points in the instructional process, particularly when children are showing and commenting about their work to the group. The children will take their own pictures of completed work during steps in the instructional process. Mr. Bivens can also quickly take a series of photos during the instructional process. All photos and video recordings can be organized into a folder, viewed and edited later, and/or sent home to the family to show a product created by each child that day. Both the recordings and photos also enable Mr. Bivens to reuse them in PowerPoint and SMART activity development in the future.

SOLVE IT During PLAN IT, Mr. Bivens knows that his student Ashley, who has Down syndrome, will have difficulty following iPad button and screen sequences without support. She does respond well to explicit instruction and prompting, and she is well liked by her peers. Ashley follows directions much of the time but occasionally looks away for extended periods, thereby missing important directions given to the class. Although she enjoys school, her peers, and class activities, Ashley is unable to perform classroom tasks at the same pace as other students. This results in frustration and occasional aggressive behavior toward her peers. When she is explicitly and repeatedly taught rules prior to the activity, Ashley's ability to comprehend and follow rules increases. Mr. Bivens also knows that while Ashley can transition between activities she sometimes has difficulty making these transitions and may benefit from supports to assist her in making targeted transitions.

To ensure Ashley's inclusion in the planned activity, Mr. Bivens uses the Break It Down process to help make decisions (see Table 9.3). Ashley needs supports to help her with transitions, routines, attending, displays of inappropriate behavior, and completing sequences of tasks during the instructional setting. Mr. Bivens knows that Ashley's developmental level is such that she needs pictures of things and events in the classroom to help her understand expectations. He uses this knowledge to create several visual supports for Ashley to help her transition in and out of her dramatic play activity. He uses his iPad to take pictures of each activity area in which students participate daily, and he arranges them in a horizontal alignment on poster board that is affixed to the wall in several places in the classroom. These pictures allow Ashley to see the routine sequence from any place in the room.

Mr. Bivens feels that Ashley's fondness for her hero Curious George could be used to his advantage to communicate appropriate social behavior expected of her in a small-group setting. Mr. Bivens decides to use power cards—cards using a picture of the child's hero to help young children follow routines or comply with directions (Angell, Nicholson, Watts, & Blum, 2011). Sometimes there are multiple steps on the card; other times, there are icon supports to cue the child on what is expected. Mr. Bivens can read the card to Ashley, incorporating a statement such as, "Curious George wants Ashley to go to the next activity. Curious George is proud of Ashley." Ashley's power card is the size of a trading card, with a small picture of Curious George on one side and four Boardmaker picture steps on the reverse side, showing Ashley how to participate in key tasks: listen, watch, answer questions, and do your work (see Figure 9.4). The power card will be carried by Ashley across activity areas. Mr. Bivens knows that he will read the power card to Ashley on a regular schedule at the beginning of a planned activity requiring group participation until she learns to use it.

Because Ashley favors pictures over text to provide her with information, Mr. Bivens takes a screen shot of each of the iPad app screens having icons that children must use in CookieDoodle, as well as each step of the process of baking a cookie. These images are then organized into a visual support wherein the icon is shown and paired with a picture of what happens when it is tapped (see Figure 9.5). Each of these solutions became part of what Mr. Bivens typically did for Ashley. Soon he found other applications of the power cards for different challenges during other activities. By taking what he learned from problem solving using the Break It Down chart, Mr. Bivens was better able to anticipate Ashley's needs and increase her participation throughout the day and school year.

Table 9.3. The Break It Down process for Ashley

Define the problem: Ashley has difficulty participating in class activities that require sequential steps in activities. She gets frustrated and acts out when she has difficulty participating.

Activity: Students will participate in a dramatic play center activity that builds on a recent field trip to the neighborhood bakery. A SMART Activity containing photos of the sequence of baking cookies will be presented, followed by introduction of an app that allows students to create their own cookies. Students will talk about their creations at varying steps in the baking process.

Planned activity steps	Planned activity requirements			Child performance	What's the answer?
	DO	SAY	REMEMBER		
To begin: Children transition to the SMART Board	See where to go Listen to teacher's instructions for transition Move to appropriate SMART Board area	N/A	Remember where to go for SMART Board activity Remember rule of staying quietly seated	Ashley has trouble with transitions Ashley went to another center when the students were asked to go to the SMART Board	Daily routine chart using photos of activity areas Peer provides physical assistance in transitioning to small-group setting
Review and discuss photos taken at bakery	Look at teacher while staying seated quietly Listen to teacher See the SMART Activity photos	Describe actions taking place in photos	Remember rule of staying quietly seated and attending to teacher Recall events of field trip	Ashley sometimes does not attend to teacher instructions Ashley was looking around the room when the first slide was shown and couldn't remember what happened in several photos	Provide Ashley with a power card of her hero, Curious George, providing rules for group participation Verbal prompt to gain her attention
Transition to dramatic play area	Hear the teacher's instructions See the dramatic play area Walk to the area Sit on floor	N/A	Recall where dramatic play area is Remember classroom rules for quiet transitions	Ashley has trouble with transitions Ashley showed some confusion when teacher said it's time to go to dramatic play	Call attention to daily routine chart using photos of activity areas

Uses app features to "bake a cookie"	Listen to and see the teacher model app steps; See the app step icons; Hold the iPad; Tap the icons for app step; Take photo of work using iPad; Show choices made to others	Describe choice made at each step of activity	Remember what teacher says; Recall where to find step icons	Ashley is sometimes confused when she must participate in activities that require more than a few steps; Ashley looked at the teacher during models but had difficulty finding app icons on the screen. Sometimes she was frustrated	Visual chart showing enlarged photos of app icons with Board-maker symbols beside them to communicate meaning of icons; Curious George Power Card providing rules for group participation; Reinforcement for active participation; Peer assistance when difficulty arises; Teacher takes photos of Ashley's work
Prepare cookies for family party at school	Listen to and see the teacher model app steps; See the app step icons; Hold the iPad; Tap the icons for app step; Take photo of work using iPad; Show choices made to others	Describe choice made at each step of activity	Remember what teacher says; Recall where to find step icons	Ashley has difficulty following directions; Ashley was observed to set her iPad aside and go to another activity area	Visual chart showing enlarged photos of sequence of icons needed to make a cookie; Curious George Power Card providing rules for group participation; Reinforcement for active participation
Make more cookies	See the app step icons; Hold the iPad; Tap the icons for app step	Request assistance if needed	Recall multistep sequence of icon selection; Remember how to save cookies to cookie jar	Ashley has problems engaging in independent play and prefers to watch others; Ashley moved toward her friend Jayme and watched her as additional cookies were being made	Allow Ashley to observe other children
To end: Return iPads to teacher and move to literacy center area	See the teacher; Hand iPad to teacher; See the literacy center area; Walk to literacy center area		Remember location of literacy center area; Remember rules for quietly transitioning	Ashley sometimes does not know where to go when it is time to change activities; Ashley went to the sand play center instead of the literacy center	Laminated daily routine chart with photos; Curious George power card providing rules for group participation

TEACH IT Based on the TECH IT-ARRANGE IT-CHECK IT steps used in the PLAN IT process, Mr. Bivens then proceeds to teach his planned activity. Mr. Bivens opens his SMART activity to the first page of the eight-page presentation as the children transition to the SMART Board area. He takes a moment to talk with Ashley about her power card (see Figure 9.4) and explains that Curious George likes students to use his rules: "Listen, watch, answer questions, and do your work." As each photo of their recent field trip is shown, Mr. Bivens says in sequence, "So what were the bakers doing here?" Ashley is looking elsewhere, so he calls attention to her power card, pointing to the picture of *Listen*. Mr. Bivens says, "Ashley, look at your card. What does Curious George want you to do?" Ashley replies, "Listen," and Mr. Bivens reinforces her response.

As students respond to Mr. Bivens' questions about the bakery pictures, he echoes children's correct responses and uses key words that summarize the image, such as *mix dough, cut cookie, bake cookie,* and *put on icing.* This provides a model for Ashley, so that when Mr. Bivens asks her what is happening in the photo, she is able to use a short response and participate in the class discussion.

When all the slides were presented, Mr. Bivens then says, "Now that we've talked about the steps in baking cookies that we saw at the bakery, let's go bake some cookies of our own! Time to go to Dramatic Play." He observes Ashley presenting some confusion with regard to what to do, so he verbally prompts her: "Ashley, look at our daily schedule on the wall. Show me where Dramatic Play is." Ashley observes the wall chart and then points in the direction of the area, whereon Mr. Bivens provides verbal reinforcement. When children are seated in the dramatic play area, Mr. Bivens explains to the children that they will use an iPad app to bake cookies. He gives Ashley a visual chart that has the icons children will tap and corresponding screenshots of what appears when the icons are tapped (see Figure 9.4).

Mr. Bivens then distributes an iPad to each child. He tells the children, "We will bake cookies together, one step at a time—just like the bakers do!" He provides instructions regarding which app to look for on the iPad and shows children the icon for *Instant,* which he taps while saying, "This is where we get our dough to make our cookies." When a *Select a Cookie Dough* window opens, Mr. Bivens says, "You see, there are many choices. I can choose dark chocolate, or sugar cookie, or chocolate chip." He chooses *sugar cookie,* and then he runs his finger back and forth across the screen to "roll the dough." Then Mr. Bivens says, "Okay, now it's your turn to make a cookie. Let's choose our cookie dough and roll it out."

As the children begin to make selections, Mr. Bivens notices that Ashley has not responded yet, so he points to the cookie on her visual chart and says, "Ashley, can you find the cookie on your screen?" She looks from the chart to the screen, smiles, and reaches out to tap the icon. Mr. Bivens then calls attention to the Cookie Dough screen on her chart and points to the iPad screen, saying, "See when

Figure 9.4. Front and back side of a power card used to help a child follow rules for participating in a group play activity using an iPad app. (The Picture Communication Symbols ©1981–2013 by DynaVox Mayer-Johnson LLC. All Rights Reserved Worldwide. Used by permission.)

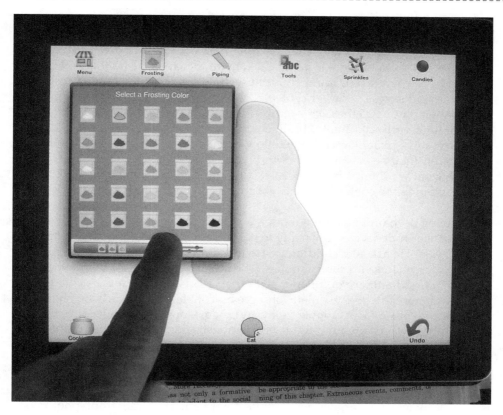

Figure 9.5. Sample visual support used to help a student understand what appears when an iPad icon in CookieDoodle is tapped. (Image courtesy of H.P. Parette.)

you tap this picture [the *Instant* icon], the Cookie Dough screen opens up and you can choose your cookie dough and roll it!" Ashley makes a choice, and as she rolls out her dough using her finger, Mr. Bivens uses his iPad to capture a picture of her working. He also captures photos of the other students as they work. He then says, "Okay, tell us what cookie you chose?" Each child holds up his or her iPad to show the rolled cookie and talks briefly about it. Mr. Bivens captures short video clips of each student talking about the cookie made using the iPad, which he later files away for assessment purposes.

When each student has shown his or her cookie, Mr. Bivens says, "Okay, let's take a picture of our cookie." He modeled how to take a picture of the completed work done by showing children how to press the *Home* button and *Power* button on the iPad. He watches as each child attempts this and provides direct assistance to several children who have difficulty, including Ashley.

Mr. Bivens systematically uses the same procedure for each subsequent step (select a cookie cutter, bake the cookie, apply extras [icing, sprinkles, candies], save to the cookie jar), while capturing video footage, photos, and student-captured photos at varying points in time. Mr. Bivens is pleased with the enthusiasm of the students and notes how quickly they began using the iPad app. Ashley seems to benefit from use of the visual chart, which helps her to understand the next steps in the process of using the app to bake a cookie.

When the children are finished creating their cookies, Mr. Bivens says, "Let's save our cookies to the cookie jar by clicking on the jar at the bottom." He shows the children where to click and children see that his cookie is located inside the jar. Each child saves his or her cookie, including Ashley, who is given a physical prompt by pointing to the *Cookie Jar* icon. After telling the students that they will prepare for a party at school, Mr. Bivens models for the students how to create a tablecloth and a plate. The children follow by making selections for both and commenting on their selections. Then Mr. Bivens says, "Now let's taste our cookies and see what we think." He models clicking the *Eat* icon and shows the children that by tapping the cookie bites are taken out of it. Each child then eats his or her cookie.

Having been provided with models and instructions for each step, Mr. Bivens feels that the students are now ready to participate in the solitary play component of his lesson. He asks the children to use the app to create more cookies for their cookie jar to share with their families. The children enthusiastically launch into this play period and are quite busy with their iPads. Ashley sets her iPad down and moves close to a peer to quietly observe his cookie creations. Mr. Bivens knows that this is an example of onlooker play and is developmentally appropriate given that Ashley appears attentive and is not demonstrating any behavior problems.

When dramatic play time is over, Mr. Bivens says, "Okay, it's time to go to large group." Students begin to transition, but he observes that Ashley looks confused. Mr. Bivens calls attention to the daily routine wall chart and says, "Ashley, look at our chart." He points to the dramatic play photo and says, "Dramatic play is over. Now we go to large group," while pointing to the large-group photo. Ashley looks around the room, recognizes the space presented in the photo, and smiles as she makes the transition successfully.

In this example, Mr. Bivens embeds both cooperative play and solitary play into his planned activity designed to develop skills related to group participation and working with others. Structured teaching using modeling and opportunities for hands-on explorations with the iPad contribute to engagement by the students. Several assistive technology supports enable Ashley to participate in the planned activity, thus providing a means of access to the curriculum.

FAMILY AND COMMUNITY SUPPORTS

Throughout this chapter, a small number of instructional technology and assistive technology tools and strategies are presented in the classroom setting. Each of these examples highlights ways that technologies can be implemented to promote the development of play skills, thus providing supports for the accompanying development of academic skills in young children. However, the use of these technologies to support development should not be limited to the classroom. When possible, teachers should work with parents and community members to extend learning in the classroom to learning at home and in the community. The following vignettes will illustrate ways that technology use can be carried over to the home and community to support children's ongoing play skill development.

After school, 4-year-old Kelsey and her mother have a snack together called "Ants on a Log." The snack was one that Kelsey learned to make at school using celery pieces, peanut butter, and raisins, after being introduced to what chefs can do in their jobs as part of a unit of study on careers. Her mother asked how Kelsey knew how to make the healthy snack. Kelsey says that she just followed the movie's pictures like a chef would do. With a confused look from her mother, Kelsey asks her mother to check the family's e-mail. The teacher had sent an attachment of the video to all the parents in Kelsey's class at the conclusion of the curriculum unit. Once on the computer, Kelsey and her mother accessed the e-mail message with the video. Kelsey proudly told her mom how the children pretended to be chefs and carried out the steps of making the snack at school. Kelsey commented that she especially liked wearing a chef's hat and eating the snack. Kelsey's mother thought that the teacher's choice of an activity was a good lesson on eating healthy, while Kelsey also was engaged in creative play with her classmates.

Another way to connect with families and the wider community is Voice-Thread, which provides a UDL means to support the classroom curriculum and connect student activities and products to be shared with families. This free web-based application allows images, videos, zoom-in capabilities, and opportunities for shared comments. For example, early in the school year of Mrs. Davidson's kindergarten class, the children built creative block structures. One in particular drew the instant attention of all the children: a spaceport created by Jacob and Ben. Mrs. Davidson took close-up photos of the inventive spaceport and allowed the structure to remain for 3 days in the block area. All the children were asked to imagine who might inhabit the spaceport. She asked each student to create a drawing of a person or space monster along with a story about the character. She then made a book of the student's pages. Next, these were scanned into a digital storybook for uploading to VoiceThread along with the photos. Family members were able to make comments directly into the edges of the pages of the storybook. Furthermore, distant relatives and community members could join in the conversations about the results of the creative play activity that led to a literacy product.

Other apps, such as Doodlecast for Kids and Educreations, allow children to record their voices as they draw and write on the iPad screen (see Figure 7.10). This work can then be shared with families in a movie format attached in e-mail.

SUMMARY

Without question, play is an essential part of the development and learning process for all children. Through play, young children learn about the world and others around them, contributing to the development of critical thinking and a cadre of other skills that will shape their lives and potential success in school in the future. Given the increased visibility of technology in the play experiences of children during the early years, the challenge for teachers is how children's interest in and preferences for technologies can be meaningfully translated into planned classroom activities. Mere availability of instructional technology is insufficient absent UDL characteristics, which make today's technologies shared, dynamic, interactive, and engaging.

Although there may be concerns on the part of some teachers and families that technology may increase the isolation or detachment of some children from others during play activities (e.g., solitary interactions with online activities, software, or apps), both families and teachers have responsibilities to ensure that developmentally appropriate technology-supported play activities are available to all young children. In the classroom, this assumes that "playful experiences in which exploration and meaning making is scaffolded and extended . . . has the potential to be a much richer learning environment" (Yelland, 2010, p. 9).

When thoughtful consideration is given to including instructional technologies into classroom activities using the EXPECT IT-PLAN IT-TEACH IT approach, developmentally appropriate play as a context for technology-supported instruction (and such richer learning environments) can be greatly enhanced.

ADDITIONAL READINGS

Blake, B., & Pope, T. (2008). Developmental psychology: Incorporating Piaget's and Vygotsky's theories in classrooms. *Journal of Cross-Disciplinary Perspectives in Education, 1*(1), 59–67.

Judge, S.L., & Lahm, E.A. (1998). Assistive technology applications for play, mobility, communication, and learning for young children with disabilities. In S.L. Judge & H.P. Parette (Eds.), *Assistive technology for young children with disabilities* (pp. 16–44). Cambridge, MA: Brookline.

Sandberg, A. (2001). Preschool teacher's conceptions of computers and play. Retrieved October 15, 2012, from http://www.highbeam.com/doc/1G1-91564858 .html

REFERENCES

Angel, M., Nicholson, J., Watts, E.H., & Blum, C. (2011). Using a multi-component adapted power card strategy to decrease latency prior to interactivity transitions for children with developmental disabilities. *Focus on Autism and Other Developmental Disabilities, 26,* 206–217.

Blake, S., Winsor, D., & Allen, L. (2011). *Child development and the use of technology: Perspectives, applications and experiences.* Hershey, PA: IGI Global.

Bowman, B., Donovan, M. S., & Burns, M. S. (2000). *Eager to learn: Educating our preschooloers.* Washington, DC: Committee on Early Childhood Pedagogy, Commission on Behavioral and Social Sciences and Education, National Research Council

Casey, L.B., Reeves, K.C., & Conner, E.C. (2012). Using technology in the world of play. In S. Blake, D. Winsor, & L. Allen (Eds.), *Child development and the use of technology: Perspectives, applications and experiences* (pp. 130–143). Hershey, PA: IGI Global.

Downey, S., Hayes, N., & O'Neill, B. (2007). *Play and technology for children aged 4–12.* Retrieved October 15, 2012, from http://www.dit.ie/cser/media/ditcser/images/Play-and -Technology.pdf

Isenberg, J.P., & Quisenberry, N. (2002). Play: Essential for all children. A position paper of the Association for Childhood Education International. *Childhood Education, 79,* 33–39.

Klugman, E., & Fasoli, L. (1995). Taking the high road toward a definition of play. In E. Klugman (Ed.), *Play, policy & practice* (pp. 195–201). St. Paul, MN: Redleaf Press. National Association for the Education of Young Children. (2009). *Developmentally appropriate practice in early childhood programs serving children from birth through age 8.* Retrieved October 15, 2012, from http://www.naeyc.org/files/naeyc/file/positions/PSDAP.pdf

National Association for the Education of Young Children & Fred Rogers Center for Early Learning and Children's Media. (2012). *Technology and interactive media as tools in early childhood programs serving children from birth through age 8.* Retrieved September 22, 2012, from http://www.naeyc.org/files/naeyc/file/positions/PS_technology_WEB2.pdf

Parten, M. (1933). Social participation among pre-school children. *Journal of Abnormal and Social Psychology, 27,* 243–269.

Piaget, J. (1952). *The origins of intelligence in children.* New York, NY: International Universities Press.

Piaget, J. (1962). *Play, dreams and imitation in childhood.* New York, NY: Norton.

Rieber, L.P., Smith, L., & Noah, D. (1998).The value of serious play. *Educational Technology, 38*(6), 29–37.

Sandall, S., Hemmeter, M.L., Smith, B.J., & McLean, M.E. (Eds.). (2005). *DEC recommended practices: A comprehensive guide for practical application in early intervention/early childhood special education.* Longmont, CO: Sopris West.

Yelland, N.J. (2010). New technologies, playful experiences, and multimodal learning. In I.R. Berson & M.J. Berson (Eds.), *High tech tots. Childhood in a digital world* (pp. 5–22). Charlotte, NC: Information Age Publishing.

10

TECH IT: Obtaining, Evaluating, and Using Instructional Technology Innovations in Early Childhood

Jason C. Travers and Cori M. More

After reading this chapter, you should be able to

- Identify considerations when choosing new technology innovations for classroom use
- Identify methods to locate information about new instructional technology for teachers
- Apply critical evaluation of instructional technology innovations as developmentally appropriate practice
- Evaluate effects of instructional technology innovations on groups of students and individuals with special needs

As noted throughout this book, an increasing array of instructional technologies is being used in today's early childhood education settings. Encouragingly, this has resulted in an ever-growing amount of information, resources, and recommendations about technology being shared among teachers. For example, many YouTube videos show how families and education professionals use new instructional technologies with young children. Readily accessible web sites and digital documents can provide recommendations and evaluative information about educational applications (apps) for use on desktop, laptop, tablet, and handheld computers.

The National Association for the Education of Young Children (2011) has focused considerable attention on apps used in early childhood settings, and a special forum stimulated discussions among professionals regarding the integration of iPod and iPad apps in classroom settings. Because of the rapid growth in the avail-

Table 10.1. Examples of current resources regarding apps for young children

Site/document	Web address	Description
Free Apps for Kids	http://bestappsforkids.com/category/apps-for-education/early-learning-apps	An array of free apps, selected by parents, that hold potential for facilitating learning
Moms with Apps	http://momswithapps.com	A collaborative group of family-friendly developers seeking to promote quality apps for kids and families; links to a wide array of apps are provided
30+ Best iPhone Apps for Kids	http://www.parenting.com/gallery/25-iphone-apps-for-kids	Provides description of highly rated iPhone and iPod touch games for young children
Best iPhone and iPad Games for Little Kids	http://www.parenting.com/gallery/eduational-iphone-apps?cid=obinsite	Parenting web site providing discussion forum related to family use of various apps
Best Kids Apps	http://www.bestkidsapps.com/	Searchable descriptions of iPad, iPhone, and Android apps for children ages 0–12 years
iKidApps	http://www.ikidapps.com/2011/09/350-best-apps-reviewed.html	Provides listing and reviews of best 350 apps

ability of apps for these devices, teachers, experts, and parents have created online communities and developed rubrics and checklists for distinguishing between high- and low-quality educational apps (see Table 10.1). Researchers also have begun to investigate how educational apps affect student learning. Such activity suggests that new instructional technologies have captured the attention of many practitioners and children. However, effectively integrating them into planned activities presents numerous challenges to teachers. Specifically, these questions may arise regarding their use:

- How do I obtain new technology when limited budgets are present?

- How do I integrate new technologies into planned classroom activities?

- How do I evaluate the effects of instruction that uses new technology?

RESEARCH-BASED INSTRUCTIONAL TECHNOLOGY AND INSTRUCTIONAL TECHNOLOGY INNOVATIONS

Throughout this book, you have read about readily available technologies and how to use the EXPECT IT-PLAN IT-TEACH IT framework to achieve instructional objectives in planned activities for young children. Readily available technologies are affordable, easily obtained, intuitively designed, downloadable or web-accessible, and/or have built-in features that are consistent with universal design for learning (UDL; e.g., synthesized speech, screen magnification, reinforcement for users; see Chapter 1). In Chapter 1, it was noted that readily available technologies are part of the core infrastructure for teaching in today's classrooms because they often have UDL features that are dynamic, flexible, interactive, and shared. Because of rapid technological innovation, readily available instructional technology can be classified into two categories: research-based instructional technology and instructional technology innovations. Unlike other fields in education, the fields of instructional and assistive technology are in their infancy. Systematic educational research is both time consuming and difficult, and research that is conducted sometimes reflects less understanding about how human beings learn than is characteristic of research done in other disciplines (e.g., medicine, engineering).

The ability of engineers and educational innovators to develop new instructional technologies having immediate application in an early childhood program outpaces the development of a research base to support the use of instructional technology in school settings. Instructional technology developers rarely conduct research with their own products before disseminating them. Although this has created a vast amount of instructional technology innovations from which to choose, few of them are evidence-based products. This presents some difficult choices for early childhood programs because of limited knowledge about the technology they are purchasing, and, in some cases, the cost.

In considering the three questions posed in the previous section regarding instructional technologies, three key obstacles in early childhood programs are presented: cost, implementation, and evaluation. Each of these obstacles is discussed in the following sections.

OBTAINING COSTLY INSTRUCTIONAL TECHNOLOGY

Frequently, new instructional technology is most expensive when it is first available. For example, laptop computers cost at least $1,000 dollars when they were first introduced. Today, one can purchase a quality laptop for $400, which is more powerful than one purchased 10 years ago at considerably more expense. Over time, a gradual decline in the price of any particular technology then occurs. This is especially true of hardware that is needed to operate digital technologies. Although many software programs, apps, and web-based programs are free or have a minimal cost, an initial investment and maintenance of hardware is required (i.e., hardware breaks down, suffers from heavy use in the classroom, and often needs to be updated every 3–4 years). Thus, teachers who are early adopters of technology innovations that require new hardware are those with greater access to financial and other resources.

In the past, programs and schools serving young children may have been slow to adopt instructional technology because it was too expensive, choosing instead to wait for the cost of technology to decrease before investing in it (Blagojevic, 2003; Fabry & Higgs, 1997). Further, teachers were initially skeptical about the value of instructional technology for young children, often resulting in hesitancy to invest in the cost of new technologies. Schools have increasingly been required to meet higher expectations and demands for educating all young children while the financial resources available to them have decreased. Thus, early childhood education programs may now be more hesitant than ever to invest in instructional technology. Indeed, finding the funds to acquire instructional technologies for early childhood education programs is often the primary problem. Despite the expense of some instructional technology, it can often be acquired by teachers at a reduced expense or sometimes without having to pay for it at all. Three resources that should be considered include anonymous donor web sites, philanthropic organizations and foundations, and recycled technology resources.

Anonymous Donor Web Sites

When thinking about where to secure funds for more costly instructional technology resources for the classroom, teachers may seek the financial support of individuals, organizations, corporations, and agencies. One strategy is to advertise one's particular classroom needs on an anonymous donor web site. These include sites such as DonorsChoose.com, DigitalWish.com, and AdoptaClassroom.org, which are used by education professionals in need of classroom equipment or materials to enhance the quality of their students' education. Donor sites allow teachers to provide background information about their classrooms along with wish lists of their instructional technology-related needs. Individual donors may then examine posted needs by reading the listings and providing either the funds or the requested items for specific classrooms. Sometimes a teacher's request may be partially funded and requires the practitioner or school to make up the difference. In other cases, requests are fully funded and instructional technology may be obtained without any cost to the practitioner or school.

Philanthropic Organizations and Foundations

Another source for funding includes a range of philanthropic organizations and foundations that may provide resources needed to acquire and use some new instructional technology in the classroom. Many organizations provide grants for classroom teachers, ranging from small, community-based organizations to large, national foundations. Teachers may find it helpful to begin their search for sources by visiting web sites such as Edutopia.org or TechnologyGrantNews.com, which collect and list grant opportunities specifically for education professionals who need technology for their classrooms. Finally, the Technology and Young Children Interest Forum web site from the National Association for the Education of Young Children (http://www.techandyoungchildren.org) is an excellent resource for learning more about technology funding sources.

Recycled Technology Resources

In some states, key infrastructure technology can be obtained at no or little cost. For example, in Illinois, any school in the state can request and receive an array of free hardware from the Assistive Technology Exchange Network. This program recycles computers and other technology donated by corporations and individuals to benefit children with disabilities. Any school in Illinois can make requests for computers, printers, and other peripherals to support instruction in classrooms.

Maintained by the U.S. General Services Administration, the Computers for Learning program (http://computersforlearning.gov) is a response to an executive order authorizing the transfer of computers and related peripheral equipment directly to schools and nonprofit organizations. These and many more resources can be located by simply typing the search term *free computers* into one's browser, reading the relevant information regarding requests for resources, and then completing necessary forms.

IMPLEMENTATION ISSUES RELATED TO INSTRUCTIONAL TECHNOLOGY INNOVATION

When teachers obtain instructional technology that is a new innovation for their classrooms, issues regarding its use may arise. These new technologies often require the user to develop the ability to use both the hardware (e.g., a new device like a tablet and its operating system) and software (i.e., the apps and features on the device). Understanding how to operate a device, how to take advantage of its features, and how to work around its limits can be challenging, even for tech-savvy teachers. Complicating this problem is the fact that young children often must be taught how to use some new technology because they may not have encountered it directly in their homes (Murphy, Depasquale, & McNamara, 2003). New hardware innovations initially may not be compatible with readily available technology (e.g., the new tablet computer may not work with a child's IntelliKeys® input system, an app designed for use on an Android device would not work on an iPad or iPhone).

The use of any new technology often requires guidance from experts on how to use it (Chen & Price, 2006; Smith & Allsopp, 2005). In addition, teachers may have difficulty capitalizing on its classroom capabilities because its implementation often occurs before scientifically validated guidance is available. Practitioners may rely on a trial-and-error approach, seek out the successes of colleagues to determine what does and does not work, misuse or underuse the technology, or abandon it in favor of more familiar and less advanced tools (Phillips & Zhao, 1993; Smith & Allsopp, 2005). Fortunately, these and other barriers to effective use of instructional technology innovations can be overcome when teachers are provided with knowledge, equipped with infrastructure resources (see Chapter 1), and have hands-on experiences using the technologies (Parette & Stoner, 2008). The Internet is perhaps the best resource for practitioners to acquire information prior to adoption of a new instructional technology.

Locating Information on the Use of Instructional Technology Innovations

Teachers who are eager to adopt technological innovations can benefit from learning about the successes and difficulties of their fellow practitioners. This information will not only guide teachers in implementing effective and efficient teaching, but it often provides direction for researchers exploring the new instructional technology. Practitioners must be able to locate and evaluate information about using new instructional technology in classrooms where expert supports are not available. There are many ways teachers can obtain this information, but the Internet is an immense information resource that should be used by all practitioners.

The most common method of finding information on the Internet is through use of search engines (e.g., Google, Yahoo!). Teachers can type keywords or phrases into the search engine to generate a list of matching web sites. Although search engines are useful and simple to use, they often produce millions of search results, with many pages that are not related to the information sought by the user. Despite using different keywords or custom search strategies, an Internet search may not provide the desired information, or it may require the user to view a seemingly endless number of pages to find relevant content. Instead of relying on search engines alone, it may be more efficient to browse the web pages of reputable organizations, search video upload sites, contribute to and read wikis, subscribe to blogs, and use other sources of information to obtain specific and useful information. These methods are explained below and are summarized in Table 10.2. Other strategies for using search engines have been described elsewhere (November, 2008).

Teachers who are seeking ways to use new instructional technology in their classrooms may also familiarize themselves with web pages of associations and organizations specifically focused on technology in education. The NAEYC Technology and Young Children Interest Forum (http://www.techandyoungchildren .org), the Center for Applied Special Technology (http://www.cast.org), the International Society for Technology in Education (http://www.iste.org), and AbleData (http://www.abledtata.org) are helpful web sites to use when searching for information about new instructional technology in education.

Information searches can also be conducted on video web sites such as TeacherTube, YouTube, or Truveo. These sites store user-submitted video clips, some of which are specific to new instructional technology in classroom settings. Also, companies often market products on their web sites, including videos that show product features and various ways the products can be used. By accessing information on new instructional technologies using video clips, teachers may see features and classroom applications of technologies that are considered during the PLAN IT phase. This provides the practitioner with an opportunity to see the instructional technology being applied—something that is not easily understood by just reading about it.

Searching the Internet can be helpful, but the enormous amount of information available can be tedious to track and organize. Web browsers (e.g., Internet Explorer, Mozilla Firefox, Apple Safari) often include a basic bookmarking feature to store and organize the user's preferred web sites. By bookmarking web sites, the browser stores key information (e.g., address, keywords, dates visited) to aid the user in navigating to the site again in the future. All that is needed is for the user to click on the bookmarking icon to reveal a list of sites previously bookmarked. Similarly, many web browsers have extensions or features to add to customize the browser and make it more user-friendly. For example, a common browser extension may be installed to block pop-up advertisements. Teachers may use an enhanced bookmarking browser extension as a means to help categorize and prioritize information about new instructional technology that they have found on the Internet. Although useful, these features still require users to look for and read through numerous web pages to locate specific information.

Other useful extensions are social bookmarking services (e.g., Diigo, Stumble Upon). These extensions allow users to organize, store, manage, and share information found on web pages. Once a web page is marked, social bookmarking browser extensions allow users to highlight information on a web page for later, tag pages with their own keywords (e.g., *ideas for Shari, outdoor play activity*), discover sites based on specific interests, filter out unwanted content, or read/post comments about the web page's content. The Diigo extension features a digital version of sticky notes, which users post on the screen for others to read. Creating or joining an online social bookmark community allows users to access information tagged by other members of the community with similar interests. Essentially, social bookmarking allows people to organize, access, collaborate, and personalize their Internet experiences. For teachers using new instructional technology, the use of these tools may result in more efficient location of relevant information on the Internet.

Perhaps more familiar than browser extensions are social networking sites and blogs. Social networking sites such as Classroom 2.0, Facebook, and LinkedIn allow people with similar interests to form groups to facilitate the exchange of information. Users of such sites can post questions, information, and ideas about new instructional technology for use by other members of the group. Many schools and companies use social networking sites to market their products and provide information updates for users.

The Internet has changed to promote a more collaborative and interactive experience. One way this change is reflected is by the use of web sites that can be easily created and maintained by users, such as wikis, which are another way to gain information about new instructional technology from the Internet. Wikis are similar to traditional web sites in how information is presented, but they are different because they can be edited by someone other than a webmaster. Most wikis allow information to be added or modified by any user, but some wikis may limit changes to approved members. Teachers may find wikis particularly useful because they allow users to read what others are doing with technologies in their classrooms, share ideas about variations of activities, suggest how to improve teaching, provide solutions to problems, and share resources. The ECETECH wiki (http://ecetech.wikispaces.com) is an especially informative resource site to help practitioners integrate readily available and new instructional technologies in the classroom.

Table 10.2 presents a set of methods that can be used to find information about using instructional technology in early childhood classrooms. Many technology enthusiasts and teachers choose to create and share web blogs or online journals, typically created by one person, to share information about a particular interest or experience. The blog author (or blogger) posts information and allows others to comment on the posting. These comments often include informative ideas sparked by the blogger and can provide guidance to classroom practitioners. Some useful blogs might include those created by teachers, consumers of new technology, and educational technology specialists.

Teachers can have information delivered directly to their e-mail boxes via Really Simple Syndication (RSS) feeds. RSS feeds and search engine alert notifications are services that teachers can use to learn about new instructional technologies and their applications in classrooms. RSS monitors a user's designated web pages (e.g., favorite blogs, wikis, organizations) for new content. Whenever new content is added to these pages, the content is collected and organized for viewing with an RSS reader. (RSS readers are built into most popular web browsers, but they may also be independent applications.) To access the information from an RSS feed, a user signs up for the feed by clicking on the RSS feed button contained on many web sites. In addition, search engine alert notifications can be used to inform a user of new content on the web related to their interests by e-mail. The user lists keywords (e.g., *iPad, preschool, autism*) for the notification service and subsequently receives e-mails with links to new content detected by the search engine. These alerts can be accessed by signing up for them from a favorite search engine.

Finally, teachers can find out information about a product by visiting the product web sites. Companies often will offer support forums, video tutorials, and

Table 10.2. Methods of finding information about new instructional technology in education

Source	Definition	How sources can be used	Examples
Search engines	Programs that search the Internet or other databases to find information based on keywords or terms	Users type in keywords, then search engines list results according to popularity (most popular sites first)	Google
		The list will provide users with the most up-to-date information	Bing
		Users may have to try several different keywords to get the best information	Yahoo!
			Excite
Social bookmarking	Web sites that allow users to mark information found on different web sites for later use, and share and benefit from other members with common interests	Go to a social bookmarking web site, such as those listed to the right	Diigo
		Follow directions to become a member of the social bookmarking service	StumbleUpon
		Download any required computer software or updates	Delicious
		Use this resource to organize, store, and manage information found on web sites for later use	
		Users benefit from others with similar interests who have marked the sites that contain relevant information	
Social networks	Online web sites that allow people to connect with other people who share common interests for the purpose of exchanging information and ideas	Go to a social networking web site, such as those listed to the right	Classroom 2.0
		Follow directions to become a member of the site and create a profile	Facebook
		Use the *search* or *find* box to input keywords and obtain results based on search	Twitter
		Sites are typically easy to access and use	
		Information posted by individuals may be biased or not based on fact	
Blogs	Web sites typically maintained by an individual that contain entries and postings, allowing people to comment and share ideas	Go to a blog, such as those listed to the right	Wordpress.com
		Search the site using keywords	Blogspot.com
		Subscribe to blogs related to areas of interest if user wants to receive future postings from this author	Blogs.scholastic.com
		Teachers can create a post/blog related to their experiences and receive feedback (on some sites)	
		Users must critically evaluate information as the information presented may be based more on perception than facts	

Technology	Description	Notes	Examples
Wikis	Web pages that can be created and edited by a user via a web browser	Go to a wiki site such as those listed to the right. Create a user profile if one wishes to make a personal web site. Add information to the web site that may be useful to others (e.g., information about classroom procedures, upcoming events, and other class updates that are traditionally contained in a class newsletter). Once information has been added to the web site, one can publish the web site to share with other teachers and parents. Use the find/search box on the site to access information posted by other people. Conducive for collaborating and sharing ideas to generate a comprehensive resource. Information may need to be critically evaluated for accuracy and relevancy.	ecetech.wikispaces.com PB Wiki Pikiwiki
RSS feeds	Subscription services that inform users when content is added or changed to the subscribed web page	Go to a favorite web page and locate the RSS feed symbol. Click on the RSS feed symbol and enter e-mail information to subscribe to the feed for this site. Updates will come directly to the e-mail address provided. Users are notified when web pages are updated so they will not have to keep checking back with the pages, saving users time. Not all web pages are equipped for RSS feeds. Users may receive numerous e-mails depending on the frequency of the updates to the site.	Grabit FeedDemon Beatnik
Alerts	Content monitoring service that notifies subscribers via email when new content related to topics of interest are available on the web	Go to a favorite web browser and locate the alert feature. Subscribe to alerts based on keywords or areas of interest. New content is emailed directly to the e-mail provided. This service can result in numerous emails that may be hard to organize. Sometimes content received may not be relevant.	Google Alerts URL Wire Yahoo! Alerts
Newsletter or electronic magazines	Newsletters and magazines published in an electronic format	Teachers can go to the newsletter or magazine web site. Users can read information published to see if it is useful for their classroom. Information can be accessed from anywhere there is an Internet connection. Users need to investigate the source of the publisher to ensure accuracy of information	ChildrensTech.org Popsci.com

(continued)

Table 10.2 (continued)

Source	Definition	How sources can be used	Examples
Videos (multimedia clips)	Video and/or audio segments that can be posted online for use by the public	To access videos, users can go directly to the sites listed to the right or to a web browser	Truveo.com YouTube.com TeacherTube.com
		Then users can enter key words to search for videos. If using a web browser (such as Google), users can add the word *video* after the keywords	
		Adding words will generate a list of video clips. Click on the video clip or the link to watch the video	
		Some videos can be saved as a video file on the computer	
		Users may gain a demonstration of new technology in use	
		Many school sites have filters blocking video content so this may not work at all school sites	
		Searches may result in irrelevant or poorly produced videos	
Product review sites	Web sites dedicated to the review and rating of new products	Users may go to the web sites listed on the right	IEAR.org CommonSenseMedia.org CNET.com
		Teachers can search the site based on entering the product name	
		A list of related information will appear providing an overview of product features	
		Users may also be able to view a product demonstration before buying new technology	
		Some information provided on pages may be biased and might be presented to highlight positive attributes at the expense of limitations. Teachers should look for reviews providing both positive aspects and limitations of the product	
Associations and organizations	Groups dedicated to the advancement of a particular topic or theme. These groups tend to specialize	Go to a group web site	JoanGanzCooneyCenter.org NationalTechCenter.org ISTE.org
		Depending on the group, users may be required to join the group and possibly pay a membership fee	
		Once a member, these sites provide the most recent information and support	
		The information obtained on these sites can be very specialized	
		Information can sometimes be obtained by nonmembers, but access to this information may require a fee	

subscription feeds for updates about specific products. These sources can prove especially useful for technical support and for keeping informed of newly available hardware and software systems. Some product web sites allow users to compare the features of different products. This is especially helpful when making purchase decisions.

How Mrs. Hearns Got a Free iPad for Her Classroom

Mrs. Hearns is very excited. She just received notice that her request for a new iPad for her classroom was funded. About a month ago, Mrs. Hearns began exploring the idea of adding an iPad to her classroom. She knew she would not be able to get an iPad for every student, but she still thought there could be ways to incorporate the iPad for the benefit of her students, even if she only had one. Mrs. Hearns lived in a small community and the nearest retailer was in a town 110 miles away and the nearest location where she could get access Apple's in-store training was over 300 miles from her home in rural Montana. She wanted more information about this technology, so she turned on her laptop and began searching the Internet.

Mrs. Hearns searched the consumer reports and ratings on the iPad and found they were favorable. Mrs. Hearns spent some time on Apple's iPad product web page to see what features it had and if preschoolers could use them. She was especially interested in ways to use the iPad with Deshawn, her student who was diagnosed with a severe language delay. Mrs. Hearns had observed how interested Deshawn was with her iPhone and noted his interest in the classroom computers. Mrs. Hearns thought using the iPad might be another way to help him learn important communication skills by interacting with peers while doing something he enjoyed. She also thought the students might be able to learn content with this new technology. While seeking information online, Mrs. Hearns found a blog by a preschool teacher who described how she was able to use the iPad with her students that had language delays during their opening circle time routine. With the information she gathered, Mrs. Hearns was convinced this instructional technology innovation held great potential to support learning activities in her classroom. However, she also knew that her classroom budget was exhausted given that she had recently purchased a digital projector for the classroom.

Mrs. Hearns decided to start seeking funding sources. She entered the search term *classroom funding for teachers* into her computer browser and generated a list of many different grant sources where teachers can apply to get funding for their classrooms. Mrs. Hearns began to apply to several different sources. When she requested the funding for the iPad, she requested a little extra funding for apps, explained how she intended to use them, and listed the ways her students would benefit from them. Mrs. Hearns submitted her request and patiently waited for a response. After about 6 weeks, she got a reply. Her request had been fully approved. She logged on, completed her order, and the iPad arrived a few days later.

Mrs. Hearns knew she wanted the iPad to be more than just a toy, but she was not sure which apps to buy. She began searching the iTunes App Store for app reviews posted by other buyers. She also read critical web site reviews of educational apps and found a rubric to evaluate the apps she purchased. Mrs. Hearns also found web sites that rated iPad apps and allowed users to leave comments.

Some of the users who left comments gave ideas of how they used the iPad with their children as well. After making a few purchases on the App Store, she began seeking more information. She had many ideas about how she wanted to incorporate the iPad into the classroom, but she knew there had to be sources where other teachers shared their experiences using iPads. Mrs. Hearns found teacher blogs and web sites, YouTube videos of children using iPads in various ways, and a forum for teachers interested in educational technology. With all of this information at hand, Mrs. Hearns knew using the iPad in her classroom was going to be a success.

EVALUATING INSTRUCTIONAL TECHNOLOGIES

Chapter 4 provided a detailed description of CHECK IT assessment strategies identified during the PLAN IT phase and used during the TEACH IT phase. In Chapter 5, the use of an activity probe strategy was described, which can be used to examine a child's ability to perform a task in a planned activity both with and without the use of assistive technology. Because newer instructional technology likely is used in classrooms before expert guidance is widely available, the decision to use new technology requires that teachers be critical of any technology selected for students. Simply because children are engaged with a technology does not mean they are learning. The newest and the latest technology may or may not be the best choices for young children. As described previously, instructional technology is selected to support the required standards of the state/program, learning objectives, curriculum, and child outcomes measured through data collection. Also, it is important to collect and analyze data to determine what changes, if any, must be made regarding implementation of the new technology. The use of evaluation tools as well as the use of a slight variation of the probe strategy may be used to evaluate teaching effectiveness and to determine what broad effects new technology has on student performance (Parette, Blum, & Boeckmann, 2009).

Table 10.3 presents considerations for teachers before deciding whether or not to use new technologies in the classroom. Just as with other developmentally appropriate practices, any new technology should have as many UDL characteristics as possible, thus supporting multiple means of engagement, representation, and presentation. Thus, all technology should enhance social engagement as well as playful interactions to the greatest extent possible. New technologies should use images and words that are developmentally appropriate and age appropriate. When text appears on a screen, it should be paired with an audio cue to assist children with understanding.

For any activity using a new technology, learning should be promoted through activities that are accessible to students with a wide variety of developmental needs; scaffolded when skills progress in a sequence; and, when possible, promote problem solving. Instructional technology will typically be more effective when used along with other strategies and activities in the classroom. Finally, the new technology should provide specific positive feedback. Many programs and games will tell children "good job" or "way to go" without providing feedback to tell the student what they did well. Teachers should examine the technology to see if it provides feedback that is specific to the learner outcomes (e.g., "you found all the items that are round," "you are a master problem solver"). If it does not pro-

Table 10.3. Instructional technology innovation evaluation checklist

Appropriate instructional technology innovation use in early childhood classes will...	Instructional technology innovation might be inappropriate if...
For students	
Enhance social engagement	Technology is only used by one child at a time
Be developmentally and age appropriate	Activities resemble an electronic worksheet
Provide a combination of visual and auditory supports	The technology does not provide visual and auditory support
Promote children's playful interactions with technology	Children's interactions with technology are rote
Scaffold learning because skills build upon each other	Children are limited in responses/it is either right or wrong
Be easily accessible by children with a wide range of abilities and skills	It is difficult for children to manage without significant adult support
Be used in combination with other strategies and activities	Technology stands alone and is not related to other activities or lessons
Provide specific feedback for students	It lacks feedback or uses general phrases such as "good job"
Engage students both cognitively and socially	Students avoid using the technology
For teachers	
Improve how teachers are able to document student growth and learning	Technology takes away from teacher's ability to document learning and growth
Help teachers to plan and implement activities	Technology makes planning difficult
Enhance communication with parents and families	It detracts from communication with families or does not allow all families to receive information

vide feedback, the technology should not necessarily be abandoned. However, the teacher should provide supplementary feedback to the children to make learning more effective. In this instance, the teacher could provide that feedback while the children are working with the technology and incorporate other effective practices discussed in Chapter 3.

In addition to considering technology from the perspectives of UDL and developmental appropriateness, evaluation of new technologies should also occur from the teacher's perspective. In choosing whether or not to use new technologies in the classroom, consideration should be given to how the technologies improve instructional ability to document student growth and learning. Teachers should consider whether these technologies assist in the planning and implementation of lessons or whether they create the need for extended time. If technologies require additional time, consideration should be given to whether this time is worth investing for the outcomes anticipated.

Time also should be a consideration when using new technologies with families. Teachers should ask if communication is enhanced with families through use of new instructional technologies. Similarly, one must be aware of families who might be excluded because of a lack of access to technologies or preferences not to use such technologies. If the technology has the potential to exclude groups of people (e.g., families who cannot afford technology), then consideration should be given to overcoming this barrier before the technology is implemented to ensure everyone has access.

LOOKING BACK: WHERE TEACHERS
HAVE BEEN WITH NEW TECHNOLOGIES

Generally speaking, many teachers may assume that available hardware or software being considered for integration into the curriculum will provide educational benefit (Higgins, Boone, & Williams 2000). The advanced features and capabilities of many new technologies may seem so amazing that there may not be a tendency to critically examine them and consider what technology should and should not do for students (Cooper, 2004). An example of this phenomenon was evidenced by poor-quality educational software marketed as having educational value during the 1990s and 2000s. The affordability of personal computers and advances in technology during this time period meant that more schools could purchase and teachers could more frequently use computers to support academic learning. Software publishers recognized the opportunity for commercialization and the market was flooded with "educational" multimedia software that did not incorporated important aspects of teaching and learning to ensure educational benefit. Major educational software publishers did not fully consider key issues such as design, instructional delivery, content, accessibility, interface, and other critical areas when developing software (Higgins, Boone, & Williams, 2000; Zane & Frazer, 1992). Although knowledge about teaching and learning via technology has since increased, the poor development of educational software remained commonplace (Boone & Higgins, 2005).

The barriers and limitations of poorly designed software may previously have been seen as an inherent cost of technological advancement (Cooper, 2004). Consequently, teachers were required to adapt their instruction to incorporate technology rather than make consumer demands to achieve software improvements (Williams, Boone, & Kingsly, 2004). This phenomenon of teachers adapting their instruction to technology rather than expecting technology to adapt to their teaching is likely due to teachers' mistaken beliefs that educational software is always carefully developed, well designed, and properly evaluated prior to being made available in the educational marketplace (Higgins et al., 2000).

LOOKING AHEAD: THE CHALLENGE
OF EVALUATING NEW TECHNOLOGIES

In a fashion similar to the educational software boom of the 1990s, the development and marketing of education software apps for mobile computing devices has increased at breakneck speed in the 21st century. In September 2009, Apple announced that over 85,000 apps were available for download on the iTunes App Store (Apple Corporation, 2009). By October 2011, there were more than 500,000 apps and over 18 billion downloads (Seigler, 2011), with no indications of a slowed growth despite the major global economic recession.

A large portion of the educational software for mobile devices has targeted toddlers and young children. An analysis of the content marketed in the educational section of the iTunes App Store, Apple's marketplace for software for devices that use the iPhone operating system, found that 60% of the 25 most frequently downloaded educational apps targeted toddlers and preschool age children as the primary user. Only 16% of educational apps targeted elementary, middle, or high school students (Shuler, 2009). The adoption of and enthusiasm for mobile technology such as Apple's iPad, iPhone, and iPod touch has yielded a marketplace filled with software that claims to have educational benefits for young children.

Although the meter and rhythm of the story of mobile device computers seems different from the software boom of the 1990s, the historical rhyme has a familiar ring to it. Teachers should consider that apps categorized as having educational value, particularly for young children, may be lacking essential design, instruction, content, and other features of high-quality educational software. Thus, teachers must be knowledgeable about and critical of educational software. Some efforts have emerged to provide guidance regarding evaluation of apps, software, and web sites (e.g., Darrow, 2011; Gerstein, 2011; Schrock, 2011; Walker, 2010), although guidance has not typically been provided regarding how they may be effectively integrated into the early childhood curriculum.

Utility of the Software Checklist for Evaluation

Boone and Higgins (2007) developed a checklist of critical features that educational software must have for students with disabilities as well as typically developing young children. They reviewed the scientific literature, recruited expert evaluation, and conducted field testing to develop the Software Checklist (http://tamcec.org/pdf/TIA%20Nov%202007%204Web.pdf). Boone and Higgins identified positive attributes of educational software for students with disabilities (i.e., qualities consistent with UDL), including instruction, directions, feedback, content, individualization, interface, and accessibility as well as additional attributes specific to young children. Importantly, the reliability and construct validity of the Software Checklist has not yet been reported, so teachers should keep in mind that the Software Checklist is not a perfect instrument. Further, the checklist was conceived to evaluate software typically used on personal computing hardware (e.g., desktop or laptop computers). However, because researchers have not yet developed tools for evaluating mobile device applications, and because the Software Checklist appears to be the only tool of its kind that exists, it holds promise for evaluating mobile device apps.

Efficiency of Teaching and Creating a Short List of Apps, Software, and Web Sites

When using new apps, software, and web sites—especially those having little evidence of usefulness with young children—evaluation of potential usefulness should be considered to make technology integration decisions during PLAN IT. One strategy used by teachers is simply be to identify a pool of apps, software, and web sites with potential to support the curriculum, thus making them available for consideration during PLAN IT. Using resources such as those noted in Table 10.1, both free and low-cost apps, web sites, and software can be systematically examined and reviewed as time allows using the software checklist. Given the staggering number of apps, software, and web sites developed for young children, these resource sites serve a very practical purpose by presenting both positive and negative reviews from families who have used them, allowing the teacher to identify a short list of apps, software, and web sites that might have utility in planned classroom activities. When a sufficient number of potential apps are identified, one may easily download the apps for use. Often, free "lite" versions are available for download, and there are many other inexpensive apps. These may be especially attractive to teachers given their limited budgets for technology purchases.

It is critical to keep in mind that many potential useful features of an app, software, or web site do not constitute evidence that young children can effectively learn when using these in a developmentally appropriate curriculum. Although evidence for any instructional strategy or technology is a complicated question, at a minimum CHECK IT assessment data should confirm that the students improved on the targeted learning objective. Ultimately, as studies become available on the various tools in early childhood settings, teachers need to guide their decision making about what to include, exclude, and how to use it based on scientific educational research on technology integration with young children.

Although having a pool of potentially useful apps, software, and web sites available provides a resource for planned activities in the classroom, whether or not the products are used hinges on evaluation of their features. However, efficiency of teaching in early childhood classrooms often requires planned activities to address more than one learning objective; therefore, teachers should keep this in mind when starting their search for apps. Historically, educational software programs (and apps more recently) have not integrated best practices in instruction and principles of learning. They are typically designed to be colorful, engaging, and entertaining. As such, there may be a temptation to be enthusiastic about features (e.g., characters, music, animation, special effects) that are not critical to one's instructional purpose in a planned activity. Tools (i.e., rubrics, checklists) can be used to evaluate the qualities of each app. Critically examining each app by "playing with" the features is important to discern whether its features match with the intended purpose of a planned activity and the lesson sequence that will be used to deliver instruction.

For example, Mrs. Hearns was excited about the grant her school received to purchase a set of 10 tablet computers. She quickly reserved them for 10 hours per week for instruction in her preschool classroom. She knew that the students in her preschool classroom would be enthralled with them, but she wanted to be sure to have an array of potentially useful apps available that might be used when planning classroom activities. She downloaded free versions of popular educational applications from an online store to her own smartphone. After exploring each of them, it occurred to her that although she knew what to look for in terms of educational content, she was not sure about other aspects of the software. Specifically, she wanted to know if her students, including those with disabilities, would benefit from the apps she decided to use. Mrs. Hearns relied on search engines, social networks, wikis, and association web sites to find out what other teachers were doing to ensure quality of software. She found a few rubrics made by university professors, some formal reviews about specific applications, thorough comments about apps by teachers and parents, and the software checklist created by Boone and Higgins (2007).

Using a process of elimination, Mrs. Hearns came up with a short list of apps that seemed very interesting and promising. She then turned to the software checklist for a more formal evaluation of the apps. Her results are in Table 10.4. Based on the information she obtained and the evaluation she completed, Mrs. Hearns decided she would keep the Martha Speaks Dog Party app for consideration in future

Table 10.4. Mrs. Hearns's evaluation results summary of apps using the Software Checklist

	App reviewed			
	Kids Can Match Animals Lite	Martha Speaks Dog Party	Monkey Preschool Lunchbox	Letter Tracer Preschool Writing Practice
Positive qualities for all students with disabilities	46% (56)	46%	38%	27%
Instruction (15)	3	5	3	2
Directions and documentation (9)	2	2	2	2
Feedback and evaluation (9)	4	5	4	0
Content (9)	8	6	5	3
Individualization options (4)	2	1	1	1
Interface and screen design (4)	3	2	2	3
Accessibility (6)	4	4	4	4
Positive qualities for early childhood	55%	65%	55%	40%
Instruction (8)	0	2	1	0
Directions and documentation (2)	2	2	2	2
Feedback and evaluation (1)	1	1	1	1
Content (4)	4	4	3	1
Individualization options (1)	0	0	0	0
Interface and screen design (2)	2	2	2	2
Accessibility (2)	2	2	2	2

planned activities. After using it for a few weeks, hoping to help other teachers, she wrote a thorough review of the Martha Speaks Dog Party app at the online store where she purchased it. She included details about the strengths and limitations encountered both during the evaluation and after using it in her planned classroom activity so that other teachers (and students) could benefit from her efforts.

EVALUATION OF APPS, SOFTWARE, AND WEB SITES FOR TECHNOLOGY INTEGRATION DURING PLAN IT

Once a pool of potentially useful apps, software, and web sites has been identified that might support the curriculum, these become readily available and can be considered along with other instructional technologies during PLAN IT. As has been discussed in previous chapters, finding the right technology starts with EXPECT IT—identifying the standards and learning objectives to be addressed in a planned activity. Once an EXPECT IT decision has been made, planning ensues wherein two interrelated processes occur: TECH IT and ARRANGE IT (see Chapter 3 for a discussion of these two components of the PLAN IT process). The learning objective, standard, curriculum sequence, tier of support (see Figure 3.3), and instructional strategy prescribed by the curriculum lead the teacher to consider a particular instructional technology.

In Chapter 3, Mrs. Hearns used the EXPECT IT-PLAN IT-TEACH IT process to make decisions about instructional technology and connect it to instructional strategies. Consider how she might do things differently using educational apps for an iPad. In this example, Mrs. Hearns uses evaluation strategies to inform her decision-making process about app selection for an iPad.

Step 1: EXPECT IT

Mrs. Hearns examines her curriculum and decides to address the standard that children should apply reading strategies to develop fluency and understanding. A learning objective connected to the curricular sequence in the state standards is the *recognition of consonant-vowel-consonant (C-V-C) words.*

Step 2: PLAN IT-TECH IT

Mrs. Hearns realizes that her children need to master identifying and blending sounds in C-V-C words before moving forward in the curriculum. She also knows that she wants to use one or more instructional technologies to help the students attain mastery. Although her curriculum does not call specifically for use of in-structional technology, she considers the readily available technologies that she has in her classroom—the computer and digital projector, PowerPoint, bookmarks of an array of web sites having ready-made classroom games and activities, and numerous apps that she has previously downloaded and evaluated. She wants to follow a prescribed curriculum lesson that involves puppets. However, she be-lieves that an appropriate integration of technology for this prescribed lesson would be to use PowerPoint to provide some additional direct instruction pertaining to blending C-V-C words. She will create five slides for the instructional component, each having a picture of a three-letter word created in Boardmaker accompanied by letters for the word. Emphasis features will be applied to each slide so that let-ters fade in as Mrs. Hearns clicks a mouse and models the blending. Students will then chorally respond by sounding out letters and pronouncing the word.

After the instruction with PowerPoint, Mrs. Hearns wants to complement the instruction with guided practice using newly acquired iPads to allow students to practice C-V-C words in the curriculum. She has 10 iPads available for practice during literacy center time. In her prior review of apps, she was impressed with Montessori Crosswords, which allows the option of simple words with three sounds. From reviewing her Software Checklist, Mrs. Hearns observed that the app pro-vided families and teachers with recommendations about using the app and on-screen visuals regarding how to use the features. The app provided a settings menu allowing control of a variety of features, such as the amount of time the child could play, and various font, sound, and pronunciation control features. Children had direct connections to content presented, varying levels of difficulty available, and there was a visually appealing interface and screen for the children.

Mrs. Hearns noted that there are signals and scaffolding elements to assist her students in learning. In her activity, each student will have an iPad and will launch the app whereon they are presented with a picture of an object having three letters, which is pronounced for them. Children see the alphabet presented below; by tap-ping any of three blank squares beside the pictured object, students have a sound pronounced representing the letter in the word. On tapping any letter in the alpha-bet, the letter wobbles and the sound is pronounced. The letter can then be dragged to the box, will expand outward to call attention to itself, and will stay in that position only if it is the correct letter; if the letter is not correct, it shakes itself and falls back to the alphabet line. On creating the correct word, each letter sound is pronounced, followed by the word and accompanied by animation activity on the screen. The iPad app complements the presentation of the instructional slides by allowing children to take turns blending sounds.

 ARRANGE IT

In the process of planning her classroom activity based on the learning objective she has identified, Mrs. Hearns knows that her core curriculum has predetermined activities and learning objectives that she will use with her students. She has noticed that the teacher's manual explains that targeted C-V-C words must be mastered prior to moving on to more advanced sounds and blending activities. She also recognizes that the curriculum is using a prerequisite sequence (see Chapter 3 for discussion of instructional sequences). She further decides that a combination of instructional strategies—direct instruction which includes modeling and guided practice—will be used in literacy center with a small group of students.

 CHECK IT

Because Mrs. Hearns has used VoiceThread in her classes before, she decides that she would like to capture video of each student showing their iPad screen and making selections of sounds. On completing the selection of letters, they hold their iPad up and pronounce the word. Mrs. Hearns wants to use the VoiceThread recordings as permanent products to document each child's performance. She will notify family members at the end of the day that a new VoiceThread is available for viewing their respective child's performance on the planned activity. This becomes part of their portfolio. Mrs. Hearns also wants specific information on errors. She has created a table with all the children's names at the top. In the left column are the identified words for the lesson. She keep track as each child responds in her iPad using the *pdf-notes* app, which allows her to upload assessment forms and data collection sheets. If children say the word correctly, Mrs. Hearns marks a check directly on her iPad screen. If the child makes an error (e.g., drops an ending sound), she makes a note by the child's name. Having this data sheet prepared will enable Mrs. Hearns to see who is struggling and with what kinds of errors. She will use the data to see patterns of errors and reteach in those areas. Mrs. Hearns then continues with the TEACH IT process.

In this example, it was essential for Mrs. Hearns to evaluate the app before she actually considers it during TECH IT. Finally, she tries it out with a small group of students to pilot it and make sure everything is running smoothly. This step will allow for troubleshooting where needed. She watches her students and her data closely to see if the children are learning from the app and planned activity.

SUMMARY

As all teachers realize, the technology used in today's schools is constantly changing. In preparing students to become successful learners, it is critical to remain informed regarding new technology developments (Parette, Quesenberry, & Blum, 2010). Although school budgets remain limited, teachers must make informed decisions when regarding how their classroom budgets are spent on new technologies. Staying informed on current research related to technologies is helpful. Accessing information on the Internet will help when conducting preliminary evaluations of current technologies prior to purchase to conserve limited classroom fiscal resources. Questions pertaining to developmental appropriateness and UDL, such as those presented in Table 10.3, may also be considered before deciding to make a purchase.

Of particular importance is to think critically about how new technologies can be used in the classroom. Young children need to not only have access to technology, but the new technologies must be used in a way that is developmentally appropriate. Once a decision is made to use new technologies, the impact of these technologies on student learning—both cognitive and social—must be continually evaluated. Finally, teachers can become leaders in the discussion around the appropriate use of new technologies so that all students can access the highest quality, up-to-date technologies in today's classrooms.

ADDITIONAL READINGS

Green, J.L. (2011). *The ultimate guide to assistive technology in education. Resources for education, intervention, and rehabilitation.* Waco, TX: Prufrock Press.

Florida Instructional Technology Training Resource Unit. (2010). *Exploring new territories 2010.* Retrieved October 18, 2012, from http://www.fdlrs.org/docs/ent 2010web.pdf

REFERENCES

Apple Corporation. (2009). *Apple's app store downloads top two billion: More than 85,000 apps now available for iPhone & iPod touch.* Retrieved November 12, 2010, from http://www .apple.com/pr/library/2009/09/28appstore.html

Blagojevic, B. (2003). Funding technology: Does it make sense? *Young Children, 58,* 28–33.

Boone, R., & Higgins, K. (2005). Designing digital materials for students with disabilities. In D.L. Edyburn, R. Boone, & K. Higgins (Eds.), *Handbook of special education technology research and practice* (pp. 481–492). Whitefish Bay, WI: Knowledge by Design.

Boone, R., & Higgins, K. (2007). The software checklist: Evaluating educational software for students with disabilities. *Technology in Action, 3*(1), 1–16.

Chen, J., & Price, V. (2006). Narrowing the digital divide: Head Start teachers develop proficiency in computer technology. *Education and Urban Society, 38,* 398–405.

Cooper, A. (2004). *The inmates are running the asylum: Why high tech products are driving us crazy and how to restore the sanity* (2nd ed.) Upper Saddle River, NJ: Pearson Education.

Darrow, D. (2011). *K-5 iPad apps for evaluating evaluation: Part five of Bloom's revised taxonomy.* Retrieved October 18, 2012, from http://www.edutopia.org/blog/ipad-apps-elementary -blooms-taxomony-evaluating-evaluation-diane-darrow

Fabry, D.L., & Higgs, J.R. (1997). Barriers to the effective use of technology in education: Current status. *Journal of Educational Computing Research, 17,* 385–395.

Gerstein, J. (2011). *Evaluating the value of apps for educational use.* Retrieved October 18, 2012, from http://usergeneratededucation.wordpress.com/2011/12/19/evaluating-the-value -of-apps-for-educational-use/

Higgins, K., Boone, R., & Williams, D. (2000). Evaluating educational software for special education. *Intervention in School and Clinic, 36,* 109–115.

Murphy, K.L., DePasquale, R., & McNamara, E. (2003). Meaningful connections: Using technology in primary classrooms. *Young Children, 58,* 12–18.

National Association for the Education of Young Children. (2011). *NAEYC technology and young children interest forum.* Retrieved October 18, 2012, from http://www.techandyoung children.org

November, A. (2008). *Web literacy for educators.* Thousand Oaks, CA: Corwin.

Parette, H.P., & Stoner, J.B. (2008). Benefits of assistive technology user groups for early childhood education professionals. *Early Childhood Education Journal, 35,* 313–319.

Parette, H.P., Blum, C. & Boeckmann, N.M. (2009). Evaluating assistive technology in early childhood education: The use of concurrent time series probe approach. *Early Childhood Education, 37,* 5–12.

Parette, H.P., Quesenberry, A.C., & Blum, C. (2010). Missing the boat with technology usage in early childhood settings: A 21st century view of developmentally appropriate practice. *Early Childhood Education Journal, 37,* 335–343.

Phillips, B., & Zhao, H. (1993). Predictors of assistive technology abandonment. *Assistive Technology, 36,* 36–45.

Schrock, K. (2011). *Critical evaluation of an iPad/iPod app.* Retrieved October 18, 2012, from http://school.discoveryeducation.com/schrockguide/pdf/evalipad.pdf

Seigler, M.G. (2011). *As iPhone sales dip ahead of 4S, Apple's earnings fall below street expectations.* Retrieved October 18, 2012, from http://techcrunch.com/2011/10/18/apple-q4 -2011-earnings/

Shuler, C. (2009). *iLearn: A content analysis of the iTunes App Store's Education Section.* Retrieved Novemeber 6, 2012, from http://joanganzcooneycenter.org/Reports-21.html

Smith, S.J., & Allsop, D. (2005). Technology and inservice professional development: Integrating an effective medium to bridge research to practice. In D.L. Edyburn, R. Boone, & K. Higgins (Eds.), *Handbook of special education technology research and practice* (pp. 777–792). Whitefish Bay, WI: Knowledge by Design.

Walker, H. (2010). *Evaluation rubric for iPod apps.* Baltimore, MD: Johns Hopkins University. Retrieved October 18, 2012, from http://learninginhand.com/storage/blog/AppRubric .pdf

Williams, D., Boone, R., & Kingsly, K. (2004). Teacher beliefs about educational software: A Delphi study. *Journal of Research on Technology in Education, 36,* 213–229.

Zane, T., & Frazer, C.G. (1992). The extent to which software developers validate their claims. *Journal of Research on Computing in Education, 24,* 410–420.

Index

Page references followed by *f* or *t* indicate figures or tables, respectively.

- -